Conversations with Chimamanda Ngozi Adichie

Literary Conversations Series
Monika Gehlawat
General Editor

Conversations with Chimamanda Ngozi Adichie

Edited by Daria Tunca

University Press of Mississippi / Jackson

The University Press of Mississippi is the scholarly publishing agency of
the Mississippi Institutions of Higher Learning: Alcorn State University,
Delta State University, Jackson State University, Mississippi State University,
Mississippi University for Women, Mississippi Valley State University,
University of Mississippi, and University of Southern Mississippi.

www.upress.state.ms.us

The University Press of Mississippi is a member
of the Association of University Presses.

First printing 2020
∞

Names: Tunca, Daria, editor.
Title: Conversations with Chimamanda Ngozi Adichie / edited by Daria Tunca.

Other titles: Literary conversations series.
Description: Jackson : University Press of Mississippi, 2020. | Series:
   Literary conversations series | Includes bibliographical references and index.
Identifiers: LCCN 2020004460 (print) | LCCN 2020004461 (ebook) | ISBN
   9781496829269 (hardback) | ISBN 9781496829276 (trade paperback) | ISBN
   9781496829283 (epub) | ISBN 9781496829290 (epub) | ISBN 9781496829306
   (pdf) | ISBN 9781496829313 (pdf)
Subjects: LCSH: Adichie, Chimamanda Ngozi, 1977—Interviews. | Authors,
   Nigerian—21st century—Interviews. | BISAC: BIOGRAPHY & AUTOBIOGRAPHY /
   Literary Figures | LCGFT: Interviews.
Classification: LCC PR9387.9.A34354 Z562 2020 (print) | LCC
   PR9387.9.A34354 (ebook) | DDC 823/.92—dc23
LC record available at https://lccn.loc.gov/2020004460
LC ebook record available at https://lccn.loc.gov/2020004461

British Library Cataloging-in-Publication Data available

Books by Chimamanda Ngozi Adichie

Listed below are the first British, American, and Nigerian editions (where applicable) of Chimamanda Ngozi Adichie's books. They appear in chronological order of publication.

Decisions. London: Minerva, 1997.

For Love of Biafra. Ibadan: Spectrum, 1998.

Purple Hibiscus. Chapel Hill: Algonquin Books of Chapel Hill, 2003; London: Fourth Estate, 2004; Lagos: Farafina, 2004.

Half of a Yellow Sun. London: Fourth Estate, 2006; New York: Alfred A. Knopf, 2006; Lagos: Farafina, 2006.

The Thing around Your Neck. London: Fourth Estate, 2009; New York: Alfred A. Knopf, 2009; Lagos: Farafina, 2009.

Americanah. London: Fourth Estate, 2013; New York: Alfred A. Knopf, 2013; Lagos: Farafina, 2013.

We Should All Be Feminists. New York: Vintage, 2014 [e-book]; London: Fourth Estate, 2014; Lagos: Narrative Landscape Press, 2018.

Dear Ijeawele, or A Feminist Manifesto in Fifteen Suggestions. London: Fourth Estate, 2017; New York: Alfred A. Knopf, 2017; Lagos: Farafina, 2017.

Contents

Introduction

"Interviews get you into trouble," I told Chimamanda Ngozi Adichie when we met in London in October 2018, as part of a conversation that was to be published in the present volume. The Nigerian writer offered no immediate verbal response, but the expression on her face suggested agreement—or, more emphatically even, something along the lines of "You're telling *me*."

To readers who have followed Adichie's career since the publication of her debut novel, *Purple Hibiscus* (2003), the above exchange should come as no surprise. Indeed, it is hardly an exaggeration to say that the author's interviews have caused greater upheaval, whether on social media or in the press, than all of her fiction put together; only the reactions to some of her nonfictional pieces have equaled the storms of controversies that her interviews have generated. The reason for this general agitation is twofold at least. On the one hand, Adichie is a writer who speaks her mind—and unapologetically so—on sensitive topics such as gender and politics, in a manner that might challenge some of her audience's preconceptions, or in a way that raises moral and social questions more easily cast aside with invective than contested on the basis of sound reasoning. On the other hand, in the case of written interviews, some of the debates have been sparked—or at least fueled—by the way in which the writer's words have been edited on the page. Well beyond Adichie's individual case, this particular point emphasizes the fact that the interview, as a genre, is not only overtly polyphonic in its inclusion of the voices of interviewer and interviewee, but also covertly so. Indeed, while the purpose of published conversations is ostensibly to showcase the voice of an interviewee, the editorial choices involved in presenting the subject's responses conceal traces of at least one other person's consciousness—hence, of at least one other set of ideologies, and sometimes even motivations. Oral interviews too, often conducted in front of a live audience, bring with them their own complications, ranging from instances of misunderstood questions (a problem compounded when simultaneous translation is involved) to cases of missed irony, sometimes with adverse consequences.[1]

However, controversies and video clips gone viral should not obscure the important reasons that provided the impetus for the present volume: namely, that the many interviews granted by Adichie over the years have allowed her to illuminate some of the most intriguing and thought-provoking aspects of her fictional and nonfictional work, and that the conversations she has held with journalists, critics, and writers have provided her with an extraordinary platform to share her reflections as a public intellectual. Most importantly, this book aims to emphasize that interviews, especially when given over a period of time, also tell a story—or, more accurately perhaps, they tell *stories*. Among the many tales contained within the pages of this volume, I will briefly outline four.

The first story retraced in this book is, quite naturally, that of its protagonist, Chimamanda Ngozi Adichie, whose opinions shared in interviews coalesce into a fascinating portrait that presents both abiding features and gradual transformations. For example, the reader who goes through the volume chronologically will soon notice that Adichie's assertiveness is a distinctive personality trait that found expression well before she acquired the writerly authority granted by her literary success. Even in early interviews, the author does not hesitate to politely but firmly disagree with the premise of a question put to her, or to resist the imposition of readings of her work that she perceives to be debatable at best. This frankness leads to constructive exchanges, for instance, in her interviews with political scientist and anthropologist Wale Adebanwi, both of which have been included in this book. Another constant across time is that Adichie, though endowed with a characteristic level-headedness, is also occasionally given to romanticization; she is, however, equally prone to recognizing this trait in herself (see Adebanwi's first interview, Wachtel, and Rifbjerg, this volume). Here is an instance where, one might say, the personality of the writer matches the content of her work, for, if Adichie's fiction sometimes depicts idealized romantic love or feelings of nostalgia, these rarely come without a critique of the political, social, or personal conditions that shape or hinder the expression of these powerful human emotions.

Continuities such as those mentioned above contrast with developments over the years—most notably, there are changes in both tone and content in the writer's observations about her position on the literary scene and beyond. Adichie has evolved from a young university graduate and freshly published author (see Daniels and Wickett, this volume) to a global literary superstar, makeup ambassador (see Wischhover, this volume), and "feminist icon," and in interviews she is increasingly invited to engage in self-reflection about her status as a public figure. If the writer herself has rejected the term "celebrity" as a descriptor, arguing that the word makes her think of "more visually public figures . . . , like actors and musicians" (Nwonwu, this volume), she has come to acknowledge and even critically analyze the impact of her success on the reception of her works—or, indeed, on the reception of her every word—and the consequences of this on her own way of apprehending the world (see Tunca, this volume).

If the first story recounted in this collection is that of the interviewee, the second is that of her interviewers. Of course, this tale is intimately linked to the first, but it is more appositely discussed under a different rubric as it bespeaks a more general trend in literary circles, especially where African writers are concerned. At the time when Adichie was writing her first short stories for American and British literary journals and releasing her first novel, she was one of a handful of young African writers who were being published internationally. The paucity in numbers was such that Adichie, when asked about the state of African literature, declared: "African literature is clearly in decline. Very few works of fiction and poetry get published these days" (Santi 2004, 69). Today, following the rise of "new" African writing on the international scene, such a statement appears oddly outdated. However, Adichie's then relative isolation as an emerging African writer largely conditioned early responses to her work in the West.[2] It was common for interviewers (in otherwise highly interesting Q&As, some included in this volume) to ask the author to provide facts about her country of origin so as to enlighten potentially clueless audiences, a tendency that effectively turned the creative writer into a "native informant" of sorts. Remarkably, Adichie often managed to infuse her answers with interesting comments about colonialism, or to make polite statements that emphasized her limited knowledge about Northern Nigeria, thereby pointing to major cultural and political differences within her home country. This "native informant" line of questioning has never entirely disappeared—witness how many times Adichie has been asked to comment on the Northern Muslim fundamentalist group Boko Haram over the years—but in recent times the writer has rather been turned into an expert whose valued *opinion* is sought out. That Adichie has come to be regarded as a serious social commentator is a largely positive development. For example, in the wake of the publication of *Half of a Yellow Sun* (2006), journalists and critics regularly solicited her views on the Biafran war, the historical event at the center of her book. This interest allowed the writer to share her analysis of the conflict and to engage in topical discussions about the war's aftermath and its repercussions in

twenty-first-century Nigeria. Thus, Adichie rapidly became a key participant in the conversation that she had hoped that her novel would initiate
(see Adebanwi's second interview, this volume, as well as the Q&A published on Adichie's website prior to the publication of *Half of a Yellow Sun*,
also included in the following pages). Similarly, Adichie developed over
the years into a vocal commentator on religion in Nigeria and abroad, for
instance offering sharp observations on the prominent phenomenon of
Pentecostalism (see especially VanZanten, this volume).

Adichie continued to be cast into the role of social commentator after
the publication of her third novel, *Americanah* (2013), a context in which
she provided insightful reflections on the topic of race in the US and,
increasingly, on American politics (see Rifbjerg, Otas, and Hall, this volume). However, there is also a sense in which the conversation around
Americanah, especially in Europe and the US, stalled more quickly than it
should have. Indeed, the author was often asked similar questions about her
book, and thus had to summon all her rhetorical creativity to endlessly riff
on the same subjects, all the while watching other important aspects of her
novel being virtually ignored. Needless to say, such a sense of repetitiveness
does not apply to conversations about *Americanah* alone as it concerns, to
an extent, discussions of *Purple Hibiscus* and *Half of a Yellow Sun* as well.
Crucially, this carbon copy effect has become pervasive in interviews with
writers and performers all over the world. In the case that concerns us here,
that of literary conversations, this fact raises an uncomfortable question:
since writers are repeatedly solicited on the same subjects, the ultimate goal
of interviews cannot possibly be to obtain new information about works of
literature or to garner novel opinions. There is, rather, an uneasy sense in
which interviews are all too often diverted from this primary function and
instead made to entertain audiences and serve promotional agendas—those
of event organizers, newspaper editors, and publishers.

In this context, one must refrain from assigning disproportionate blame
to interviewers for any possible lack of imagination, for the problem is
more often than not a shortage of time (needed for preparation) or finan-
cial resources (needed to enlist the help of a research assistant). Moreover,
one might further argue that the contemporary situation, in which writers
are increasingly requested to participate in events and festivals for publicity
purposes, has ultimately contributed to the rise of a new brand of interviewer: the live audience member. Indeed, if a journalist's or literary critic's questions are uninspired, general readers—regardless of geographical
location and cultural background—will jump in as soon as the discussion

is open to the floor and submit the writer to various interrogations that are often tailored to their own personal needs. With regard to Adichie, this tendency has no doubt been encouraged by the publication of her two very practical feminist texts, *We Should All Be Feminists* (2014) and *Dear Ijeawele, or A Feminist Manifesto in Fifteen Suggestions* (2017). In any case, this trend provides an interesting illustration of how paying attention to literary interviewers of all kinds ultimately also allows us to appraise the changing role of the writer in society. As I put it to Adichie in our conversation, there is a sense in which she appears to have become a therapist for her readers—a role that the Nigerian author, who has always favored pragmatism over abstract theory, appears quite happy to fulfil.

Alongside these stories of interviewee and interviewers, this collection also leaves pride of place to the story of Adichie's work itself. Indeed, the volume deliberately includes multiple tales of genesis and inspiration—by this, I mean not only the classic question related to literary influences and genealogies (see Jelly-Schapiro and VanZanten, this volume, for interesting discussions of this), but I also refer to the open-hearted answers given by the writer over the years about the family stories and anecdotes that have inspired her fiction. The existence of these stories confirms what the author has often said about her creative process, namely that her writing is usually driven by observation and by arresting real-life events (however implausible they may be) rather than by a wish to make overt political statements. Beyond the level of anecdote—and disregarding the misguided compulsion to ground *all* fiction in fact—such episodes provide windows onto the worlds that have seized the writer's imagination; occasionally, they also allow readers to substantiate connections that might have been instinctively felt. For example, hearing Adichie talk about the strong spiritual bond that she shares with her great-grandmother Omeni, who inspired the short story "The Headstrong Historian" in the collection *The Thing around Your Neck* (2009a), may prompt a rereading of this text as an oblique autobiography of sorts. Ultimately, because fiction is also, and perhaps primarily so, an act of emotional connection, this volume features several interviews in which Adichie discusses her feelings toward her own characters (see Spencer and VanZanten for comments on Eugene in *Purple Hibiscus*, and Rifbjerg for Adichie's take on Obinze and Kosi in *Americanah*).

The final story contained in this collection is one that readers themselves are invited to put together. If so inclined, they may indeed engage in detective work in order to spot, and then possibly account for, the odd discrepancy in Adichie's replies over the years. Conversely, the consistency in some of the writer's answers reveals an unwavering approach to certain issues whose significance readers are at liberty to assess. In my own experience of reading and listening to Adichie's interviews, I have found the author to be refreshingly outspoken, witty, and funny, but also bitingly sarcastic and impressively skillful even when defending opinions that diverged from my personal beliefs. Readers are, in any case, invited to approach this collection from their own critical vantage point, mindful also that an unreliable narrator-cum-editor has chosen which interviews to include, and has shaped the multiple narratives outlined above. In Adichie's words, "What the journalist [or, here, the scholarly editor] chooses to include or exclude is much more about the journalist [or the scholarly editor] than it is about the subject" (Nwonwu, this volume). This statement quite naturally leads to an important disclaimer, namely that all inadequacies, undue emphases on certain topics, and possible omissions of others, are entirely the result of editorial—not authorial—choices. Chimamanda Ngozi Adichie, who has kindly lent her support to this project and granted me an interview now published in this volume, has neither censored material nor requested that specific conversations be included.

It has thus been a deliberate *editorial* choice to leave out so-called "controversial" interviews—which, in any case, are available online—and instead privilege selected material featuring the writer's responses to the vigorous discussions in which she has been involved. For example, in her interview with Mazi Nwonwu, Adichie addresses at some length the commotion that followed an interview published in the *Boston Review* (Bady 2013), in which issues of editing, along with the loss of tonal nuance involved in the conversation's transcription to the page, obscured the intention behind some of the writer's declarations. In her interview with Tom Hall, also included in this volume, Adichie is given the opportunity to comment on another controversy, which was sparked by her declaration that the experiences of trans women differed from those of women who had been born female (Newman 2017). Finally, in my own interview with the author, I invited Adichie to expand on the reactions that she met following her interview with Hillary Clinton (Adichie 2018b). In this public conversation, the writer had indeed told the former Secretary of State and presidential candidate that she felt "just a little bit upset" that the first word in the politician's Twitter descriptor was "wife," whereas the first word in Clinton's spouse Bill's was not "husband." Clinton responded that, "Well, when you put it like that, I'm going to change it" (Adichie 2018b)—which she did. Adichie's intervention, which was mainly perceived as an amusing feminist anecdote in the West, created a storm of controversy in Nigeria, where many accused her of disrespecting the institution of marriage.

The many passionate reactions provoked by Adichie's declarations over the years—whether these responses be favorable or hostile—undeniably testify to the considerable public influence that the writer has come to exert. While the ramifications of this influence are still being debated, its existence can hardly be doubted. For example, in an extensive profile article published in the *New Yorker* in June 2018, Larissa MacFarquhar wrote that "[Adichie's] publisher tells her that the most pirated books in Nigeria are her novels, books by T. D. Jakes (the pastor of an American megachurch), and the Bible." The mildly blasphemous conclusion to this statement is left unwritten, but the suggestion is explicit enough to allow readers to get a clear sense of Adichie's clout in Nigeria. Internationally too, her works have come to be prominently displayed in countless bookshops, and her two TED talks, "The Danger of a Single Story" (2009b) and "We Should All Be Feminists" (2012), have currently accumulated over thirty million views across YouTube and the TED website. No wonder, then, that Adichie's words have given rise to such large numbers of discussions—vigorous debates that, above all, testify to the provocative nature of the writer's pronouncements. As Matthew Lecznar puts it, Adichie's "intellectual interventions, in all their varied shades, represent a vital resource and provocation for those struggling to live ethically in this globalised and precarious age" (2019, 44). Meanwhile, as scholars and general readers are intensely debating the philosophical and political foundations of Adichie's worldview, thereby consolidating her status as a global superstar, the writer more modestly describes herself as "a storyteller" (e.g. 2009b, 2018c; see also Jelly-Schapiro and Wachtel, this volume). Even if, as mentioned in the opening of this introduction, interviews are always shaped and framed by external agents, it is hoped that the specific conversations included in this volume leave enough room for Chimamanda Ngozi Adichie to be precisely who she wishes to be: someone who tells her own stories, not through the lives and minds of her characters this time, but in her own voice.

References

Adichie, Chimamanda Ngozi. 2003. *Purple Hibiscus*. Chapel Hill: Algonquin Books of Chapel Hill.
Adichie, Chimamanda Ngozi. 2006. *Half of a Yellow Sun*. London: Fourth Estate.
Adichie, Chimamanda Ngozi. 2009a. *The Thing aound Your Neck*. London: Fourth Estate.

Adichie, Chimamanda Ngozi. 2009b. "The Danger of a Single Story." *TED: Ideas Worth Spreading*. http://www.ted.com/talks/chimamanda_adichie_the_danger_of_a_single_story.

Adichie, Chimamanda Ngozi. 2012. "We Should All Be Feminists." *TED: Ideas Worth Spreading*. http://www.ted.com/talks/chimamanda_ngozi_adichie_we_should_all_be_feminists.

Adichie, Chimamanda Ngozi. 2013. *Americanah*. London: Fourth Estate.

Adichie, Chimamanda Ngozi. 2014. *We Should All Be Feminists*. New York: Vintage.

Adichie, Chimamanda Ngozi. 2017. *Dear Ijeawele, or A Feminist Manifesto in Fifteen Suggestions*. London: Fourth Estate.

Adichie, Chimamanda Ngozi. 2018a. "On Bookshops—Not Libraries—in Nigeria." *Facebook*, 26 January. http://www.facebook.com/chimamandaadichie/posts/10155852122695944.

Adichie, Chimamanda Ngozi. 2018b. "2018 #FreedomToWrite Lecture: Hillary Rodham Clinton with Chimamanda Ngozi Adichie." *YouTube*, uploaded by PEN America on 23 April. http://www.youtube.com/watch?v=-kemFB24Xhs&.

Adichie, Chimamanda Ngozi. 2018c. Speech delivered at the opening press conference of the Frankfurt Book Fair, 9 October. http://www.publishersweekly.com/pw/by-topic/international/Frankfurt-Book-Fair/article/78342-frankfurt-book-fair-2018-why-chimamanda-adichie-will-not-shut-up.html.

Bady, Aaron. 2013. "The Varieties of Blackness." *Boston Review*, 10 June. http://bostonreview.net/fiction/varieties-blackness.

Broué, Caroline. 2018. "Nuit des idées 2018—Quai d'Orsay ." *YouTube*, broadcast live by Ministère de l'Europe et des affaires étrangères on 25 January. http://www.youtube.com/watch?v=oNLQfXOoodM.

Lecznar, Matthew. 2019. "Intellectual Interventions: Chimamanda Ngozi Adichie and the Ethics of Texture and Messiness." *Wasafiri* 34(1): 38–45. doi: 10.1080/02690055.2019.1544762.

MacFarquhar, Larissa. 2018. "Chimamanda Ngozi Adichie Comes to Terms with Global Fame." *New Yorker*, 4 June. http://www.newyorker.com/magazine/2018/06/04/chimamanda-ngozi-adichie-comes-to-terms-with-global-fame.

Newman, Cathy. 2017. "Chimamanda Ngozi Adichie on Feminism." *Channel 4*, 10 March. http://www.channel4.com/news/chimamanda-ngozi-adichie-on-feminism.

Santi, Behlor. 2004. "*Writers Notes* Speaks with Chimamanda Ngozi Adichie, Author of *Purple Hibiscus*." *Writers Notes Magazine* 1: 65–70.

Notes

1. A well-known incident in this regard occurred when Adichie gave a public interview in Paris in January 2018, during which she was asked whether there were any bookshops in Nigeria. The writer, along with most of the people in the audience, missed the irony that was supposed to hide behind the interviewer's mock-impersonation of an ignorant French person, and offered a scathing reply: "I think it reflects poorly on French people that you asked that question" (Broué 2018). To make the misunderstanding complete, the word "bookshop" in the journalist's question, an interrogative sentence uttered in French, was mistakenly translated by the interpreter as "library," due to its closeness to

the French word for "bookshop," *librairie*. The video of the exchange immediately went viral on social media. Shortly thereafter, Adichie posted a clarification on her Facebook page, which explained her initial reaction to the question and came to the defence of the unfortunate journalist—whose "genuine, if flat, attempt at irony" did not warrant for her to be "publicly pilloried" (Adichie 2018a). However, this did little to appease the commotion at the time. Perhaps the awkward exchange was, for some, too good a story to let go. In any case, this incident demonstrates the limited control that public figures such as Adichie have over the dissemination of their own declarations in interviews. For a discussion of the controversy, see Lecznar (2019).

2. I deliberately use the term "West" as opposed to the more contemporary "global North" to signal the relevance of colonial history to the patterns that have surrounded the reception of Adichie's work. I am aware that, in using such a general label, I am lumping together vastly different cultures and territories, but I do believe that Western countries share enough commonalities in their responses to Adichie's writing for this association to be valid in the present context. Needless to say, an in-depth study focusing on the reception of Adichie's works would need to be more nuanced in making territorial demarcations. A similar comment applies to references to large countries such as Nigeria, where responses have been influenced by internal differences.

Acknowledgments

First and foremost, I would like to express my deepest gratitude to Chimamanda Ngozi Adichie for her generous support of this project. Her help has taken many forms, from granting me an extensive interview for this volume, to dealing with copyright issues that would otherwise have made it impossible to reprint previously published pieces. My thanks also go to Ms. Adichie's assistant manager at the time when this book was in its editing phase, Mureji Fatunde, who ensured the smooth running of all our interactions, and attended to numerous organizational and administrative matters.

I wish to express my appreciation to the individual interviewers whose pieces appear in this book, many of whom either personally granted me permission to use their work or liaised with editors and publishers to clear copyright: Wale Adebanwi, Eve Daniels, Tom Hall, Joshua Jelly-Schapiro, Mazi Nwonwu, Belinda Otas, Synne Rifbjerg, Daniel Spencer, Susan VanZanten, Dan Wickett, and Cheryl Wischhover.

I am also indebted to my colleagues and friends Bénédicte Ledent, Izuu Nwankwọ, Rebecca Romdhani, and Malica S. Willie, for providing crucial help at various stages in this project. Finally, I would also like to thank my coworkers at the University of Liège in Belgium, especially the members of the postcolonial research group CEREP, for indulging me while I obsessively brought up Chimamanda Ngozi Adichie in nearly every professional conversation that we had over the past fifteen years.

Chronology

1977 Chimamanda Ngozi Adichie is born on 15 September in Enugu, Nigeria, the fifth of sixth children to Igbo parents, Grace Ifeoma and James Nwoye Adichie. Her mother, a graduate in sociology, was the first female registrar at the University of Nigeria, Nsukka; her father was Nigeria's first professor of statistics at the same institution, where he also served as Deputy Vice-Chancellor.

1983–95 Attends the University of Nigeria Primary School, and then the University of Nigeria Secondary School, where she wins several awards for her academic excellence.

1995–97 Studies medicine, and then pharmacy, at the University of Nigeria, before deciding to quit and pursue her education in the United States.

1997 Publishes her first book, the collection of poems *Decisions*.

1997–99 Is awarded the Anthony J. Drexel Scholarship for Academic Excellence and attends Drexel University in Philadelphia for two years, studying communication.

1998 Publishes her first play, *For Love of Biafra*.

1999 Moves to Connecticut and transfers to Eastern Connecticut State University.

2001 Graduates *summa cum laude* from Eastern Connecticut State University with a major in communication and a minor in political science.

2003 Publishes her first novel, *Purple Hibiscus*, and obtains an MA in creative writing from John Hopkins University.

2004 Is shortlisted for the Orange Prize for Fiction, for *Purple Hibiscus*.

2005 Is awarded the Commonwealth Writers' Prize for Best First Book, for *Purple Hibiscus*.

2005–06 Holds a Hodder Fellowship at Princeton University.

2006 Publishes her second novel, *Half of a Yellow Sun*.

2007   Is awarded the Orange Broadband Prize for Fiction, for *Half of a Yellow Sun*.

2008   Earns an MA in African studies from Yale University, and is awarded a MacArthur Foundation "Genius" Grant.

2009   Publishes her first collection of short stories, *The Thing around Your Neck*, and delivers the speech "The Danger of a Single Story" at the TED global conference in Oxford.

2011–12   Holds a fellowship awarded by the Radcliffe Institute for Advanced Study at Harvard University.

2012   Delivers the speech "We Should All Be Feminists" at the TEDx-Euston conference in London.

2013   Publishes her third novel, *Americanah*, earning several awards and distinctions, including the National Book Critics Circle Award for Fiction. *Americanah* is also listed as one of the "Ten Best Books of 2013" by the *New York Times Book Review*.

2014   *We Should All Be Feminists* is published in book format.

2015   Wins the "Best of the Best" of the second decade of the Baileys Women's Prize for Fiction (formerly the Orange Broadband Prize for Fiction), for *Half of a Yellow Sun*.

2017   Publishes *Dear Ijeawele, or A Feminist Manifesto in Fifteen Suggestions*.

2018   Is awarded the PEN Pinter Prize.

Conversations with
Chimamanda Ngozi Adichie

A Q&A with Chimamanda Adichie

Eve Daniels / 2003

From *Talking Volumes*, Minnesota Public Radio, 21 August 2003. © 2003 Minnesota Public Radio®. Used with permission. All rights reserved.

Eve Daniels: What led to your decision to pursue a writing career?
Chimamanda Ngozi Adichie: I didn't ever consciously decide to pursue writing. I've been writing since I was old enough to spell, and just sitting down and writing made me feel incredibly fulfilled. I may have considered other careers to make a living, since I wasn't sure I could do it from writing, but I have never thought actively about my choice to write. I just write. I have to write. I like to say that I didn't choose writing, writing chose me.

ED: What or who inspires you as a writer?
CNA: This may sound slightly mystical, but I sometimes feel as if my writing is something bigger than I am. There are days when I sit at my laptop and will myself to write and nothing happens. There are other days when I have things to do but feel compelled to write. And the writing just flows out. I am never sure what triggers these "inspirations," if that is what they are. More mundanely, the rituals and geography of specific places inspire me—the chaotic energy of Lagos, the sereneness of Nsukka, the insular calm of Mansfield, Connecticut. And I love observing people and tiny details about them. I often get the urge to write from imagining or inventing lives for people I don't know.

ED: What's the significance of your book's title?
CNA: Purple hibiscuses feature in a symbolic way in the novel. Also, we had different species of red and white hibiscuses back home in Nigeria, but I had never seen a purple one. In fact, I thought I had invented the purple hibiscus until my editor told me they are quite common in the US!

ED: How much of your novel was drawn from real people and experiences in your life?

CNA: I grew up in a university town, in a close-knit, moderately Catholic family, and I observed many of Nigeria's political upheavals. So the themes in the novel—family, religion, politics—are drawn from real life. But the characters are mine and are not based on anybody I know, at least not consciously. The exception is the character Mama Joe, the eccentric, interesting, and sweet woman who braided my hair for many years. I wanted to pay tribute to her!

ED: Since much of your writing is set in Nigeria, what are the challenges in writing for an American audience?

CNA: There are things I have to make a little more of an effort to make clear, things I have to find subtle ways to explain, since they would be unfamiliar to an American audience. That said, I do think that *Purple Hibiscus* tells a universal story, one that we can all identify with because of that basic human quality that we have.

ED: Do you think that your writing has potential to broaden American perspectives of Africa and its cultures?

CNA: Absolutely. There is very little knowledge of contemporary Africa in the US. In addition, the "war and hunger" kind of coverage Africa gets in the news distorts reality. Of course there are wars and there is hunger in many African countries, but there are also millions of normal people who are going about their lives, with gains and losses, love and pain, just like everyone else. I hope my fiction will enable Americans to see those human, and in many ways ordinary, lives of Nigerians. I hope also that more contemporary African fiction will be published in the US, because fiction, I think, is one of the best ways to open our eyes to cultures different from ours.

ED: Was it challenging to write about politics and religion from the perspective of a fifteen-year-old?

CNA: It is always challenging to write about politics and religion while telling an interesting story that will hold your reader. I think a younger narrator made me more careful not to overburden my fiction with polemics, or with my own politics. It is also more believable to see the complexities and absurdities of religion through the eyes of a younger person who is not cynical or jaded.

ED: Past *Talking Volumes* authors have included Salman Rushdie, Margaret Atwood, and Amy Tan. What's it like to be among such literary heavyweights? **CNA:** Flattering. But really, I am more excited simply to have an opportunity to open my world to people who would never have read about Nigeria otherwise. I am thrilled that there are people who will get to "see" the lovely, declining town where most of the novel is set, who will laugh and cry with an Igbo family, and who will, hopefully, look out for my next book!

Interview with Chimamanda Ngozi Adichie

Dan Wickett / 2004

From *Emerging Writers Forum*, April 2004. Reprinted by permission.

The following is an interview with Chimamanda Ngozi Adichie, author of the novel *Purple Hibiscus*, as well as many shorter works, both fiction and non. She is currently at John Hopkins University in order to obtain her master's degree. Born in Nigeria, she now splits her time between the United States and there.

Dan Wickett: Thank you very much for spending some time answering these questions.
Chimamanda Ngozi Adichie: You're welcome.

DW: You originally hail from Nigeria. For those of us uninformed, what is Nigeria's history? Was it at one point a colonized nation? If so, by whom? When did it gain independence and was it done so peacefully? What sort of government is in place nowadays?
CNA: Nigeria was created by a British governor in 1914. It became independent in 1960 and yes, it was a relatively peaceful independence although I am wary of this idea of a "peaceful independence." What I think is important is not so much how independence was achieved, as what independence meant. It meant that a country clobbered together for British imperial purposes and run for decades by an authoritarian colonial government was now supposed to pull a perfect democracy from the air. Of course that didn't happen. After a few years of so-called democracy, the cycle of coups began, and we have mostly had military governments. We have a democratic government now, which is just as ineffective as the preceding military ones.

DW: You came to the United States in 1997, having switched from a path in medicine to studying communication at Drexel University. What led you to this big move? Was it in part due to your change of majors?

CNA: Yes. I'd been on the "science track" back home and I couldn't just switch to the arts or social sciences. I was very keen to leave medicine and do something very different from the sciences.

DW: You then switched schools again, finishing your degrees at Eastern Connecticut State University. What prompted that change?

CNA: My sister lived in Connecticut. I wanted somewhere to live rent-free.

DW: Did you avoid getting a degree in English or creative writing for any specific reason?

CNA: I wanted to learn more than just what to read into what I read, if that makes sense. I have read books since I was a toddler and I rather like the sense of independence that comes with simply loving books and developing an individual sense of what works and what doesn't. I am not a believer in canons; I am a believer in strong character and strong prose. Besides, I am very much interested in the media and politics.

DW: Your father was the Deputy Vice-Chancellor. What does that position entail?

CNA: It meant, I suppose, that he played second fiddle in university administrative affairs. He worked for more than thirty years as a professor of statistics at the University of Nigeria and happens to be the most interesting man I know. He is retired now.

DW: You have always done very well in school, attaining top grades in your junior and senior year in high school, and graduating *summa cum laude*. Do you think that this has helped you out at all in your writing career?

CNA: It probably hindered my writing, considering that many nights I could have spent writing fiction were wasted on studying for exams.

DW: I understand that you're writing a second novel about Biafra, and the war that went on in the past. Is this something that is taught well in Nigerian schools, or are children growing up over there as poorly informed about their country's history as those here are?

CNA: Yes. But I would be circumspect about drawing such direct parallels with American children because I think the Nigerian case is a little more insidious. There is a deeply politicized feeling among many Nigerians that Biafra should be forgotten, that we should all behave as if it never happened and that those who do bring it up are troublemakers, or secessionists or whatever. Biafra is a very important part of our history, and many of the issues surrounding the war are still unresolved, but what worries me most is that we seem to think these issues will go away if we simply pretend they are not there.

DW: You've also written poetry, short fiction, short nonfiction, and your novel, *Purple Hibiscus*. Do you prefer writing in one of these forms over the others, and if so, why?

CNA: No. I think different subjects call for different forms, and I enjoy all, although I don't write much poetry now.

DW: You've seen a certain amount of success with your short fiction, winning the PEN/David Wong Prize for short fiction, receiving an O'Henry Award, and being nominated for the 2002 Caine Prize for African Writing. Is there a collection of short fiction in the near future?

CNA: Not in the too-near future. I want to be certain about what stories belong together in a collection first and that sort of thing.

DW: How did winning any of the aforementioned awards, or in the case of the Caine Prize, the nomination, affect your writing, if at all?

CNA: The Caine Prize not much really, because although it may have given me the opportunity to find an agent, I already had an agent and a book contract when I was shortlisted. The PEN award was a lovely surprise. I sometimes think that writing often becomes a pathetic little exercise of seeking validation, and to be chosen by J. M. Coetzee and Michele Roberts, both of whom I much respect, was definitely a good source of validation! That said, I'm not sure it really affected my writing. Nor did the O'Henry Prize, which also came as a very pleasant surprise and validation.

DW: In both your short fiction and your novel, you have had characters speaking Igbo. In cases where you use a character's native language like this, do you feel a need to add the English translation for the reader to more easily be able to understand what is going on in the story?

CNA: I use Igbo words or phrases to remind the reader, from time to time, that the characters are not speaking English. I don't always translate these because I don't think they come in the way of understanding the dialogue itself. Of course, I'll find a subtle way to explain some things that I think do come in the way of comprehension.

DW: Am I misinterpreting your having trouble with the institution of marriage based on the works that I've read? There doesn't seem to be any examples of good marriages in your fiction—the short story "Transition to Glory" has a case of adultery, and *Purple Hibiscus* has an abusive husband. Am I reading too much into that?
CNA: Perhaps. I do have what I think is a healthy skepticism about marriage, indeed about most social institutions. That said, my parents have a wonderful marriage (so I am not lacking for good models), but bad marriages really make for more interesting reading than good ones, don't they?

DW: In *Purple Hibiscus*, you bring up a situation I've seen before, both in fiction and nonfiction, that of an elder relative remaining a believer in the gods of the culture, and not becoming Catholic. Is this very common, and does an opposite situation ever come forth—that where a father and mother adopt Catholicism as their religion, but their offspring want to follow the traditional religion of their grandparents and before?
CNA: Yes, it is fairly common and if the opposite situation exists, then I haven't seen it. What I have seen are cases where people like me come to learn how wrong they have been to condemn their history in the name of a colonized Christianity. But we have already been too Christianized and so we then exist in this gray area of being Christian of sorts but trying to hold on to a slice of our past which we perhaps do not entirely understand. I don't know enough about the way Igbo religion was practiced in precolonial times because the old ways are often labeled "satanic," even more so now with the wave of fundamentalist, materialistic, self-absorbed Christianity that is sweeping across Nigeria. Born-again Christians at home often claim that everything "traditional" from the kolanut to the village herbalist is the spawn of Satan.

DW: *Purple Hibiscus* has been, or will be, published in the UK, Australia, Spain, Germany, and in Dutch. Do you actually have at least one of each of these editions, or plan to? What was it like hearing that your book would be available to so many more people than if it were just being printed in English?
CNA: I have the UK edition but the rest don't come out until this fall (it will be published in France and Israel as well). It was exciting hearing about

the foreign rights sales, but I suppose it will be even more so when I see the actual books printed in languages I can't read.

DW: Do you have a regular writing routine?
CNA: No. I write when it comes, so to speak.

DW: It seems that in the past few years, there have been more books written about Africa that avoid the clichéd looks at warring nations and starving children. Have you had the chance to read any of the following: *Slim* by Ruth Linnea Whitney, *He Sleeps* by Reginald McKnight, or *The Road Builder* by Nicholas Hershenow? Is this something that you hope to see more of in the future?
CNA: Of course. But I think we have to understand that although warring nations and starving children may be clichéd and a little crude, the mindset that supports these stereotypes still persists. That is the problem. Have you wondered why reviewers and blurb-writers are quick to reassure readers that a book about Africa (usually one written by a Black African about Black Africans) is NOT JUST AN AFRICAN BOOK BUT IS UNIVERSAL, as well? As if "African" and "Universal" are mutually exclusive. Nobody ever informs the reader that a great English or American novel is universal because the assumption, of course, is that it is.

The Heart of Darkness image of Africa, where Africa is the possibly subhuman "other," a place for the West to test its humanness, is still very apparent in many books written about Africa. The difference today is that the Africans are given an odd quirkiness that we are supposed to read as the politically correct "dignity," and they are not called "savage," although the subtexts usually suggest that they are. (Perhaps not in the books you mention, although I have only read Reginald McKnight's.) I find it troubling that people like Ryszard Kapuscinski are hailed as the definitive voice on all things African, although many Africans would disagree.

I wish that the West would stop wanting to see Africa though West-tinted eyes and that they would confront Africa in all its complexity through the eyes of Africans themselves.

DW: Thanks again for taking the time, and good luck with the novel!
CNA: Thanks.

"Nigerian Identity Is Burdensome": The Chimamanda Ngozi Adichie Interview

Wale Adebanwi / 2004

This Day, 9 May 2004. Reprinted by permission of Wale Adebanwi, who is the Rhodes Professor of Race Relations and the Director of the African Studies Centre at the University of Oxford, UK. He was a Bill and Melinda Gates Scholar at Trinity Hall, Cambridge University, UK, when he had the interview with the author.

The initial announcement that *Purple Hibiscus*, the debut novel by young Nigerian writer Chimamanda Ngozi Adichie, had been shortlisted for the prestigious British literary award, the Orange Prize, worth £30,000 (about ₦ 6 million), alongside award-winning writers, delighted Nigerians across the world. She was yet another example of the abundance of literary talents in the country, literary enthusiasts affirmed. This was to be further confirmed when the book made the final list of six shortlisted books, including *Oryx and Crake* by Booker Prize winner Margaret Atwood, *The Great Fire* by US prize-winning Shirley Hazzard, *The Ice Road* by Gillian Slovo, *The Colour* by multiple prize winner Rose Tremain, and *Small Island* by Andrea Levy.

Twenty-seven-year-old US-based Chimamanda is the daughter of a former deputy vice-chancellor of the University of Nigeria, Nsukka. The family once lived in the house where one of Nigeria's best-known writers, Chinua Achebe, also once lived. She studied medicine in Nsukka before heading for the United States at nineteen to study communication and political science at Eastern Connecticut State University. Presently, she is attending writing seminars at Johns Hopkins University, in the US. A bookseller's website praised *Purple Hibiscus*, which revolves around fifteen-year-old Kambili, as "a stunning debut that captures the fragile beauty of a young woman's awakening at a time when both country and family are on the cusp of change." The winner of the prize will be announced in June. She had the following chat with UK-based Nigerian scholar and writer, Wale Adebanwi, through the net.

Wale Adebanwi: You seem to be conscious of plugging into a cultural tradition in *Purple Hibiscus*. I mean, you start with "Things began to fall apart . . ." And then one can see a no-longer-at-ease paradigm running through the narrative, and the arrow of God piecing some people, with a few becoming men of the people. Are you in the course of reproducing Achebe with an eye on late twentieth- and early twenty-first-century sociopolitical dynamics in Nigeria?

Chimamanda Ngozi Adichie: No, at least not consciously. I am certain that a different reader may see other paradigms running through the narrative. The first line is indeed a tribute to (Prof. Chinua) Achebe, who remains the most important writer for me. But I am not interested in reproducing him, or anyone else. I am interested, rather, in writing about Nigerian issues in a way that acknowledges my influences and yet remains entirely mine.

WA: One gets, at best, a very soft irritation with Kambili's father's religiosity in the narrative. By overrepresenting this religiosity, are you offering a critique of the understated socioreligious fundamentalism that hides behind many of the so-called "God-fearing" public figures in Nigeria?

CNA: I don't think his religiosity is overrepresented. Or if it is seen as being overrepresented, then perhaps that is the point; he is, after all, a fanatical believer. Neither do I think that the religious fundamentalism in Nigeria is understated. I think it is troublingly overt. More so because religion in Nigeria has become insular, self-indulgent, self-absorbed, self-congratulatory. Churches spring up day after day while corruption thrives as much as ever and God becomes the watchman standing behind you while you seek your self-interest at all cost. God loves you more than others. God wants you to be rich. God wants you to buy that new car. That sort of rhetoric probably has a lot to do with the state of our economy and the experience of living in a place of scarce resources, but it is self-defeating. There will never be social cohesion or social consciousness. We will all never be rich. Even morality—I mean that simple idea of right and wrong where "wrong" is judged by whether or not your action hurts another person—will not exist. Kambili's father, for all of his fundamentalism, at least has a sense of social consciousness that is expansive and proactive and USEFUL, so while his character may be seen as a critique of fundamentalism, the God-fearing public in Nigeria can learn a bit from him as well.

WA: I look at the social condition of Kambili's aunt as a mirror of the crisis of higher education in Nigeria. A university lecturer long overdue for senior lecturership cannot afford milk! Is this the future?

CNA: The hope, of course, is that it isn't. But it may well be, if we continue to neglect higher education and build a university for each village in order to sate political egos and then use interesting words like "autonomy" to insist that these universities pull funding from thin air. I had a wonderful childhood in the university town of Nsukka, my parents retired as dedicated and passionate university people and so, naturally, I feel very strongly about the rapid decline of higher education.

WA: Your story mirrors the multilayered and multifaceted decadence in Nigeria, but you seem to sidestep what the future holds in stock. Two issues. One, is it that you don't want to be a prophet (whether of doom or gloom)? Two, do you think literature—as Seamus Heaney wishes for poetry—can be "strong enough to help"?

CNA: I have no wish to be a prophet of any kind. I am interested in reflecting my own version of reality and more so in the past and present than in the future. I am not familiar with the Seamus Heaney quote. But I suppose I do wish that literature can be strong enough to help. But help in what way? If literature can affect the way one person thinks, then perhaps it has helped.

WA: On the heels of my last question, you try in this book to tell the terrifying story of Nigeria in a very subtle way. Does the telling heal you too, as an individual who lived under those terror regimes and who also has to carry that increasingly burdensome Nigerian identity around the world?

CNA: I am ambivalent about this idea of writing only as therapy, because if so I might as well just write in a private journal. I don't claim to write just for myself. That said, the Nigerian identity is burdensome, what with the suspicion at airports and being told you can't pay with a credit card for Nigerian-related things, and the total lack of dignity we encounter at embassies and things of that sort, but I have never wished that I had a different identity. Instead what I have wished—and what I often insist on in my life and in my writing—is that my identity be treated as having a different—and much lighter—baggage.

WA: What are you trying to say with the physical possibilities between Kambili, an adorable young girl, and the boyish Catholic priest? Are you, as a secular Catholic—if you could be called that—deconstructing the religious order? Or is this a statement of the impossibility of asexual life?

CNA: I think celibacy is a plausible choice. However, I am not convinced that it is a necessary requirement for the Catholic priesthood. I question this even more in the context of African Catholicism where there is incredible hypocrisy on this subject. Still, I don't think I'm deconstructing the priesthood at all; I don't quite feel equipped to do that. For all its faults and hypocrisies—and there are quite a few—there is much to admire in the Catholic priesthood. I think that the boyish Catholic priest is simply a human being, one who does not claim perfection of any sort, who is clearly running the race just like any other member of his congregation and who is not beyond or above human desires. As for the physical possibilities between him and Kambili, I think that your question in itself is telling—it shows that we persist in seeing priests as incapable of any physicality. That, of course, is simply untrue. The possibilities, then, are no different from the possibilities between any two characters in fiction.

I'm not sure what secular Catholic means. I AM Catholic. It is an identity that, although I didn't have much of a choice in, I have since taken ownership of. I am very much a Vatican II enthusiast, and think that the Church should make some more changes on its stance on a number of issues. Still, there is much I admire and love in the Church, the rich rituals, the traditions, the commitment that some orders have to social justice and scholarship as well as the sort of outward-looking faith that holds to some vision of a fairer world.

WA: In some sections of your narrative, you seem to be reproducing the Nigerian stereotypes: a Yoruba is editor of a crusading newspaper, a Hausa man is the gatekeeper and the Igbo are all Catholics—except the "heathen" Papa-Nnukwu. How do you respond to this?

CNA: I don't agree at all that a Yoruba as editor of a crusading newspaper is a stereotype. Clearly, Ade Coker is loosely modelled after Dele Giwa, whose death moved me very much, but I'm not sure that qualifies it as a stereotype. The Igbo are not all Catholic in the book, or Kambili's father would not be so disparaging of Pentecostalists in Enugu. That said, I am not a believer in "explaining" my fiction and respect that people will read different things into one book. I think that there is a thin line between literary requirements and the need for authenticity in depicting a particular time and place. I am more interested in authenticity. For me, stereotyping becomes a problem when it is on the character level, so that it is Kambili's mother who I have recently thought to be close to a stereotype, as the rather familiar Battered Woman.

WA: It is interesting how you handle the "banality of evil" in this story, retelling what would seem to be the stories of the killings of Dele Giwa, Ken Saro-Wiwa, Alfred Rewane. But, at the end of your narrative, it is unclear what triumphs. Evil or good? The tyrant dies and the symbol of democratic freedom, Kambili's father, is also killed, even though he had stopped publishing his crusading newspaper. Are you deliberately problematizing (human) consequences?

CNA: I don't need to deliberately problematize them. They are already problematic, aren't they?

WA: I love the metaphor of *aku*, but I wonder if it is not a dangerous metaphor in the context of social change. After *aku* flies, it will still fall to the toad and you only have to wait till the evening when the *aku* would lose its wings and fall down. The evening may not always come, and if it comes at all, it does not come for everybody. While the *aku* flies, millions of lives are being destroyed. When will evening come?

CNA: That will be left to the literary theorists. I wrote that scene out of a sense of nostalgia and nothing else. I wanted to capture the sense of rain-drenched innocence I remember so well from my childhood. There was no intended metaphor.

WA: On the question of exile broached in the narrative, is this the option? Or, is there another option for the thoroughly disillusioned and repressed such as the university lecturer, Aunty Ifeoma?

CNA: Aunty Ifeoma leaves because she is left with no choice. Whether that should be read as a general statement is, of course, debatable. I think each person's condition and context is different and I don't want to make sweeping generalizations about exile.

WA: You can be very romantic in a somewhat off-handed way, Chimamanda. Your character, Kambili, says that the priest is the one "whose voice dictated my dreams." Is there such a person in real life for you? Is someone using his maleness well with you rather than wasting it like the Catholic father in your story?

CNA: "Using his maleness well?" Ha. That is an oddly interesting expression that begs for deconstruction! I don't like to talk about my personal life, Wale. I think that my worldview, on the whole, is a romanticized one, in the sense that I am constantly wishing that the world were safer, kinder, fairer, more honest.

WA: What would you do with the £30,000 Orange Prize if you get it? Would you, like Kambili, give a chunk of it to charity?
CNA: Kambili didn't win a prize. She simply gave away part of a large inheritance. As for the Orange Prize, "if" is the operative word. Let's wait and see, although I have to say that while being on the shortlist has been very good for my novel, I have always hoped for the opportunity to reach higher with each successive book.

WA: What is in the horizon? What's your outlook in life?
CNA: In addition to waving a magic wand and changing the world? Writing.

Morning Yet on Creation Day

Daniel Spencer / 2005

From *Semper Floreat Online* 2 (2005). Reprinted by permission.

Chimamanda Adichie's first novel *Purple Hibiscus* is as quiet as it is brave. The novel explores the tension between Christianity and traditional African spirituality through the eyes of a fifteen-year-old girl. It is the story of Kambili and her father, the zealously religious businessman Eugene. Eugene is respected in the community for his philanthropy and brave support for those who stand up to the dictators that rule Nigeria. At home he is a tyrant and no lapse in religious observance will go unpunished. Kambili finds a new world while visiting the home of Aunty lfeoma and her children in the university town of Nsukka. Though they are so poor they can't afford gas for their car, Aunty lfeoma's family has a dignity and joy in their poverty that Kambili finds invigorating.

Purple Hibiscus is one of those rare novels that highlights and articulates simply and perfectly a societal ill that is not usually spoken about. I had assumed that large chunks of the novel were autobiographical, that the tension between Christianity and so-called idol worship had played on Adichie's mind since she was a child. I was surprised to learn that she is more interested in telling other people's stories.

Daniel Spencer: I understand you lived through some of the events of the book. What was the importance of that particular coup and why did you set the novel at that time?

Chimamanda Ngozi Adichie: What I actually did in *Purple Hibiscus* was to merge events from two periods in Nigerian political history: a number of things that happened under Babangida, who was a dictator we had from 1985 to 1993, and also some things that happened under Abacha, who was there from 1993 to 1998. So the coup is a collage of two coups. I think that period when Nigeria had a series of dictators was very important because it signaled so many things. For me, growing up on a university campus as the daughter of a professor, it meant that my father was no longer paid his salary. So we didn't eat like we used to in the past and we couldn't go shopping as often as before. That's what it meant for me as a child growing up.

DS: So your childhood was quite like that of Aunty Ifeoma's children in your book?

CNA: It wasn't as extreme. Aunty Ifeoma, when she was paid—which wasn't often—was a junior lecturer; she was paid considerably less than a professor. So we did eat slightly better than Aunty Ifeoma's family. It was very important for me to write her story because it really is the story of many people who were at the university at the time. Just because it wasn't my story necessarily, doesn't mean that lots of people didn't live through that.

DS: Another character I wanted to ask about in the book is Eugene. Why has his brand of religious fundamentalism taken root so strongly in Nigeria?

CNA: What I wanted to do with Eugene really was to show how the faith that came with empire produced a lot of extreme confusion. I think he personifies that. This is a man who clearly had issues, issues within himself, but also through the religion that came with colonialism, which came with so much baggage. This was a man who went to school at a time when Christianity was aligned with education. You learned there was a new God, superior to your old God, and this God was white. You had to prove how loyal you were to this new God by how much you could turn your back on the old ways. I think that he is an example of a person who took all this in and his way of handling it was to become an extremist. There are people like him, lots of people like him. When I come across people like him, I often say that they are proof that the empire did a fantastic job.

DS: You refuse to condemn any of the characters in the book. How do you maintain that sort of equipoise in relation to a character like Eugene, when he behaves so foolishly?

CNA: Really, it's because I felt empathy for him and I feel empathy for people like him in real life. I'm the sort of person who tries to understand where people are coming from. I really do care about all my characters because I spend time with them. I was very keen for him not to be easy to dismiss. I think that if you write somebody so extremist and you are not careful to infuse other qualities into him, readers won't take him seriously. They will simply say, "Oh, he's a monster," and that's it. I think people like him are not just black and white monsters, there is a lot of grey in there. It was a conscious effort; it was work to make him have that other side, but I wanted to do that. It was something I set out to do from the beginning.

DS: He is a stark illustration of the dichotomy between our private and public lives. Do you think there is something of Eugene in everyone?

CNA: I think so, I really do. I think that what we call civilization is what teaches us to pretend. Of course it's a question of degree; I mean, he is crazy and extreme and I wanted him to be. I think that when we think we are civilized, we have learned the rules of pretence.

We go out and we do what we are expected to, but inside of us there is something that isn't the same.

DS: Another thing I noticed about the book is that it is quite gentle in its tone. Even when Eugene is unspeakably cruel to Kambili she reacts in a very measured way and she never complains much. Why did you choose to write the book that way rather than perhaps more dramatically?

CNA: I think that for fiction to succeed, the worse the violence is, the quieter the telling voice has to be, so that your reader is overwhelmed. As a reader I've never really been drawn to fiction that is overdone. I really wanted this to be very quiet and to show through Kambili that you can love people who hurt you. She adores her father, and he also loves her and loves his family. He thinks he's doing the right thing.

DS: Is Aunty lfeoma's hand-to-mouth existence still the way academics live in Nigeria?

CNA: Things for academics in Nigeria have not become better, they have become worse. Now people who are professors are close to living like Aunty lfeoma lived. The tragedy of it is really that they are often not paid what they should be paid. If they were paid maybe life would be slightly better, but then you constantly have ridiculous stories about how the government hasn't released the funds for their salaries or someone has taken the money and put it in some account. That sort of thing. It's not so much that they aren't paid well; they are sometimes simply not paid.

DS: What is the state of women's rights in Nigeria? We hear all sorts of stories about women being stoned to death for adultery.

CNA: In Nigeria, the North is Muslim and quite different from the South, which is mostly Christian. The North is savannah and the South is rainforest. The geographical differences illustrate the political and social differences. I really don't know much about the North, where the stoning occurred, which was also very political, I think. In the South, where I come from, women are a mix of Aunty Ifeoma with her fierce independence and Kambili's mother with her domestic reticence. The women who are like Aunty lfeoma were the kind of women that I knew when I was growing up.

We have a Finance Minister who is a woman, who has a lot of respect. She is probably the only minister who is really respected in Nigeria. We have women who are in top positions in banks and companies. At the same time, you have women who are teaching their daughters to find good husbands and then settle down and stay home and be good wives. There are lots of women who believe that a woman's place is to sit at home and wait for the man. So, on the one hand there is hope, and on the other there are many things that I find very frustrating in the way that we continue to bring up young women.

DS: Is there an intellectual exodus from Nigeria? Do the best and brightest move away to work overseas?

CNA: Absolutely, we have an incredible brain drain. Most of them, like Aunty lfeoma, leave because they have no choice. If you are a professor in Nigeria and you are really bright, you start working in a university and you are not paid, the labs don't have the chemicals you need, and the roads are full of potholes. If you get an offer from the US of course you are going to take it. You think, "I want my kids to have a good education, I want to practice what I know in the best possible environment." The best and brightest of Nigeria are gone.

DS: I read that you don't read reviews. Is that an act of willpower or is it that you just don't want to read reviews?

CNA: I really do not read reviews; in total I've read three, two of which were not very pleasant. That's probably one of the reasons why I don't read them. [*laughs*] Now that I am in the middle of my second book, I think reading reviews of the first might be distracting for me. I don't mean just bad reviews, I mean good and bad. If I read a good review and somebody wrote that "she writes very simple, clean sentences," I might then have it my head and think, "Oh, I have to write simple, clean sentences." That will get in the way, so I just simply will not read them. I get people to send them to me and I keep them. Maybe at some point, when I'm sixty-five and on my deathbed, I'll read them.

DS: What was it like to grow up in a university town like Nsukka?
CNA: Nsukka was, and still is, very dusty. It's not a necessarily beautiful town, speaking geographically. It's the sort of town that nobody would know about if they hadn't decided to build the university there. We lived inside the campus, which meant it was secluded from the town itself. Life was very safe. You knew everybody else because everybody's parents worked in the university. My life was centered around my family, school, church, the library. Life really was very happy. I get very nostalgic about my childhood now. We went to church; I really liked church growing up. I only started to ask hard questions when I was older. And there was the library, of course, where I fell in love with books and reading.

It's only when you get older, when you start to look at things with the eyes of adult, that you start to realize things. For example, I realized that Nsukka is very much in decline. When the university started off in 1960, things worked. As time went past and we had a string of military dictators, things really started to go downhill.

DS: Do you think the place will steadily decline or is it saveable?
CNA: I don't know about saveable, it is going to take a lot. It only takes a year or two for things to fall apart. If you think about not funding a lab, and then not funding a lab for ten years. Everything becomes rusty and horrible. It will take a long time and a lot of money, which I don't know that Nigeria has. Nsukka is very much in decline and it's sad for me and I worry, but I really don't know if things will pick up.

DS: How hard was the decision to become a writer initially? I read that you wanted to become a doctor.
CNA: I didn't want to become a doctor, it was decided for me that I would be a doctor. I always wanted to write, I have always been writing. Of course, in the beginning I wrote really bad poetry and bad stories. With time and with reading more I guess I got better. Even when I was taking classes in pre-medicine I was writing. I think I just realized I would be a very unhappy doctor and so I left.

In Nigeria when you do well in school, and I think this is the case for most countries that have a history of colonialism, to get jobs that are lucrative it had to be practical; there was little room for the arts. If you go back to

Nigeria and asked a class of kids what they want to be when they grow up, I don't know that anybody would say a writer. All of them would say doctor, engineer, lawyer. I did well in school and my teachers said, "She's going to be a doctor." I just went along with that.

DS: You've said that if you were first published in Nigeria you don't think you would have had the same success. Why is that?

CNA: Because in Nigeria, we really don't regard literature anymore. It's interesting, I wrote about this in a piece for the *Guardian* and lots of Nigerians wrote to me and told me I was wrong. My case really is that, while I recognize that the economy plays a huge role, we can't remove religion. I have been published in Nigeria now, but if it had happened first, I probably wouldn't be speaking to you now, because I probably wouldn't have had the book published in other parts of the world.

DS: A Nigerian writer you've spoken about quite a bit is Chinua Achebe. I understand that you reread his book, *Arrow of God*, when you need to rekindle your writing spirit. Why is that book special to you?

CNA: I read it when I was very young and it just did something for me. For the first time I saw people who were like me and who felt like I did, in a book, and it was magical. Before that I had only read British books for kids. I really started writing stories about white people because I was reading stories about white people. I felt books by nature had to have white people in them. Until I read Chinua Achebe. Reading him then was this discovery and this shift for me. I think that magic has stayed with me and is connected to the book now.

DS: How important is a writer like Achebe in Nigeria and Africa in general?

CNA: He is very well-known; he is also widely read by people in Africa. Actually not just in Africa, but in the world. When I meet people outside of Africa, when I mention Nigeria, the next thing they say is "Oh yes, Achebe." He is quite important in Nigeria; he has become a moral voice. He is no longer just Achebe the writer, he is also Achebe the man of integrity.

DS: Colonialism is a prominent theme throughout *Purple Hibiscus* and you have said that you think in English. Do you ever resent that your thoughts are in some way a legacy of colonialism?

CNA: Yes, I do. I often resent it. It is a very complex kind of resentment. I'm very much aware of a sense of loss. We lost a lot. Lots of people say that colonialism had to happen. While I don't particularly agree, I wish, even if it had to happen, that it was slightly more benign. That we had retained more of our culture and traditional ways while being part of the British empire. I think that British colonialism seems to have been harsher in Africa than it was in Asia. Somehow the people in India are lucky enough to have retained their ways a little more than we did. I think about it very often. I think about the fact that lots of people can't speak Igbo anymore. I think about the fact that I don't fully understand the traditional religion, the traditional way of life, the fact that I can't speak Igbo without slipping in a few words of English. For me that is sad.

DS: Did you, like Kambili, have a sense of fascination with those traditional ways when you were younger?
CNA: Yes, I did. I would often ask my grandmother questions. I was a very keen observer when I was young, I guess I still am; I would just watch people and things. That's when I came to question the divide that exists. Christians in Nigeria are often very condescending towards people who have retained the old ways. Even as a child I remember thinking something wasn't right about it.

DS: You have spoken openly about your desire to change the world, or at least part of the world, with your writing. How powerful do you think litera-ture is in that regard, can it bring real change?
CNA: I don't know. I honestly don't know. I often say when I am in my darker moments, that it is all so useless and hopeless. When I am hopeful I think that it can. I really was changed by literature. I think if I hadn't been a reader as a child the little that is good in me probably wouldn't be there. Literature really did teach me to have an open mind, that the rest of the world isn't like mine and I have to tolerate that. I'd like to think it can change things, but I really don't know.

Q&A with the Author

Anonymous / 2006

From *halfofayellowsun.com*, 2006. Reprinted by permission.

Interviewer: What led you to write a book about the Nigeria-Biafra war?

CNA: I wrote this novel because I wanted to write about love and war, because I grew up in the shadow of Biafra, because I lost both grandfathers in the Nigeria-Biafra war, because I wanted to engage with my history in order to make sense of my present, because many of the issues that led to the war remain unresolved in Nigeria today, because my father has tears in his eyes when he speaks of losing his father, because my mother still cannot speak at length about losing her father in a refugee camp, because the brutal bequests of colonialism make me angry, because the thought of the egos and indifference of men leading to the unnecessary deaths of men and women and children enrages me, because I don't ever want to forget. I have always known that I would write a novel about Biafra. At sixteen, I wrote an awfully melodramatic play called *For Love of Biafra*. Years later, I wrote short stories, "That Harmattan Morning," "Half of a Yellow Sun" and "Ghosts," all dealing with the war. I felt that I had to approach the subject with little steps, paint on a smaller canvas first, before starting the novel.

I: Given that, at the time of the war, you hadn't yet been born, what sort of research did you do to prepare for writing this book?

CNA: I read books. I looked at photos. I talked to people. In the four years that it took to finish the book, I would often ask older people I met, "Where were you in 1967?" and then take it from there. It was from stories of that sort that I found out tiny details that are important for fiction. My parents' stories formed the backbone of my research. Still, I have a lot of research notes that I did not end up using because I did not want to be stifled by fact, did not want the political events to overwhelm the human story.

I: Was it important to you that you get all the "facts" of the war correct for this work of fiction?

CNA: I invented a train station in Nsukka, invented a beach in Port Harcourt, changed the distance between towns, changed the chronology of conquered cities but I did not invent any of the major events. It was important that I get the facts that mattered right. All the major political events in the book are "factually" correct. But what was most important to me, in the end, was emotional truth. I wanted this to be a book about human beings, not a book about faceless political events.

I: Are memories of the Nigeria-Biafra war still alive in Nigeria, talked about on a regular basis, or do you feel that the conflict is being lost to history as time passes and that it becomes less important to Igbo culture?

CNA: The war is still talked about, still a potent political issue. But I find that it is mostly talked about in uninformed and unimaginative ways. People repeat the same things they have been told without having a full grasp of the complex nature of the war or they hold militant positions lacking in nuance. It also remains, to my surprise, very ethnically divisive: the (brave enough) Igbo talk about it and the non-Igbo think the Igbo should get over it. There is a new movement called MASSOB, the movement for the actualization of the sovereign state of Biafra, which in the past few years has captured the imagination of many Igbo people. MASSOB is controversial; it is reported to engage in violence and its leaders are routinely arrested and harassed by the government. Still, despite their inchoate objectives, MASSOB's grassroots support continues to grow. I think this is because they give a voice to many issues that have been officially swept aside by the country, but which continue to resonate for many Igbo people.

I: The book focuses on the experiences of a small set of people who are experiencing the conflict from very different points of view. When we step into their individual worlds, we don't exactly know their every thought—the narrator who follows them isn't omniscient—but rather we seem to see and understand them through a film. Can you describe your narrative style and why you framed these characters the way you did?

CNA: I actually don't think of them as being seen through a "film." I have always been suspicious of the omniscient narrative. It has never appealed to me, always seemed a little lazy and a little too easy. In an introduction to the brilliant Italian writer Giovanni Verga's novel, it is said about his treatment of his characters that he "never lets them analyze their impulses but simply lets them be driven by them." I wanted to write characters who are driven by impulses that they may not always be consciously aware of, which I think is true for us human beings. Besides, I didn't want to bore my reader—and myself—to death, exploring the characters' every thought.

I: The character of Richard is a British white expatriate who considers himself Biafran, drawing a certain amount of quiet—and some loud—criticism for his self-proclaimed identity. Another key narrator, Ugwu, is a thirteen-year-old houseboy who reacts rather than acts. Both are interesting choices for characters for the narrator to "shadow." Why did you pick them?

CNA: Ugwu was inspired in part by Mellitus, who was my parents' houseboy during the war; in part by Fide, who was our houseboy when I was growing up. And I have always been interested in the less obvious narrators. When my mom spoke about Mellitus, what a blessing he was, how much he helped her, how she did not know what she would have done without him, I remember being moved but also thinking that he could not possibly have been the saint my mother painted, that he must have been flawed and human. I think that Ugwu does come to act more and react less as we watch him come into his own. Richard was a more difficult choice. I very much wanted somebody to be the Biafran "outsider" because I think that outsiders played a major role in the war, but I wanted him, also, to be human and real (and needy!).

I: Are there other characters based on real people?

CNA: "Harrison" is based on a real Harrison who lived with my family until very recently. What the character does with beets is, in fact, what the real Harrison told me he did during the war.

I: There is a conflict in this story between what is traditional and tribal versus that which is modern and bureaucratic. What is the mix today? How worrisome is it that some of the tribal ways have been lost?

CNA: Cultures evolve and things change, of course. What is worrisome is not that we have all learned to think in English, but that our education devalues our culture, that we are not taught to write Igbo and that middle-class parents don't much care that their children do not speak their native languages or have a sense of their history.

I: We see snippets of a book written by a character in *Half of a Yellow Sun*—it is an account of the conflict depicted in *Half of a Yellow Sun*, written after the fact. Its authorship may come as a surprise to some at the end of the story. What effect did you want this book within a book to have on *Half of a Yellow Sun*?

CNA: I wanted a device to anchor the reader who may not necessarily know the basics of Nigerian history. And I wanted to make a strongly-felt political point about who should be writing the stories of Africa.

I: What is next for you in your career (or careers, as the case may be!)?
CNA: The next book. And I've just started graduate work in the African Studies program at Yale.

I: You must have come across many books on Biafra. Are there any you would recommend in particular?
CNA: *Surviving in Biafra* by Alfred Obiora Uzokwe is a marvelous memoir of war seen through the eyes of a young boy. Chinua Achebe's *Girls at War* contains three sublime Biafran stories. Adewale Ademoyega's *Why We Struck* is a fiercely ideological look at the events that led to the war. *A Tragedy without Heroes* by Hilary Njoku and *The Nigerian Revolution and the Biafran War* by Alexander Madiebo are fascinating personal accounts from top-ranking Biafran Army officers. The writing in Ntieyong Akpan's *The Struggle for Secession* has a formal beauty and he presents—inadvertently, I suspect—a complex, flawed and sympathetic portrait of the Biafran leader. Wole Soyinka was imprisoned during the war and records this period in his magisterial memoir *The Man Died*. George Obiozor's *The United States and the Nigerian Civil War: An American Dilemma in Africa* is informative, albeit brief, and has an interesting foreword by Walter Ofonagoro. Herbert Gold's stark account of his visit to Biafra, *Biafra Goodbye*, moved me to tears. *The Biafran War: Nigeria and the Aftermath* by Herbert Ekwe-Ekwe is a concise and clear-eyed look at the conflict. Chukwuemeka Ike's *Sunset at Dawn* and Flora Nwapa's *Never Again* are novels that convincingly portray middle-class Biafra. John De St Jorre's *The Nigerian Civil War* presents an excellent view of Biafra from the outside. And *Sunset in Biafra*, the bitter and beautifully written memoir by Elechi Amadi, looks at the war from the point of view of an anti-Biafran minority.

"My Book Should Provoke a Conversation"—Chimamanda Ngozi Adichie

Wale Adebanwi / 2007

From *The News*, 9 January 2007. Reprinted by permission of Wale Adebanwi, who is the Rhodes Professor of Race Relations and the Director of the African Studies Centre at the University of Oxford, UK. He was a Bill and Melinda Gates Scholar at Trinity Hall, Cambridge University, UK, when he had the interview with the author.

In her latest novel, *Half of a Yellow Sun* (London: Fourth Estate, 2006), Chimamanda Ngozi Adichie, twenty-nine, bravely takes on the subject of the Nigerian civil war, encountering the ordinary people who lived through the tragedies of that dark era of Nigeria's history. After her highly successful debut novel, *Purple Hibiscus* (Chapel Hill: Algonquin Books of Chapel Hill, 2003)—which won the Hurston/Wright Legacy Award 2004 (Best Debut Fiction Category); the Commonwealth Writers' Prize 2005, Best First Book (Africa Region); the Commonwealth Writers' Prize 2005, Best First Book (overall); was shortlisted for the Orange Prize and longlisted for the Booker Prize—Adichie's new work will reconfirm her place as one of the fresh, but strong, voices emerging from the African literary firmament. In these email exchanges with Wale Adebanwi, Adichie, who is currently pursuing postgraduate studies in the United States, discusses why she took on the difficult subject of the civil war, the Nigerian tragedy that preceded and succeeded the war, and the textual dynamics of her engaging narrative.

Wale Adebanwi: It is interesting to read *Half of a Yellow Sun*, a narrative of the civil war by someone who was born seven years after the formal surrender. But there is no doubt that your life as an Igbo and as a Nigerian was already conditioned, in particular ways, even before you were born, by what led to that war and the consequences. As a daughter of the postwar era, why do you think it is important to tell this story which constitutes an indirect "witnessing," if you will, to a history that remains traumatic?

Chimamanda Ngozi Adichie: I did not choose this subject; it chose me. Both my grandfathers died in Biafra. My parents survived Biafra. I grew up in the shadow of Biafra. I grew up hearing "before the war" and "after the war" stories, all the time knowing that the war had divided the memories of my family. I had to write this book to digest for myself this legacy that I carry. *Half of a Yellow Sun* is fiction based on fact. I state in the author's note that I took some liberties for the purposes of fiction which means that I played with small things—I invented a train station in Nsukka, for example. But I did not play with the big things. I did not let a character be changed by something that did not actually happen. All the major political events in the book are factually correct.

WA: You seem to provoke or invite some harsh criticisms in this narrative from both the Igbo and, particularly, the non-Igbo interpreters of the civil war. Was this deliberate?

CNA: It is really sad that there is such a thing as an "Igbo" interpretation and a "non-Igbo" interpretation of a history that is supposedly common to all. I don't think anybody ever sets out to invite harsh criticism. I set out to write a story that deals with the realities as I understand them. I am a fiction writer, a teller of human stories, and this implies that I grapple with the good and the bad. I have also learned that one cannot please everyone and one should not try. I do realize that people have strong ideas of what the narrative of the war should be, but if this novel pushes some out of their complacency, then it is a good thing. I want this book to provoke a conversation. We need to talk about a history of events we too often minimize or dismiss or speak of in meaningless clichés. We need to talk about it honestly.

WA: There are some topics that would seem to be taboo topics about the war, at least publicly, among Igbo intellectuals that you seem to raise here. For instance, there is the whole question of the official assurances that "No power in Black Africa can defeat us!" which Colonel Madu dismisses as he realizes that there are no arms stockpiled as expected. What gives you the courage to raise these questions? Fiction?

CNA: My courage, if we can call it that, comes from a need to tell a human story. I was interested in portraying that time as it actually seemed to have been. That bit was inspired by Biafran Army Commander General Madiebo's book, *The Nigerian Revolution and the Biafran War*. I'm not convinced that the subject of Biafran propaganda is taboo among Igbo intellectuals. I think propaganda is a war tactic that has been used in all wars; it is the psychological equivalent of bombing and shooting. The Biafran leadership possibly overrelied on propaganda because they were not as well-armed as the Nigerian side. The official assurances you refer to were intended to do for Biafra what, say, Winston Churchill's broadcasts to the English people during the Second World War did, even when the actual prospects of victory were dim for the English. Propaganda buoyed and encouraged people and kept them sane. Propaganda also resulted in needless death and suffering because people were not always prepared to flee their towns when they fell.

WA: Let's talk about textualities. What precisely are you trying to say with this work and how would you want it interpreted—even though you have no absolute power over the interpretation? Your project is obviously beyond mere fiction—if there is anything like that, in the first instance. That's a difficult subject you chose. It is possible to do a double reading of this: at one end, you can say this is an affirmation of a particular identity, a beleaguered identity, indeed, one that was savaged in a particular context of history. But there is the other side of the book that says to that identity that it has got to do more to account for itself and its inherent, if disastrous, contradictions. You veil the grounds for the second reading—as Edward Said said, the text is always hiding something; but by unveiling the first reading, you already provided the possibility of unveiling or revealing the second reading. How do you think the Igbo would react to this?

CNA: I have no power at all over how this book is interpreted. I realize that many people will come to it differently. I hope that it will be judged first as a work of art, a human story, a story about love above all else, and that readers will keep their preconceived notions aside and enter the world that the book creates. As for how the Igbo should react to this, I don't think there will be one "Igbo reading." We Igbo after all are infamous for our distaste for uniformity. Perhaps it might make the Igbo interrogate their history and ask questions about how the civil war has affected their general psyche. It seems to me that it is the Igbo in general, among the larger Nigerian groups, who have the least sense of a cultural identity. The indignities that came after the Biafran defeat clearly contributed to this.

WA: When Chief Emeka Ojukwu published *Because I Am Involved*, which many thought would be "the book," but which turned out to be an indulgent narrative where, among others, a beauty queen was praised—long before the world knew why—I remember a senior colleague publishing, in a newspaper, a short story entitled "Sandra," in response to Chief Ojukwu. It was about a young Igbo woman who was personally devastated by the war. It was to say that this is the true face of the war, those who were "really involved." I kept thinking of Sandra as I read about Olanna and the other women in *Half of a Yellow Sun*. These characters perhaps speak to us more honestly and more clearly than the key actors in the war—and their memoirs. Is this reading plausible?

CNA: Yes. In Chinua Achebe's *Girls at War*, he writes of true Biafran heroism often happening "below the eye level of the people in this story, in out of the way refugee camps, in the damp tatters, in the hungry and bare-handed courage of the first line of fire." I believe that the true war heroes are the ones about whom nobody writes books, and especially the Biafran women who showed remarkable bravery in keeping families together. I think the reason that the ordinary person's story is more engaging is that it is in those lives that we see the real effects of war—the indignity of starvation, the struggle to hold on to their humanity.

WA: Much of the emerging literary works in the new generation of Nigerian writers—and poets—have as a central theme social anomie—as occasioned by historical, sociopolitical and economic conditions that we, the "(Anti-) SAP [Structural Adjustment Programme] Generation," faced from the early 1980s Nigeria to this period. They deal with these conditions in different ways, from Helon Habila's *Waiting for an Angel*, Chris Abani's *Graceland*, Sefi Atta's *Everything Good Will Come* to Akin Adesokan's *Roots in the Sky*, and your *Purple Hibiscus*, among others. You seem to have left this subject a little aside to deal with the civil war which you must imagine is core to the crisis of the last two decades of devastations wrought by military rule and the attendant democratic struggle. How does *Half of a Yellow Sun* relate to these works that I have mentioned and others in that category?

CNA: I don't think Nigerian writers of my generation necessarily set out to address social anomie in that overt way. As storytellers, we set out to reflect our lives, and our lives, unfortunately, are circumscribed by social unrest and this invariably emerges as a theme. I think you are right in suggesting the connection between our present and our past. We cannot begin to make sense of our present and of our future until we have engaged properly with our past. Many things that are politically important today, from the concept of geopolitical regions to the question of oil revenue allocation, are better understood (and perhaps resolved?) if we take into account the years before and during the civil war.

WA: When I finished reading this book, I kept thinking of James Baldwin, the African American author of *The Fire Next Time*—among other great works. He is my favorite African American writer, by the way. Baldwin was provoked in one of his books to describe the African Americans as a "bastard people" in the context of their history and what they had made of that history. Isn't that what we have become, against the backdrop of your narrative and what we witness daily in our fatherland—if we can still call it that? Look at what we have made of the stupendously endowed country that Nature gave to us. What is the matter with us as a people?
CNA: I wish I knew the answer to that. There are times when, observing Nigeria, I am filled with both despair and disgust. We set such low standards for ourselves. Politically, there is much that is cyclic about Nigeria. The same things (and people) are repeated over and over again. But we also have to look at ourselves and our culpability—we are a country of people who complain that the roads are dirty and yet throw rubbish out of our car windows. I am a James Baldwin fan, too, by the way. I especially admire his novel *Another Country*.

WA: We can leave textualities behind and consider eventualities. At the close of *Half of a Yellow Sun* there is the euphoria that the war is over. Some understandable relief in the collapsed Republic of Biafra, given the horrendous, and indeed unspeakable, suffering. But, when one reconsiders things in the context of our post-civil war experience, one might like to suggest, without being irresponsible, that the euphoria was misplaced. Is the war really over? Compare and contrast, if you will, the decapitation of the fleeing body of Ikejide, Kainene's steward, by shrapnel in your narrative of war with the beheading of Gideon Akaluka in December 1994 by Muslim fundamentalists in Kano, who then placed their victim's head on a spear and danced around Kano chanting, "Allahu Akbar." And you say the war is over? Take some of the key elements who assassinated General Ironsi and his host, Colonel Fajuyi, in 1966, thereby provoking the conditions that produced the genocidal rage in the North. Some of these elements were to feature prominently in the now regrettable recruitment of General Obasanjo—a civil war hero who received the Biafran surrender—to head a collapsing enterprise in 1999, thirty years after. After seven years of a scandalous presidency, complete with the massacres of Odi and Zaki-Biam, do you still say the war is over? Think of the Tarok-Fulani war; the war that OPC [Oodua People's Congress] has levied against the Hausa-Fulani, the Igbo or the Ijaw in Lagos, which President Obasanjo had to describe at a point as "total madness." Not to even talk of the cruel derision that the idea of "Igbo presidency" provokes in the inner recesses of certain quarters, even as MASSOB leader, Ralph Uwazuruike, languishes in jail for reraising the Biafran flag. And they say the war is over?

CNA: This is a great question—and answer—Wale! I think it is clear that in a metaphorical sense, we are still at war. What amazes me about Nigeria is how willingly and easily we forget, or pretend to forget, our recent history. I have always believed that we Nigerians can live together but it is (sometimes artificial) scarcity that politicizes identity. Remember that it was the idea of the Igbo "taking over everything" in the event of a unitary decree that was partly used to fuel the massacres of Igbo people before the war. If we had a real middle class, if jobs and security and energy were things we could fairly take for granted, then I think the conflicts that masquerade as ethnic or religious would reduce. But of course I realize that there will always be identity-based conflict. Religious fundamentalism is a dangerous thing that is sweeping not only the North but the South of Nigeria. I suspect it has a lot to do with uncertainty, with a country that seems to be spiraling out of control. Ours is a country in which the individual is abused and made to feel helpless by the state—old pensioners fall down and die while pleading to be paid their well-earned and meagre pension, for example—and so it is not surprising that Christianity has become a prosperity-preaching enterprise, that we constantly talk about God, but do very little to act what we say. This religiosity worries me very much because it shuts off debate and makes it impossible for people to take responsibility. People steal money and say, "We thank God." Our planes crash because of a substandard aviation and we say, "It was God's will." Disasters happen and instead of public officials demanding accountability, they say we need to fast. Churches spring up everywhere and yet corruption remains the order of the day. We should ask our politicians never to mention God but to work in such a way that we citizens will see what they have done and attribute it to God. I hope that Uwazuruike and leaders of other so-called ethnic militias will be released. Dissent is not treason. Problems only fester if we suppress them. We need to ask why these groups exist in the first place, why MASSOB has such wide grassroots support, for example. If people are disenfranchised, they will look for alternative ways of political expression. And history shows us that the strategy of using might to deal with issues of justice is doomed to fail.

WA: Still on Ikejide's Head (of State), if you can call it that. It is said that, "His body kept running and it didn't have a head," until it eventually collapsed. Is the slain steward a metaphor for our country?
CNA: I don't consciously use metaphors in my writing. I suppose it could be read as that. For me, it was simply Ikejide's body running without a head. It was a story told me by an acquaintance in London whose family had left Nigeria after the war. He had not been back since but he said he was haunted by this image: he was a little boy and his town was about to fall and there was an air raid and he and his family members were running when he saw a man beheaded by a piece of shrapnel but the body kept running for a while before it fell. It broke my heart, imagining a little boy seeing this.

WA: Let's talk about the "goat sound" that one of the key leaders in the First Republic is said to have made while begging the soldiers not to kill him in 1966 and the ways in which your characters seem to enjoy telling the story over and over again. It reads like one of those unforgivable things we say across ethnic groups in Nigeria about one another. Don't you think we have been, in part, cruelly sundered by such grotesquely malicious statements? "A goat begging not to be killed: mmee-mmee-mmee." Did we not all become, in the end, goats begging not to be killed by either General Buhari, Babangida, or Abacha and the murderous soldiers who seized our country?
CNA: Not all the characters enjoy telling this story and I think it is important to note that. It is also important to note that for the people who did enjoy it, it was an admittedly sad way of voicing their resentment about their political exclusion when Igbo children were not allowed to go to Northern schools and the Igbo Union had to start its own school. It is a shame, however, how we seem to delight in ridiculous stereotypes of one another. What colonialism has done is that it has made us ashamed of our tribal identities. I find it risible that our politicians talk of being detribalized. It really is a meaningless word in that context because the dictionary definition is that one does not belong to a tribal group. Rather than demonize tribe, our politicians should accentuate fairness, honesty, meritocracy. It does not matter to me where my president comes from as long as the president does not steal, can read, listens to people and cares about the lives of ordinary citizens. I do understand that ours is a history made fractious by politicized

ethnicity. But it is not tribe that ruined us. It is injustice. It is corruption. The fact that ethnicity has been used in politicized ways in the past should not be a reason for us to deny who we are. A Korean friend recently spoke about how being Americanized and not speaking proper Korean was considered a *faux pas* in Korea. I was impressed. In Nigeria, we would be admiring people who did not speak their native languages. Our self-confidence is so fragile that it is frightening. My version of an ideal Nigeria is one in which we celebrate who we are, in which the Ijaw and Hausa and Tiv teach their children to speak their languages, in which we learn our culture and history first and then possibly that of other groups, in which Nigerians don't keep trying to prove how European they can be, in which we understand that English and our native languages are not mutually exclusive. I have often been asked why I identify so strongly as an Igbo woman. It is a question that baffled me because it assumed that I shouldn't identify as Igbo and therefore had to explain it. Shouldn't the presence, rather than the absence, of that identity be the norm? I would not be who I am today if I had not grown up in an Igbo-speaking family, surrounded by Igbo norms and values.

WA: The image of Chief Ojukwu—who you call "His Excellency" in the book—that comes out of *Half of a Yellow Sun* is not all flattering. But, Chimamanda, what you do is to make your fatal jabs at "The Leader" so subtle that one could miss it. Of course, there is no denying the gallant efforts of standing up to mass murderers and those who shielded them and benefited from the edifice of blood, and the sheer mass appeal of Ojukwu's elocution in that era . . . The narrative recognizes all that and does not gloss over them. Yet, in interesting ways, we are also told that "His Excellency" was also "His Excellen-Sleaze"—my word! Chief Ojukwu was having a ball, literally and metaphorically, while thousands perished! Remember the talk in the book about "His Excellency" taking a ranking soldier into detention because he wanted to sleep with his wife? This is fiction, no doubt—and perhaps it has no relation to actual living persons! However, one is struck by the capacity of leaders for the most capricious acts that were raised here. For me, it may have been someone else and not Chief Ojukwu, but to have had a ball in the middle of all that suffering could only be the preserve of "The Leader." How do you react to my reading?

CNA: We often easily judge characters who have played major roles in historical events and condemn them in ways lacking in nuance. I do not at all think that Chief Ojukwu is an ogre who was having a good time while people died. I think he was a complex man who made mistakes and who, like most men thrust into war leadership, was unwilling to face defeat even when it was sitting beside him. I don't think he enjoyed the fact that so many people died but he, again like most leaders, was removed from day-to-day refugee camp realities. There is much I admire in Chief Ojukwu. I respect the idealism that he seemed to have in his younger days, when he made choices that went against his life of privilege. I admire the courage it must have taken to make the choices he did before the war. I understand—and to understand is not to excuse—his fears and uncertainties, which made it difficult for him to trust, as the accounts of ex-officers show, his own army. He was only a few years older than I presently am when he became the popular leader of a country of independent-minded people. Read Ntienyong Akpan's account of the war *The Struggle for Secession*. It is quite beautifully written and is in some ways an obvious "anti-Ojukwu" account, if not a self-exculpatory one, but it presents an interesting portrait of the man Chief Ojukwu was. There were rumors of his affairs during the war among the Biafran middle class, and I wanted to portray how he was seen by the different characters—Kainene is cynical, Olanna and Odenigbo are respectful, Richard is adoring, Madu is contemptuous. But this is not a book that is concerned with the leaders of Biafra, it is concerned with how the choices these leaders made affected ordinary people. I'm pleased to hear that word "subtle" because I am convinced that fiction, especially that based on historical fact, has to be subtle to succeed.

WA: In a way, your narrative can be described as part of the elaborate attempts by intellectuals to have closure as regards the civil war. But this seems a repeatedly failing enterprise. Take even the institutional attempts like the Oputa Panel. Some people took especial exception to Igbo claims presented to the panel; even the acrimony that ensued reinscribed the whole social and political technology of injustice and inequities that, in the first place, predisposed the country to war in 1967. Can we ever have closure? And, are we not walking towards another cataclysm?

CNA: For me this book is not an act of closure, it is an act of remembering. I don't believe in the concept of closure. I think that the traumas we have experienced remain an indelible part of who we are; we carry it with us always. However, I do believe in constructive dialogue and reaching some rapprochement. I think that people who took "exception" to the Oputa Panel as well as those who refused to appear, are people for whom their own personal interest trumps everything else. We should acknowledge what happened in Biafra. We should accept that injustices occurred. Often people have said, "but it wasn't only this group who suffered," as if we should somehow have a competing of injustice narratives or as if that means ignoring one group because others suffered too. There is room to acknowledge everyone and we should do so.

WA: You set much of this story in the University of Nigeria and university town of Nsukka, like much of *Purple Hibiscus*. Are you done with this much-beloved environment of your birth and upbringing or are there more stories coming from crazy academics?
CNA: Nsukka is a town I love and more important for fiction, a town I know well. It is easier to write about what you know. I am certainly not done.

WA: There is Europe all over this book, either in the Walter Rodneyian *How Europe Underdeveloped Africa* sense or in the Bill Ashcroftian sense of *The Empire Writes Back*. Why are you counterposing Africa to Europe? It sometimes reads like you are reversing Hegel, capturing Europe as the savage Other. At other times, it reads as if you are deliberately encountering Europe through its abjected and derided Other—Africa.
CNA: I wanted to engage with the presence of Europe, perhaps not continental Europe but the UK. How can one write about postindependence Nigeria without engaging with the British presence? I believe firmly that independence, if we can call it that, set Nigeria up to fail. What we Nigerians have to take responsibility for is the extent of that failure.

WA: Let us talk about sexualities, adult-rated and sometimes adulterated in this narrative. I find it interesting the ways in which sex is underscored in the book as people climbed the bed even in the middle of the war. In the end, our basic humanity survives even the most horrendous circumstances. One could read the exhibited sexualities as an affirmation of life in the middle of mass slaughter. How do you hope that it will be read—I mean, beyond the relief that the sex acts give the reader in this, for the most account, psychologically draining and intense book?
CNA: Interesting word play, Wale. I hope the sexuality in this book will be read as the characters' holding on to their humanity in the midst of death and uncertainty. It is also a celebration of love, particularly the complex, flawed love between Olanna and Odenigbo. It is also about the ability of love to transcend sexuality, in the case of Richard and Kainene. It is an atrocious violation, in the case of a war rape. It is central to what (and how) we are human and never more so, in my opinion, than in war situations when our very humanity is in question.

WA: At the risk of your accusing me of seeking for stereotypes in your stories, I think the image of the effeminate, undersexualized white male is initially overplayed here. Was this counterposed to the thoroughly sexualized—and routinized—world of the black male (with a capital M)? Also, there is something distinctively feminist about the way you practically sanctioned some sexual transgressions in this work. I suspect that is why at least one scene of such transgressions by a woman and her sister's husband is a bit unreal.

CNA: Or, perhaps because you approached that scene with certain preconditioned ideas? I am happily feminist, but I never start my fiction with ideology. There are obvious suggestions in earlier sections about the attraction between the two characters and so the act is not entirely unpredictable. It is up to the reader to decide whether it was an act of revenge or not. Olanna is a character that is in many ways NOT a feminist, at least in the earlier sections. I don't think Richard is a stereotype. In the world of the book, we see that his diffidence comes from a keen search for identity. His being "undersexualized" says more about Kainene and their relationship than it says about him, really. I find the question of a "stereotype" often problematic on the whole. Sometimes in running away from the idea of "stereotype," in a manic desire to be "original," writers produce completely contrived fiction. I can sense this when I read. Writing from a place of imagined and experienced truth is what I am interested in. A familiar image may result but it is the freshness that one brings to it that matters. Every story has been written before, anyway.

WA: In *Half of a Yellow Sun*, the initial reluctance and eventual raping of the poor bar girl strikes me powerfully. War does not only savage us, it is also capable of making savages of even the best among us.

CNA: I think that one of the great horrors of war is how brutalizing it can be to ordinary good people, how choices are reduced to the barest of minimums, how easily what we call "civilization" slips away.

WA: Olanna's earlier protests and protestations against marrying Odenigbo were based on avoiding the "prosaic partnership" that marriage flattens relationships into. It is a protest against the everyday-ness of things which eventually catches up with everyone, as it did Olanna. We can't hear her complain about that banality when she eventually settled into it. Did she grow up?

CNA: But we don't get a chance to see if it does become a prosaic partnership in peacetime. Remember that her decision was made in the context of the uncertainty of war. But Wale (and yes, I am needling you!), isn't she being stereotypical by agreeing to marriage? Isn't ascribing her ostensible peace with marriage to her "growing up" too familiar and stereotypical? Perhaps my point is made.

WA: To be praised by the ultimate wordsmith, Prof. Chinua Achebe, must feel cool—excuse my lingo. You came almost fully made, says Achebe, in the blurb of the book. What's in that making?

CNA: I was so pleased, so grateful, to get Achebe's seal of approval. I've never met him. My editor in New York sent him the book and I remember the afternoon she called to say she had heard from him and that he could not believe someone my age had written this book. It was not just that he said something, it was WHAT he said that meant so much to me. What's in this "making" he refers to? I think I have been blessed with a gift and that I made the conscious decision to work very hard to make something of this gift. I am an incredibly hard worker, perhaps a bit of a perfectionist—I will revise a single sentence fifty times until I am pleased with it. I have a singular commitment to my work and I am fortunate to have the support of loved ones; my parents, my sisters and brothers and close friends are an incredible source of support. An artist always needs to know that there is a safe place that one can turn to.

WA: You always play with cross-cultural marriages and relationships. I know you have a brother who is married to a Yoruba lady. Chimamanda, it will be interesting to see how you go yourself in real life—or how you are going already!

CNA: You forget my nephew, the wonderful, smart, adorable thirteen-year-old Tokunbo Oremule, from my sister Ijeoma's first marriage. Yes, it will be interesting to see how I go or how I am going in real life, indeed. As for playing with cross-cultural relationships in my work, I think it is my way of simply making a point about possibility. Relationships where both people are of a common culture are generally easier, but sometimes joy and love come clothed in a different culture and it is our responsibility to grab it. This is the only chance we have to live in this complex, wondrous world.

Chimamanda Ngozi Adichie

Joshua Jelly-Schapiro / 2009

From *Believer* 7.1 (January 2009): 54–61. Reprinted by permission.

"Things began to fall apart at home," go the first lines of Chimamanda Ngozi Adichie's acclaimed first novel, *Purple Hibiscus*, "when my brother, Jaja, did not go to communion and Papa flung his heavy missal across the room and broke the figurines on the étagère." The reference to *Things Fall Apart*, Chinua Achebe's masterpiece about colonialism destroying tradition, marks Adichie's debt to her Igbo forebear but also signals her differing concerns. The sentence could perhaps be read to distill the larger ambitions of Adichie's work thus far: to engage the themes that long defined African literature—the legacies of colonialism, the cause of nation-building—but to do so in a way expressive of a new generation's ironic view of these questions, and in a way attuned to the intimate lives of her characters.

Purple Hibiscus, which won the Commonwealth Writers' Prize in 2004 for best first book, depicts a teenage narrator and her brother coming to terms with their authoritarian Catholic father as Nigeria begins to fall apart under a military coup. Adichie's second novel, *Half of a Yellow Sun*, is set during the Biafra war, the horrific 1967–70 conflict begun when South Nigeria's Igbo citizens declared independence from their new country's government in its Muslim North. The novel depicts the war through a story about how it is lived by a small coterie of characters—a pair of middle-class sisters (one pretty, one plain) and their respective mates (a revolutionary mathematician, an English ex-pat); a houseboy and a university master. Last year it was awarded the prestigious Orange Prize for Fiction.

Adichie was born in 1977 in Enugu, a small village in Anambra state, in Southeast Nigeria. She grew up, though, in the university town of Nsukka, where her parents still work, and where she spent her childhood in a house that was once home to Achebe himself. (Of discovering his work at the age of ten, she has recalled: "I didn't think it was possible for people like me to be in books.") She briefly studied medicine ("It's what educated Nigerians are supposed to do"), but having hoped from a young age to be a writer, she soon quit her course and moved to the United States to finish college. Joining her sister, a doctor living in Connecticut, she completed a BA in communication and political science at Eastern Connecticut State University. Since that time Adichie has studied creative writing at Johns Hopkins, spent a year teaching the same at Princeton, and returned to Connecticut two years ago to complete a masters in African studies at Yale. In addition to the two novels, she has written numerous short stories and essays for publications including the *New Yorker, Granta*, and the *New York Times*. In September 2008, she was named a MacArthur Fellow.

Adichie speaks in a sonorous voice inflected with the Nigerian-British cadences of home, her precise diction joined to a ready laugh. Our conversation took place on a warm May day in New Haven across the street from the Yale University Art Gallery.

I. "I have Nigerian friends who can list every monarch in England from the ninth century, and know nothing about Nigeria in 1954."

Joshua Jelly-Schapiro: You're just finishing school, eh? Congratulations! What brought you back? How has it been?
Chimamanda Ngozi Adichie: Oh, must we? [*laughs*] I'm glad to be done. It was an ill-advised decision to come. It's not that the program is a bad program so much as it is that I'm just not a good fit for it. I don't like academia, in a way; I find it constricting. I started the program because I wanted to learn about Africa. It's one thing to be from a country in Africa, but there's just so much that you don't know; our education system just doesn't prepare us for knowing who we are. I have Nigerian friends who can list every monarch in England from the ninth century and know nothing about Nigeria in 1954. So I wanted to make up for that. I probably would have done better simply continuing my own self-directed reading. Academia is often about academia and not about the real, messy world.

JJS: Your fiction is overtly engaged with these themes of history, and politics—the history of Nigeria; the legacies of colonialism; Biafra. What does approaching these questions as a novelist afford that might differ from how a historian does?

CNA: I think it's probably that I'm interested in the exceptions. One of the things about historical work—some of it, not all—is that it's very much interested in generalities: that this is what people in general did. Sometimes historians refer to countries as though they were people—they'll say: Britain did this. As a novelist, I'm more interested in that particular human being living in a particular part of Britain, and how they felt, and what they understood, and how they approached their realities. I remember when I was researching *Half of a Yellow Sun*, I was reading this book about the war, written by an American, and there was this section about how people were being unreasonable—about how they weren't eating the food brought by the Red Cross. And the writer couldn't understand why the Biafrans did not want to eat the food; they were starving, and they just wouldn't. And talking to people who were there, I realized it was because there was a myth that the Nigerians [the other side in the war] had poisoned the milk. People believed this—it wasn't true, but people believed it. And it deeply affected how they approached their reality, why they chose not to eat the food. It's easy, you know, to sit in your academic chair and say you know, that was quite irrational. But it's what I'm interested in, the little stories, less the generalities than those details.

JJS: *Half of a Yellow Sun*, though, is at least as much about memory as history—less about the history of Biafra than about how Biafra is remembered (or perhaps not remembered). One of the ways you do that is in the structure: the narrative moves back and forth in time—it reads like we remember things, not necessarily in the order they happened.

CNA: I think so, too. Though you know, it's interesting—I spoke at the University of Ife, in Nigeria. And usually when I do these events in Nigeria, I tend to divide the questions in categories. There are those people whose family were Biafran, who are still burning with this kind of neo-nationalist zeal. And there are those who are like me, who are sort of skeptical of things, but who feel strongly that we should talk about it. And there are those who are just furious with me for writing this book, because "let's let the past be the past"—and it was one of these people who was saying: "Why do you insist on bringing up the past, that is gone?" And I remember thinking: For you it's past, but for so many people I know it's living memory. And I think that's the approach I brought to the book.

Talking to my parents, their friends, my relatives, it's still very present. They don't talk about it unless you bring it up. But then you do, and you realize, my God—there's so many things that haven't been dealt with. You know my uncle, he's a farmer, in my village. Things aren't going very well for him, he's poor—and he feels very strongly that this would not have happened if Biafra had won; he wants Biafra to come back. He's projected his hopes on this phantom Biafra, and it's moving, and also funny. But he fiercely believes this. And he'll tell me: well, look, I'm very poor, my farm is not going well, and if Biafra had won this wouldn't happen. And my aunt, his wife, who's also a farmer—she's told me that about two years ago, she went to till the farm, and did so in the field, and dug up these bullets from the war. I wish I'd had that story before I wrote the book.

JJS: The book reminds me in some ways of those books by the kids of Holocaust survivors: Art Spiegelman's *Maus*, for example—stories that deal with "remembering" traumatic events your parents lived through, with the ways in which their memories become yours, in a way.
CNA: I think those of us who didn't experience the trauma, but have somehow inherited it—I think we're fortunate to have that. I think one of the reasons that writing about the Holocaust is still coming out, for example, is that the people who experienced it just couldn't write about it. People ask: Why hasn't Chinua Achebe written a novel about Biafra? He was in the thick of it. And I think, Well that's why he couldn't—he was in the thick of it. I listen to what my father went through and think: My God, if all that happened to me, I would be a bitter, bitter person. I'd just be angry with the world, and I wouldn't be able to write anything.

JJS: I heard Amos Oz say recently that he's tried to write of his experience as a soldier, but that he never could; that whatever language he's tried to give those experiences in analogy to everyday life, it doesn't accord with what he remembers—the smell, noise, everything.
CNA: Right, and I understand that.

JJS: People tend to talk about the "historical novel" like it's a unitary form, but of course there are a million ways to tell a story related to a historical event or era. Was it immediately apparent to you how you had to approach Biafra, how you had to write it as an intimate story about sentiment and relationships?
CNA: It's so difficult to have proper answers to questions like that, because when you're doing it, you're not really very consciously analytical, or justifying the choices you make. But the idea of a historical novel—I don't really like the label. Because it evokes for me books I read when I was growing up, about Renaissance Florence, and it was usually really bad romance, with

the women in really tight dresses. They were these books called Historical Romance, it was a series. And there's always been something about the label "historical novel" that just puts things in my mind.

I suppose the thing I was most certain about, though, with that book was that I wanted it to be about human beings. There is quite a bit written about the war, of course, but usually it is sort of about battalions and things of that sort. And I don't much care who won this town or commanded this battalion and took that town. I wanted to write about people. And I think there's something always contemporary in that—there are people who have written to me and said, these people seem like they could be in the year 2000. And I say, well, you know people don't really change; people's motivations don't really change. The circumstances change, but people don't really change. People have the same motivations.

II. "I don't think it's so much about what sex organs we have as it is about what we write."

JJS: How do you feel about the distinction that's often made between "female novels" and "male novels"? Both your novels seem in many ways to collapse the way those labels are applied. And you write some very empathetic and fully realized males in *Half of a Yellow Sun*—Ugwu, the houseboy, but also Richard the Englishman.
CNA: Well, you know, I do think *Purple Hibiscus* was sort of a girl book— and *Half of a Yellow Sun* sort of crossed over. [*laughs*] My friend Binyavanga [Wainaina] said the problem with *Purple Hibiscus* was the cover of the book. That he'd be so embarrassed to have this on the train—that he can't read a book with a flower on the cover. And I thought, Well, you know I understand that. I hated that cover, too.

But the male-female dichotomy is all quite silly when you think about it seriously—though there are writers, both male and female, who are less engaged with emotion. And I'm sort of old-fashioned in my taste—I like emotion, and I like the story, I like humanness. And there are people like Cynthia Ozick, for example, who's a writer I really respect, but I don't really want to curl up and read Cynthia Ozick. It's like I often don't remember Cynthia Ozick after I've read her—you sort of read it, and think, Oh! She's brilliant. But then at the end, or weeks later, I just really don't remember.

But then Michael Ondaatje, who's male, I think has that human thing. I read him, and I'm just in love. . . .

JJS: He writes good women, too.
CNA: Yes! And I read him and I'm crying. I remember I was crying when I read *Anil's Ghost.* So, I don't think it's so much about what sex organs we have as it is about what we write.

JJS: Your characters' physical selves play an important part in how we come to know them, their interactions with each other. I wonder if you could talk about the place of bodies in your work.
CNA: I think it's a key part of the way I understand the world. I think people are very physical beings. I was doing a reading in Lagos, and someone said, "You know, for an African book, so much sex in it!" And I said to him, "So Africans don't have sex?" And he said, "No, they do—but for an African book, so much sex!" I suppose it's an expectation that we're supposed to be restrained. But it's just not my vision. And I think particularly, when I was writing *Half of a Yellow Sun,* I remember listening to my parents—who lost everything, had to run from town to town, much like the characters in the book—and realizing that my brother was born during that war. And my parents speak of going to weddings during that time, of laughing. I really loved that, and I hoped that I could show it in the book—the ways in which people can be running for their lives but also laughing. And I was thinking as well about how the way in which you relate to the person you love changes, the way you have sex changes, the way you look at sexuality changes. I don't know, I guess it must be that girl thing, that I'm such a girly girl. . .

JJS: But it matters! How do you approach the challenge of writing about bodies—be it sex, or also violence—in a subtle way? How do you approach it in a way that doesn't feel pornographic?
CNA: I think I actually struggled more with the violence. Because I wanted it to be stark. I didn't want to be euphemistic about it; but at the same time I didn't want to be pornographic about it. You don't want your reader—or you—to feel like you're taking advantage somehow. You're writing about this killing that makes no sense, and you just don't want a reader to feel manipulated. And really, the violent scenes—the massacre scene, the rape scene—were so hard. I rewrote them so many times; I was obsessive about them. I was going crazy.

III. "I think: let's just tell our bloody stories."

JJS: You use bits of Igbo dialogue in your fiction. But most often when your characters are speaking in Igbo, you render their speech in English, with some Igbo words thrown in. I wonder if you could talk about how you've thought about language. There was a time when debates around writing in a "colonial language" were a big deal in Africa—the whole polemic around Ngũgĩ's *Decolonising the Mind*.

CNA: Well, the first thing for me is that I belong to a generation of Africans, really, who no longer speak only one language—I go back to Nigeria, and I'm speaking Igbo, and I can't speak two sentences in Igbo without throwing English words in there. And that's become the norm for my generation. I'm very sympathetic to Ngũgĩ's argument, but I think it's impractical. And I think it's limiting. The idea that only Gĩkũyũ, for example, can capture the Kenyan experience is just no longer true.

JJS: Language itself is always changing; it's living.

CNA: Right. And you have a great many people, urban Africans, who don't even speak those languages, who speak only English. But again—it's an English, I've often argued, that's ours. It's not British English. It may have come from there, but we've done things with it. I went out recently in Nigeria with a friend of mine who's an Englishman, and we went out with friends, and afterward we got in an argument—not an argument, but Nigerians are very good at shouting at each other more than necessary—and I hadn't realized that we had lapsed into this kind of very Nigerian English. And my friend said to me, "What's going on?" I said, "We're speaking English." And he said, "I don't understand a thing." And I thought, Ohhh, you don't understand. And I felt very pleased at that moment. Ahh, you don't understand, fantastic . . .

In writing, I just always want to capture that—that living in two languages, the negotiating back and forth. And of course I can't do it as much as I might; I have to think about my readers who don't speak Igbo, which is why I'm constantly doing a back-and-forth with my editors, who say, "Take a little more out." It is always a balancing act, but I can't ever see not doing it.

JJS: Achebe has that line about how it's the price English pays for being a global language—people make it their own.

CNA: Yes—and it's why academics these days talk about "Englishes" rather than English. In Achebe's fiction, I think what Achebe does that I find interesting is that he really uses that Nigerian English—he writes these constructions that are deliberately awkward; and you realize, Oh, he's doing the Nigerian English. I think his generation spoke it more. I think my generation is more likely to actually use Igbo words, or Yoruba, or whatever, in the English itself. So Achebe actually doesn't have so many Igbo words in his work, and I have more—but I think that does reflect a generational change. We're freer in a way; we're fortunate, we don't feel the need to divide them.

JJS: One of those other longstanding debates in African literature is around the place of the novel in so-called "oral cultures." There was that idea that an authentic African novel had to be an "oral novel" in some sense—people speak of Amos Tutuola, for example, that way: that in using pidgin, he wrote *The Palm Wine Drinkard* in spoken language. One thing I never quite understood about that debate is that good prose is always about writing sentences that sound good—whether we read them aloud or not—wouldn't you say?

CNA: Absolutely. That's exactly my feeling. When people start to talk about the Novel, and the Origin of the Novel . . . I think: Look, it's just storytelling. And just because it's written down, or somebody's saying it, it's just bloody storytelling. You know, my friend Binyavanga says, "Anything an African makes is African." And there is still this stupid thing, that people argue: "Is this authentically African?" And Binyavanga, you know, he has a friend in Nairobi—a street artist, who paints only white people. And someone's asking him, why do you do this? It's not really African. And the painter says, I'm Kenyan, this is what I paint, it's Kenyan. And Binyavanga says: Exactly. Why should we be prescriptive? This African authenticity becomes this really contested thing, and I think: Let's just tell our bloody stories.

JJS: It seems that's in some ways a real generational change.

CNA: I think so, too. But I think of course it's also easy for me to sit here and say that. Because there are people who fought the fights before.

JJS: Are there particular books you go back and read again and again—novels or anything else, before you write or anytime?

CNA: I often go back to *Arrow of God*, Chinua Achebe's book. That's really a book I love. I like Jamaica Kincaid—so I've read *Autobiography of My Mother* a few times. I like her sentences. I like the rhythm of them. I like Philip Roth. I've read *The Counterlife* a few times. I quite like how he deals with . . . the sociological? [*laughs*] I just feel that he's very engaged with the world. Sometimes I think there are a lot of writers who hide, in a way, behind the idea of the aesthetic, and art, and don't really grapple with things, and the world. And I think he does. And he's also just a really good writer. I like his sentences.

JJS: One doesn't often hear Kincaid and Roth mentioned together. I suppose there are common themes—memory, family, fictional autobiography. But Kincaid's style is so much more about literary effect—those poetic, visual sentences; Roth is more about character and story, libido—getting the sentences to move. What is it that's important about those two for you? How do they shape your aims as a stylist?

CNA: I like the energy of Roth, the use of repetition, the sense of story without undue self-indulgence. It's a little amusing that his characters speak in improbable blocks of text though. Kincaid is more self-consciously interested in language and I admire that unabashed lyricism because it's done really well.

IV. "I've never considered myself an immigrant."

JJS: You've been going back and forth between Nigeria and the United States for a while. How do you think that's impacted your work? Is it easier to write about a place when you're not there?

CNA: I think that one of the advantages of coming here when I did—I was nineteen, I came for university—was that I had the opportunity to see Nigeria in a way that I never would have. And it had to be America. It had to be this really strange country of extremes, and also this country that gives you space. I mean, if I had gone to England, it would have been so different; England would have been so close, in so many ways. And the US just gives me space. I quite appreciated that, and still do—that I suddenly was looking at Nigeria and could write about things. I think if I hadn't left Nigeria, *Purple Hibiscus* wouldn't have been the book that it is. There's something about it that is both consciously sentimental—and also, it's just the kind of book that one writes looking from the outside. If I'd been in Nigeria, I don't know that I would have been able to have the measure of . . . love?

JJS: Distance is important.

CNA: Yes, I think so.

JJS: You've written about the actual migrating, the travel back and forth, both in your fiction and nonfiction. You did that op-ed in the *Times* about waiting in line for a visa at the American Embassy in Nigeria; showing up at 4 a.m., the way everyone is treated . . .

CNA: Yes—you know, I was terrified when I went back. I was convinced I'd be blacklisted and no one was going to give me a visa!

JJS: But it's such a universal experience—at US embassies all over the world.

CNA: In Nigeria now they have special Pentecostal church services entirely for dealing with American visas. But I should say too that in my case, I've never considered myself an immigrant. Because I'm not, you know—I have temporary visas, I go back very often. So I do see myself as sort of a bridge between those real immigrants in America—people like my sister, for example, who moved here fifteen years ago, who made lives here, her kids are American—and people at home. And I'm just fascinated by things like my sister celebrating Thanksgiving; she doesn't even know what Thanksgiving is. She'll go through the thing, she'll cook the turkey—she doesn't even like turkey—and she'll do cranberry sauce. And it's fascinating to watch. And she'll turn to her kids, like immigrants everywhere, to explain the reality of this place to her. And a lot of these immigrants have this vision of: we're going home someday—although I really don't think they will.

JJS: It's interesting, this difference between generations, around going back—whether or not one does return, there is that idea that one could. And that's so different from a couple generations ago, when to emigrate was to emigrate—you went and that was it. The old country was the old country—past.

CNA: I think we were also quite lucky in that way—there isn't that same pressure on my sister and newer immigrants, that pressure many once felt to assimilate immediately—to speak English right away, all that. Now you can speak the older language with your children, you can build communities. You do have that choice, which is good.

V. "I happen to love this bloody country I come from."

JJS: You're one of a number of younger African writers who have gained some wonderful visibility in the US recently—Dinaw Mengestu with his book on

Washington DC's immigrants; Ishmael Beah and his memoir from Sierra Leone; Chris Abani and his fantastic novels on Lagos and Los Angeles. These seem to be writers who aren't doing stuff overdetermined by the national drama, who are engaging a really wide range of themes and problems.

CNA: I think it's very exciting. And when I talk about this sort of thing with my friend Binyavanga—we're quite close, we have these conversations where we disagree fiercely about these things—I often say to him that I feel that I am one of the younger people in this generation, but also in some ways I'm the most old-fashioned—I'm still very keen on history, on the state of this bloody country I love. But much to my excitement, people like Chris [Abani], he'll do this marvelous book about LA. And I love that. Or Helen Oyeyemi, she writes of mythology, about Cuba. And I think, Well done! I love that we have this diversity, that African literature no longer means everyone is simply fighting colonialism. Which isn't to say fighting colonialism is still not very legitimate. The idea that we gained independence in 1960 in Nigeria, for example—all you have to do is go there and look at the school curriculum, or watch the Senate, and realize that the whole thing is just deeply messed up. But I really like that—I love the diversity, of approaches, of subjects . . .

JJS: There seems to be less of that pressure that's existed for "ethnic" or "third-world writers"—the idea that every time out you're meant to write allegory about one's people. But still there's that sense that you don't always have the same license to write "universal" stories, to write of places or cultures not one's own; a pressure that "nonethnic"—white—writers don't necessarily have.

CNA: I think it has to do simply with the fact that white American remains the norm, so it's never questioned. And then everything else is "ethnic," which is hilarious to me. It becomes the one story that becomes the every story. We can read a white American and not be expected to see it as their white American story. It's sort of like James Baldwin, writing for the race—where some of his work becomes "the African American story," not a story about these characters. And even though I really resent it at times, I think that more and more, as I'm increasingly aware of having an audience, I find myself thinking about things I don't want to be thinking about. Such as: My vision is dark. I like to write about violence; for some reason I'm drawn to horrible things people have done. And then I realize: Am I somehow adding to the stereotype of my continent? Because I'm angry about the stereotype. But on the other hand, I'm also horrified by people killing each other in

Lagos, and I want to write about—but if I do . . . And it's that kind of thing that I wish I didn't have to consider. Like everyone, I want just to be allowed to follow my artistic vision. On the other hand, you do think: I happen to love this bloody country I come from, and I don't want to contribute to it being seen only in horrible ways.

JJS: Biafra's important in this respect too, isn't it—that sense in which Biafra isn't just an Igbo story, or a Nigerian story, but also inaugurated the way Westerners have seen "Africa" since. It was the first time that those images were on TV everywhere—of starving children, of black people from the same country killing each other for no apparent reason.

CNA: It started it all. Part of me wishes someone had kept those photographers and TV cameras away from Biafra! The image of Africa would be different. Because it is the image—it's been modified in some ways, but the thinking behind it has been passed down to the coverage today. It's still Biafra when CNN is covering the Congo. And it's this sort of coverage that doesn't deal with African actors. Which is why I get so depressed when I'm outside Nigeria. I think, My God, we're finished. And then I go back home—and yes, things are messed up. But you see people doing things, and making an effort, and pushing back, which you never see in the way that it's covered outside Nigeria. It's frustrating.

JJS: One of the clichéd questions asked of African writers—in part, I suppose, because so many African writers have felt moved to write on it—is that question about "the future of the African novel." So I won't ask it.

CNA: Good. [*laughs*]

JJS: But I wanted to mention that essay of Nadine Gordimer's from a few years back where she engages that old concern around having more African readers to read African books. She wrote that "African literature will either make history . . . or be history."

CNA: Again, it's that discourse of the "future of the novel"; and I'm just not that concerned—we'll always tell stories. People will find ways. If it's not through novels in two hundred years—if it's PowerPoint or whatever—well, well and good. But the point is that people will tell stories. When people call me a novelist, I say, well, yes. But really I think of myself as a storyteller.

Writer Chimamanda Ngozi Adichie Interview

Eleanor Wachtel / 2009

From *Writers & Company*, CBC Radio, 14 June 2009. Writers & Company with Eleanor Wachtel / CBC Licensing. Reprinted by permission.

Eleanor Wachtel: I'd like to ask you first about something that you said in an interview. When you were asked, "If you could go back in time, where would you go to?," you answered, "The West Coast of Africa, around 1650." Why? What would you want to see or do at that point?

Chimamanda Ngozi Adichie: I'd like to capture some Portuguese traders and put them in a cage.

EW: [*laughs*] I wondered, because it was the beginning of the slave trade. Is that really, is that though . . .

CNA: It wasn't just about the slave trade. I mean, at that time, you had Europeans trading on the West Coast, trading in things other than people. So, people had exchanges of cloth and beads and oil—palm oil, of course—and that sort of thing. There's something about that period that I find fascinating. Also, a lot hasn't been recorded about that period. So, really, it was just more about wanting to go back to a time when, I imagine—this is something that I might have invented—there seemed to be some dignity in trade, apart from the trade in human beings of course, and maybe some equality. People met on those coasts and exchanged goods and hopefully left with mutual respect. Or I'm just romanticizing things, but that's really what I had in mind.

EW: And if you could capture Portuguese traders on the side, that would be okay . . .

CNA: And keep him, yes, in a royal cage, and feed him and . . . no, I'm just joking.

EW: In your new collection, *The Thing around Your Neck*, your story "The Headstrong Historian" focuses on a traditional but unconventional African woman whose life takes some unexpected turns. You've said that this story was inspired by tales that you were told about your own great-grandmother. Can you tell me about the woman behind the story, or what you know about her?

CNA: My father's grandmother—her name was Omeni, and I have since asked my family members to call me Omeni, which they do sometimes—my father talks about her. She died when my father was eight, in 1940. My father says she was very old at the time; of course he didn't know how old. I remember being struck by stories of her being called "the troublemaker" by people in my village, because she wouldn't shut up. Her husband had died, and his relatives were very keen to take away the things that he owned from her, and she wouldn't let them. My father says that she was also known to attend the meetings that were supposed to be for men, and that she would go there and speak her mind, and make them all listen to her. I was just really drawn to the idea of this woman—my father says she was quite fierce. He says she was a really small woman, but quite fierce. He remembers going to visit her; her friends would come, and she would just talk, and everybody sat there and listened to her. So I just loved the story of this woman, who was supposed to be a troublemaker and who was supposed to be headstrong and stubborn—all of these things that are ostensibly bad, I thought were fantastic. She just challenged all the stereotypes of the long-suffering, silent, oppressed woman. So she's always been in my imagination; I've always sort of imagined that she's somewhere, urging me on to write.

EW: Do you think you take after her?

CNA: I like to think so. I know that I have been considered a bit of a troublemaker sometimes. One of the reasons I wanted to write about her—and I think I will in a longer form at some point, hopefully—is also that she was unusual, in the sense that she would go to these meetings for men. But I don't think she was necessarily unusual in the kind of strength she had and in how innovative she was. My father says that she was a potter, so she would go off to the river and collect clay and make pots. There is a sense in which I think the kind of new idea of femaleness in Nigeria today—which I think has a lot to do with Victorian Christianity—doesn't quite . . . I don't think that woman, that great-grandmother figure, is something that people would recognize. The idea of the woman living in Igboland in 1890—if you ask the average educated Nigerian woman, she would say that that woman in 1890 sat at home and cooked for her husband and worshipped him. But actually, she was making pots; she was selling her pots and making money. So, I think also there is a sense in which she [Omeni] was unusual, but she wasn't all that unusual. I was very keen to celebrate that and to write about that.

EW: It's interesting, because I have this sense of—particularly *West*—African women as being very strong and selling things and working and being in the markets, and that kind of thing . . .
CNA: Yes and no. There's a very strong class component to it. Today, in 2009, if you talk to educated West African women, middle-class women, it's a little worrying what their ideas of female[ness are] . . . I mean, there are people who are very well educated, but who still will say to you, "I won't work because my husband won't let me work, although I want to work." And then, when you point out that it really doesn't make sense to feel this way, they say, "Well, the man is the head of the family, this is what the Bible says"—that sort of thing. I really think that, in many ways, femaleness was a much more empowering thing a hundred years ago in West Africa than it is today.

EW: Grace, the granddaughter in the story, also has a fighting spirit and has this special bond with her grandmother. As an adult, she reclaims African history and identity, even her own name. I wondered how that awakening, or that journey of discovery, relates to your own sense of yourself or your own work.
CNA: I was educated in Nigeria. I was very fortunate to have a good education, but at the same time I felt that my education didn't equip me well. I didn't learn about precolonial West African history, for example. My education didn't prepare me to visualize the life that my great-grandmother might have lived. This is something that is common to people who are educated in societies like mine, and I think there is a sense in which I imagine myself on a kind of semi-crazed quest to understand my own past. I find myself really drawn to reading a lot of history, and wanting to know, "How did we get where we are?" I sometimes think that in Nigeria, we're so myopic about the past; we're very present-focused. People don't make many connections between past and present. There's a sense in which our present is disconnected from our past, and it's something I question. So, a lot of my work is about seeking, about trying to reclaim. I mean, the stories have been told, but I want to tell them my own way; I want to tell my version.

EW: Your own story begins in 1977. You were born in Enugu, in the Southeast, and raised in the town of Nsukka, where your parents both held positions at the university. Your family's roots were in Abba, in the South. How did you experience your ancestral hometown when you were growing up?

CNA: Like many Igbo families, we spent Christmas at home, in our hometown, and sometimes Easter, and then we would go visit my grandmother some weekends, before she died. I loved going to my hometown. I mean, I was the child who was very interested in our history, so I wanted to know. I would ask my grandmother questions; I would follow her around. When I became a teenager, I was much given to romanticizing, so I would walk down towards the stream and think, "My great-grandfather walked on this land." But I also noticed things—it's something one can't help but notice: the clash, in some ways. Well, "clash" is a little dramatic, but the "old" sitting side by side with the "new." And not just in terms of architecture, for example. You would see a hut that might be a hundred years old, and next to it you would see a perfectly modern house. But it was also that you saw traditions trying to find a fit. We had, in my extended family, a man who hadn't converted to Christianity. My grandfather had converted, so my family is Christian, but one of his distant cousins hadn't. We have quite the strong sense of extended family, so you had all of these people coming to our house at Christmas, but I remember being very clearly told not to eat at his house. If we went to visit this man, who wasn't Christian, and if he gave us food, [we were told] not to eat, because he had sacrificed his food to idols, and therefore it was bad. This man was funny and nice and kind, and laughed. The idea that because he didn't go to church with us, he was automatically . . .—you know, he was your family, but you couldn't eat in his house—I remember questioning [that] even as a child, and it's the sort of thing I continue to question. So for me, going to my hometown was fun. I loved it, I had tons of cousins—we laughed and all of that—but also, it was for me a learning thing. I was always watching, always storing up questions in my head.

EW: So you were the repository of the family history in some funny way, even as a little kid?

CNA: Well, in an odd sort of way. Most families have the child who's just interested in their story, and I think I was that child.

EW: In an essay that you wrote about your father, you talk about asking him to explain ornate Igbo proverbs. Can you give an example?

CNA: Oh, I can't. I mean, I grew up sort of easily bilingual—so I consider both Igbo and English my first languages because I really spoke both at the same time, and often in the same sentence, as I continue to do when I'm home. But the difference of course is that my father, having grown up in my hometown, surrounded by people who had been speaking this language for centuries and who had it passed down, speaks a very rich kind of Igbo. My siblings and I speak a very anglicized version, so sometimes my father—and Igbo is so rich in proverbs—is telling a story, and he says something and we're all looking at him; we don't understand what he said. So now, he says that and he immediately explains. I mean, I really couldn't give an example because I don't know how.

EW: I remember, when I talked to the great Nigerian writer Chinua Achebe, he talked about how important proverbs were for him when he was growing up, and there's even a line in his first novel that [reads], "Proverbs are the palm oil with which words are eaten." And I wondered, does that have resonance for you, or is it more of a generational thing?

CNA: It *is* a generational thing. For me, proverbs have become the kind of thing you deeply admire, and you just don't have it. I really don't know how. I mean, there are a few people of my generation [who do]; they're the people who are fortunate to spend a lot of time in their ancestral hometowns, and spend time with relatives who are still connected to that life. But we just didn't get it, unfortunately.

EW: The central trauma in your recent family history is, of course, the Nigerian-Biafran war of 1967 to 1970, in which over a million people died. I want to talk to you about that and about your novel covering that period, *Half of a Yellow Sun*. But first: both of your grandfathers died in the Biafran war, eight years before you were born, and you've described them as proud, strong men, determined to educate their children. Can you tell me about them?

CNA: I know a bit more about my father's father, because my father talks about him much more than my mother talks about her father. Actually, my mother has never really talked to me about how he died in the war. When I was researching the book and I was talking to everybody and being obsessive about things, I drew a line at my mother and her father. I realized she just wasn't ready, and she probably will never be ready to talk about it, and I didn't push. So I don't know how she felt. I mean, I knew that he died in a refugee camp; I knew that somebody came at six in the morning to tell them that he had died, days after he had died, because it was difficult to go across occupied roads. But she's never talked about it. She did tell me a story about her father, and sending her to school. My mother is the first of originally ten siblings—now five. My mother was born in 1942, and her father was determined that she would be educated. His relatives said to him, "Why are you wasting your money educating a girl? She's just going to cook and clean for her husband." And her father said, "Leave me alone, I want to educate my daughter." My mother says that once, when she was in secondary school— she was away at boarding school—he wrote her a letter in English, which he didn't speak very well—but he was an aspirational man—and started with "My dear son." My mother assumed that he'd made a mistake, and so she wrote him back and said, "Papa, it should be 'daughter.'" He wrote back and said, "I know. I *know*. I meant that you're just like a son; that I don't value you any less." I loved that story. There's just something about it that I love, that he refused to let people tell him that a female child is somehow less than a male child. My mother sometimes says that she wishes that he had lived to see her become the first female registrar of the University of Nigeria. And I too wish that he had lived, but . . .

My father's father . . . My father describes him as fiercely moral, and it's so moving for me to go back, even now, to my hometown, and people still talk about him. People still say things like, "If only Adichie was alive, he would tell the truth about this matter." Or, "If only Adichie was alive, people would go to him to . . ." If people had a dispute, for example—I mean, he was supposed to be a peacemaker and a truth teller. That that legacy lives on is something I just feel so proud of. He was a carpenter and herbalist and didn't have much money. But my father says that his father was such a visionary. I mean, he recognized early on that colonialism was here to stay. The white man was going to be in power for a long time, and if you wanted your child to succeed, the old ways had to give way to things such as Western education. My father did quite well in school, and so his father was just really determined. My father tells all sorts of stories about going to this town far off, because my hometown didn't have a secondary school; [he talks about] all sorts of sacrifices that his father made. For my father, I'm assuming that one of the most painful things about losing his father—who was relatively young, only in his sixties—during the war was that he just didn't get to see what his son would become.

My father also tells a story about when the war was just starting, and his father, my grandfather, who was very much an Igboman, wanted to stay in his home—"you don't run away from the enemy, this is my home, I will protect it." So my father says his father went in and brought a rusty old gun, then dug a hole outside and climbed into the hole and said, "Now, I'm waiting for the Nigerian soldiers." My father said to him, "Papa, this is ridiculous!" And he's like, "No, I can't leave my home." My father said it took a while to convince him to leave, and that some people didn't. Some of my grandfather's friends refused to leave, and of course died. It's actually something that I write about in the novel. I have a character whose mother just refuses, because . . .

EW: Exactly, yeah.

CNA: Looking at it in a clinical way, you think that's silly, but then when you realize that for some people, it's their entire identity; the way that they make sense of the world is in that space, and to ask them to just up and leave . . . they just refused.

EW: How did your father's father die?

CNA: He died in a refugee camp, he was sick. My father didn't know about it, again, until about a week had passed. Then, when my father finally went to the refugee camp, nobody could tell him exactly where his father was buried. People were dying every day, so they just buried them outside somewhere. Somebody waved vaguely and said, "Oh, it's somewhere around there." And my father, who is not at all dramatic, says that he went there and took a handful of sand, which he still has—[this,] for me, was actually one of the most moving stories he had ever told me about the war. All he was told is that his father had been sick, and that he died. I mean, it was probably something minor, but then, of course, nobody had access to medication.

EW: You've described your father as wise and wonderful, and how as a child you thought him invincible, but you also say you found him remote. In what way?

CNA: As a child, I did. I mean, Daddy was the man who was in the study. My mother was a lot more approachable. My mother knew our friends; my mother was the kind of mother who was cool, and so all the friends liked her. So, people wanted to come to our house. My mother would remember your nickname, and my mother thought it was fine for teenagers to go off to parties. She was a very cool mother. My father, on the other hand, . . . I mean, when I was growing up, sometimes I thought he was a stranger who went upstairs to his study and spent time with his books. I think it's probably that teenage thing when you just think, "My dad doesn't get it; he's odd, he's talking to himself in the study." I was maybe sixteen when I completely fell in love with him. I guess I became a human being. So, at last, I realized the world was not about me . . . [*laughs*]

EW: Sixteen is relatively young, actually.
CNA: I started to talk to him and, I don't know, we just really, really bonded. I adore him. He's not just my father; he's my friend, and we have conversations. In some ways it's sad, because my mother and I don't have the conversations that my father and I do now; it's very odd.

EW: What does he make of your work as a writer?
CNA: He's a very honest person, but also very supportive. When I started off writing, I would give him my stories to read, and he was always honest. Sometimes he would say, "I didn't understand this," or he would say, "This doesn't make any sense." When he read *Purple Hibiscus*, he liked it. He did say, rather dryly, that he was worried that people would think that the abusive father character was based on him—which they did.

EW: Because it [*Purple Hibiscus*] features a strange relationship between a narrator, who's a quiet, bookish teenager, and her domineering and abusive father . . .
CNA: And my father's nothing like that! I mean, the reason I could write that character is because my father was nothing like that. But then, people did make that assumption. But *Half of a Yellow Sun* was the novel that I was most worried about. I mean, it was so different for me, that book. It took a lot from me, emotionally, to write. And because I had used my father's memories, in some ways I was worried. I was thinking, "Have I done it well? Have I done justice to what he remembers, and how he remembers?" I remember leaving the manuscript with him. I had the manuscript for a while when I was visiting them [my family] in Nsukka. I waited the day before I left, and I gave it to him, then I took off. I was like, "I don't want to be there when Daddy's reading this," and waited for him to call me. Then, of course, I was calling my brother, who was there, and asking him, "Well, is he reading it? Can you tell from his expression?" My brother said, "I can't tell you, but all I can tell you is that he's always with the manuscript, everywhere, he's not doing anything else." Then finally, my dad called, and—I will never forget—he said: "Nne m ocie"—he calls me "Nne m ocie," which means "my grandmother"; it's sort of a fond thing, I'm supposed to be his

grandmother come back. He said, "Nne m ocie, I expected this to be good, I did not think it would be this good."

EW: Aah . . .
CNA: And I, given to stupid emotional outbursts as I am, I started to cry.

EW: Whoa, that's not stupid. That's really touching.
CNA: He's a good man.

EW: Your parents, you've said, were very committed to the Biafran cause and were deeply affected by the war—not just through losing their fathers, but everything that happened. How did they experience the war? What happened to them? How did they deal with the losses?
CNA: I don't know. I mean, my parents [were] much like many of the middle-class and academic people—in Nigeria, there is a particular class that I like to call the academic middle class: they have different concerns, they're a strange bunch. But they all really supported the cause, the Biafran cause. Biafra had grassroots support, mostly because people from Eastern Nigeria had been massacred in Northern Nigeria, which meant that Eastern Nigerians said, "We want our own state." Really, that's sort of the basic bones of it.

EW: The precipitating factor . . .
CNA: Yes. But I think that what the intellectuals did, [what] the academics did, was that they turned it into a narrative, into songs and stories, and all of that. My parents are very much a part of it. They believed fervently. My father says that until the war ended, he had convinced himself that they would win. Looking back, in retrospect, you think, "Well, Daddy, how could *you* have thought you would win? I mean, it was obvious that you wouldn't." And he said, "Well, we just believed." I think that kind of blind, almost delusional faith made it possible for them to absorb the loss of their fathers. They lost cousins. My mother was always terrified that her baby was going to die. My brother was born during the war, and she said she lived in terror that something would happen to him. But that kind of crazy faith made them survive.

EW: And afterwards?
CNA: Afterwards, I think it was difficult for them. I know that they went back to the campus in Nsukka where they had lived. I mean, a lot of the stories of *Half of a Yellow Sun* are really my parents' stories.

EW: Hmm, I'm already recognizing it. [*laughs*] Your father and Odenigbo a little bit, and . . .

CNA: Yes. My parents went back; their house had been really desecrated, and many friends had died. I think it was quite difficult for them—just to go back to pretending that things were normal when things weren't. My father says that he focused on things like, "We need to get the water running again," because, by focusing on that, you really didn't have to think too much about [the fact that] your neighbor next door had died; on the other side, he'd been arrested . . .

EW: Your novel *Half of a Yellow Sun* is set during the first decade of Nigeria's independence, which includes the civil war of 67 to 70. You said that you grew up in the shadow of Biafra. Although the war wasn't discussed at school or anything, *Half of a Yellow Sun* was the book you had to write. Why is that?

CNA: I really don't know. I do feel that Biafra has haunted me for a long time, and I can't explain it. I mean, I can't explain why it was me, for example, and not my sister, Ijeoma, who lived through it—my sister was four, or five, or six, and she still . . . she remembered, and I used some of her memories for the Baby character in my novel. It meant a lot to her, obviously, but it didn't haunt her like it did me. So I don't know why. I've just always known that I wanted to make sense of this history. I wanted to try and understand. I wanted to . . . yeah, I was just a little crazy.

EW: Because even now, you say, almost forty years later, Biafra remains a sore subject, and you say we should be asking why. What answers have you found to that question?

CNA: I am still asking. But one of the things that I am very happy about is that I'm no longer the only one asking; I no longer feel alone. I have a lot of hope in my generation of Nigerians. When this book came out in Nigeria, I really felt happy that, for them, it became a book that served as a starting point for a conversation about what happened. It's not always polite, the conversations—[they are] often spirited—but we're talking. And I think it's a starting point, because it's impossible for us to move forward in any way that makes sense if we don't engage with what happened.

EW: It's still not taught in schools?

CNA: No. There's still a formal silence around it. People who were active in the war are still very much active in Nigerian politics. There are questions still unanswered, and I think it makes people nervous. For example, the man who was Head of State, who was murdered, it's sort of general knowledge: we all know who is supposed to be responsible for his murder, but you don't really talk about it. This man who is said to be responsible for his murder is active in Nigerian politics. And our former president, for example, was very active in the war, and there are people who have accused him of, if not supporting, [at least] looking away when massacres were committed. It's how present it is that just makes people not want to talk about it.

EW: You describe in your novel the terrible massacres of Christian Igbo people by their Muslim Hausa neighbors in the North that actually triggered the start of the war, the secession of Igboland in Eastern Nigeria. Then, of course, this multiplied during the war in terms of death and destruction. Given that the country stayed together and that people have to live [together], is it just too hard to face?
CNA: I think it is hard, and it's also that people have . . . I mean, we are Nigerian. There are regional differences and regional resentments about, but I think that we've convinced ourselves that we've adopted this Nigerian identity. There is a part of us that's terrified, that [thinks that] to start digging into the past is to question the very idea of that identity; it's too fragile. I sometimes think that maybe, if we had a stable and good government that actually made every region feel included, then we might start to talk about our history. But this just might be my wishy-washy idea.

EW: Well, no, it's an idealistic idea . . . because, I mean, *is* it too dangerous? I wonder, what are the relationships now between, say, Hausa and Igbo?
CNA: It's a very complicated thing, because sometimes I think that too much is made of ethnic difference.

EW: Religious difference?
CNA: That too. Religious difference is often intertwined with ethnic difference, because the general idea is in the South, the Igbo and Yoruba people are mostly Christian; in the North, the Hausa people are mostly Muslim. So, sometimes you find that people attribute things that are actually cultural to religion, and the other way around. They'll say, "Oh, those women do that; that's what Islam made them do." And you think, "Well no, actually it's not Islam." But there's a lot that's politicized. It started with the way that the British managed Nigeria. It made sense for the British colonial government,

instead of trying to create and forge a national identity, to encourage the idea of regionalism, to encourage competition, and then to have people see difference not in political or ideological terms, but in ethnic terms. Our politics, from the beginning, was never ideological. It was always "the Northern party." And nobody knew, is the Northern party to the left or the right? Nobody [knew], it's just "the Northern party." And it continues today. My dream—and I'm such a dreamer, but hey—is that if we have a government that actually is about ideas, there are lots of people for whom it really will not matter. For example, I remember when our present president became president. He's a Northerner, and there are lots of Nigerians who resent the idea of a Northern domination, because for very long the North has been in power; I think there's good reason to feel that way. But I remember thinking, "I don't care that he's from the North, I want him to not be a thief; I want him to actually care about people; I want him to create people-centered policies, and I'll be fine." Now, that's not happening *but* I think there are lots of people who are like me, for whom ethnicity is not the point; they want good governance. The reason ethnicity continues to trouble us is because we haven't had good governance.

EW: *Half of a Yellow Sun* is told from three perspectives, and one of the main characters is a beautiful, educated, politically engaged young woman named Olanna, the partner of a math professor with revolutionary ideals. She has a twin sister, and they couldn't be more different. Both are interesting, but why twins? What did you want to explore?
CNA: When I started, I wanted to write about sisters who have a complicated relationship, and I didn't want age to complicate things further. In a culture like mine, age always does, because the older sibling has to have a certain kind of respect and you have to do a bit of sucking up. I didn't want that to come in at all. I wanted them to start off being the same age, so that age could be discounted. So, that's really why.

EW: But aren't twins problematic in Igbo culture?
CNA: They used to be. My people killed twins until . . .

EW: That's what I was thinking!
CNA: No, now twins are supposed to be a blessing, and women want twins. But until a hundred years ago, we were putting them in a pot and taking them out to the evil forest.

EW: Another character whose point of view you give us is an Englishman, Richard, who's a would-be writer. When we first meet him, he's a writer without much of a subject, but then he comes to be more Biafran than the Biafrans. He's certainly very different from the rest of the English community in postcolonial Nigeria. What do you make of him? How do you see his place in this story?

CNA: I wanted to have an outsider. Richard is a character I've been asked about a lot by Englishmen—I'm not sure what that says. I noticed as well that many Englishmen don't seem to like Richard, and that's something that I'm curious about.

EW: That's because he's periodically impotent, I think. That would put some men off!

CNA: [*laughs*] I'm often asked, "Were you trying to say something about colonialism?" And I think, "No, he was just impotent, I wasn't saying anything about anything!" But it really was important for me to have the outsider point of view. I wanted to play with it a little. I had read quite a bit about journalists in Biafra, and Richard was inspired by a number of accounts, particularly of the people who came to Biafra and somehow stepped across that "objective"—although I'm not sure there is such a thing—line and became emotionally involved. In a larger sense, the British were really disliked, strongly disliked in Biafra, because the British were seen as arming Nigeria, and the reason Nigeria was winning was because they had British support. So, the British were very unpopular in Biafra, but you did have individual British journalists who came to Biafra and just really threw themselves into the cause. That's where Richard started. Obviously, there's a lot of colonial baggage, and I wanted to have that. I wasn't going to make Richard a Frenchman, because that would be a different thing. I mean, the fact that Nigeria is, in many ways, a creation of his ancestors was important.

EW: The servant, Ugwu, is, as you say, the "soul" of the novel. His perceptions are charming, and funny, and totally persuasive. We see him at the opening of the story; he's just thirteen years old and he's leaving his rural village to work for the professor and his partner. What was it that interested you in his experience and his perspective?

CNA: I've often said that Ugwu is the character who's most like me, who I most identified with. I mean, obviously, our lives are different, but Ugwu is really me in the way that he looks at the world, and in the way that he's so keen to learn. Ugwu came from my mother telling me about the houseboy she had during the war, whose name was Mellitus. The book is partly dedicated to him.

EW: I noticed that. You say, "wherever he may be." Do you know what happened to him?

CNA: No, we don't know. My parents tried to find him; we just don't know. My mother talked about him, and I just remember thinking, "I wonder what it was like for him." I mean, my mother's stories were interesting—how useful he was, and all of that. But I remember thinking, "Well, I wonder what *he* would think." I wonder what *he* thought about things. And so, that's really where Ugwu came from. Then, part of the motivation for Ugwu also came from a houseboy we had when I was growing up, who really became sort of like a brother, and who had come from his rural hometown when I was maybe eight. I look back now and I see it as the moment when I realized the entire world wasn't like mine. Because this person had come to live with us, and he had never seen a telephone, and he did not know what a refrigerator was. I was there looking at him and thinking, "My God!" Then he became family, and later he died. He joined the Nigerian army and went to fight in Sierra Leone. It's still very painful for all of us. So I think that Ugwu was my way of paying tribute to Fide—Fide was the houseboy we had who'd died—because in many ways Fide was like Ugwu: he came from his rural hometown, [was] extremely intelligent, very funny, but just not familiar with the trappings of the modern world. But also, it was amazing how quickly he learned, because in a month, he was fixing the stereo. [*EW and CNA laugh*]

EW: The stories in your new collection, *The Thing around Your Neck*, were written over a number of years, and many are set in the United States and reflect the experience of African women immigrating to the United States. You first lived in the US with your family when you were eight, when your father was a visiting professor in San Diego, and then you returned at nineteen on a student visa. You've talked about having a complicated affection for America. What does that mean?

CNA: I think there's a sense in which—and I've often been told different versions of it—"You are an immigrant, we let you in, so shut up and be grateful." I like America very much. There's a lot I like about it, and I do feel that the trajectory of my life so far happened because I went to America. It wouldn't have happened if I'd gone to England. The space that America gives you and—whether or not it's true—the sense of possibility one gets was very useful for me. But then, on the other hand, there's a lot that I don't like. For me, affection means that you like something and you're grateful for a lot, but it doesn't mean that you shouldn't talk about the things you don't like.

EW: In your story, "Imitation," you write that it's one of the things she [the protagonist, Nkem] has come to love about America, "the abundance of unreasonable hope." There seem to be some contradictory ideas right there. What about this abundance?

CNA: I think it *is* true; I think America is a country full of unreasonable hope. It's also one of the reasons that there's very little class resentment in the US. There's a lot of unreasonable hope—it's also why you have people voting against their own interests in large numbers. *There's* somebody who can hardly feed her children, but she's voting for a party that really isn't looking out for her. But why is that? Because she aspires to that class that's being looked after. I mean, it's a dangerous thing in many ways, but also there's something that one has to admire about it—that America is this country that has created ideas that people have bought into; whether or not the idea is true is irrelevant. And I admire that. The social engineering of it is interesting.

EW: The balance of power between men and women is another of your subjects, and it seems to shift for some of the characters with the move to America. For example, in that story, "Imitation," the husband enjoys the status of having a wife and a house in the US, meanwhile installing a mistress in their home in Africa, where he mostly lives. But in the story, the wife, left alone with the children in America, becomes resistant to this arrangement and refuses to compromise. Similarly, in the title story, "The Thing around Your Neck," a young woman rejects the attitudes of her uncle, who is not actually her uncle but is imposing sexual favors on her. She just leaves and wants to make her own way. And I wonder, is it the characters' inner strength that allows them to stand up for themselves, or is it the move to America, a new country, that empowers them?

CNA: I think it's both. It's the idea of going to a new place and discovering things about yourself you didn't know you had. I mean, I have observed this in people I know. There's a sense in which living in Nigeria can sometimes make a woman think that it's impossible to do anything without a man to do it for you. As a middle-class woman, you go to university, then you find a husband; if possible, you don't work, you stay home, and he supplies you with the car and the driver, and all the trappings. Then you come to the US and you realize, "I can actually do it for myself. In addition, it feels rather good to do it for myself." I think it's also the reason that some marriages haven't survived. There are Nigerian marriages that haven't survived the move to the US; it's the balance of power shifting. So I think it's both. I mean, America is certainly important in the narrative, at least for me and what I've observed. That story, "Imitation," was about a woman discovering that she can, in fact, have a voice, no matter how small; she *can* have a voice.

EW: You've said that being a black African woman who writes realistic fiction automatically puts you in a political role, and that you feel a responsibility to accept that role. Why?
CNA: It's a role that I feel very ambivalent about. I mean, I'm a storyteller—that's all I want to be; that's really the only thing that I do relatively well, tell stories. But I also realize it would be dishonest for me to say that I'm just a writer and it doesn't matter, and my stories don't mean anything. Maybe in a fantasy world, yes. But one has to be realistic. I'm writing about a place of scarce resources. I'm telling stories that are set in recognizable places, and a lot of things there are contested. I realize that my fiction becomes political, whether or not one intends it to be. There is a sense in which I accept that, but I don't let that define me and define my work. So, in Nigeria, for example, I have been told that I am a "role model," and therefore should not say certain things in public. I just think that's rubbish.

EW: And you feel free to express explicit opinions about the politics of current Nigeria?
CNA: I do. I like to say what I think.

EW: Have you thought of going into politics yourself?
CNA: Yes, but I'm not sure I will. I think that politics is just too hard; it involves too many compromises. I don't think I could. But there are many times I have thought about it. I've thought about running for governor of my state, because my state is just a disaster zone and it's really difficult for me to understand why we have leaders who don't seem to have a sense of their people, who don't seem to care. But then, I don't know, because I haven't been there. But there are times when I've thought about it. I've thought, "I'm going to run for governor; I will prove that one can be governor without stealing a penny; I will prove that one can be governor and fix the schools; I will prove that one can be governor and make sure people have healthcare." But maybe it's easier said than done; I don't know.

EW: You've said that you feel despair when you're outside Nigeria. How is it different when you're back at home? How do you see things then?

CNA: Because you see that people are striving, that people are doing. When [I'm] outside Nigeria and I read the news on the internet, I sometimes think, "Oh, things are terrible, it's just hopeless." Then I go back and talk to people. I mean, it's not to say that things are good, because they're mostly not. There's a lot that needs to be done, and I don't think we have a government that's doing very well. But then, on the other hand, you see that people are doing, and it just makes you realize that . . . it just moves me out of my despair and takes me to a place of great irritation instead, which is preferable to despair.

EW: You recently won the MacArthur Genius Award, which is $100,000 a year for five years, no strings. So, you don't have to teach or anything. Where will you live?

CNA: I want to keep spending time in the US and in Nigeria, and I think that's probably what I'll do for the rest of my life, the back and forth. Nigeria is the home of my heart, but I like America very much, so I want to keep doing both.

EW: Well, your heart belongs to somebody in America, which is, as I understand, part of why you're staying in America. Or would you stay anyway?

CNA: I think so, yes, because I had imagined that that would be the life I would have even before I met this wonderful man.

EW: I wonder, could you read a passage from your new collection? This is from the title story, "The Thing around Your Neck."

CNA: [*reads from the beginning of the story*]

EW: Chimamanda Adichie, reading from her story, "The Thing around Your Neck." Thank you very much. It's great to have had the chance to meet you.

CNA: Thank you. Thanks. I've enjoyed this.

Q&A with Chimamanda Adichie

Lia Grainger / 2009

From *National Post*, 17 June 2009. Material republished with the express permission of: National Post, a division of Postmedia Network Inc.

Though the title of Chimamanda Ngozi Adichie's new book of stories, *The Thing around Your Neck*, might indicate something as sinister as a noose or as innocuous as a necklace, it is revealed in the seventh of twelve stories to be something more abstract and indefinable. That thing that "would wrap itself around your neck, something that very nearly choked you before you fell asleep" is the loneliness and alienation felt by a girl that is far away from her home in Nigeria, living in the United States entirely alone.

Though these stories are fiction, the territory they explore—life in a Nigerian university town, moving from Nigeria to America, a writer's workshop—mirror many of Adichie's own experiences. Her personal and studied knowledge of the characters in her stories lend them the richness and believability that are consistent features of this young writer's work. *The Thing around Your Neck* is Adichie's third book, and is already garnering the same critical acclaim won by her first two novels, *Purple Hibiscus* and *Half of a Yellow Sun*. In clean, simple prose, Adichie tears through preconceived notions of both Nigeria and America to tell deeply personal stories of violence, tenderness and understanding.

LG: Have people in North America and Africa reacted differently to your work?

CNA: *Half of the Yellow Sun* is the book that is most widely read. In Nigeria it wasn't just a novel, it was history and it was also politics. I think people took it much more seriously in Nigeria. People often stepped across from fiction and said things like, "Why did she choose to write about this and not that?" It became very contested, but often in a good way. That made me very happy, because I had hoped that people would talk about this history after reading the book, and for me it was fantastic—both the good and the bad. I would be really happy to get an email saying, "You taught me my history and I've gone back to my parents to talk about 1960," and also the emails saying, "Why did you write about this, you're a troublemaker, leave it alone."

I think also that people in the rest of Africa and in countries like India, countries that have similar colonial histories—and this I can only speak about from the emails that I get from people—is that they read the book as if it could also have been the story of their country. People in India will say it's very familiar. In the US, not so much. I was actually really surprised by [my work's popularity in the US]. I hadn't imagined that anyone would want to read it. I remember joking with my editor and saying to her, "I should be writing about Darfur, if I write about Darfur people will read it. The Biafran war happened forty years ago, nobody will care." But they did care. But I don't think that outside of Nigeria and maybe outside of most of sub-Saharan Africa it was seen as the contested political and historical thing that it became.

LG: Did you get a strong reaction to the patriarchal themes that you confront in this book?

CNA: I think if anything it was my first novel, *Purple Hibiscus*, which was very popular in Nigeria. I am told that lots of men didn't like it because it's obviously a very feminist book, and at the end you have a wife who kills her husband. Some men, I am told, said, "She's teaching our women to kill our men!" But writing about gender politics in a place like Nigeria is always going to be fraught, you are going to have to tackle it. You go into it knowing that people are going to say that sort of thing and it doesn't stop me. I have things to say and I'll say them.

LG: You've said, "I don't think all writers should have political roles, but . . . I, as a person who writes realist fiction set in Africa, almost automatically have a political role." Is "political writer" a title you embrace?

CNA: I feel ambivalent about it, because I'm very often asked about my "political fiction," and I think, "Can we just talk about the characters and how they love each other?" Because for me sometimes political fiction means it's the kind of book that you don't finish because it's boring. It's the sort of book that is like medicine: it's good for you to read it but you don't really care. But that's just my perception of political fiction, the sort of fiction that isn't about character. It's about ideas, and the ideas push the narrative and the characters are sacrificed, and it's not the kind of fiction I want to do. But then on the other hand, I realize that writing realistic fiction set in a place like Nigeria where everything is contested makes it political in its own way, so I feel ambivalent about it. There are times when I think, "Why can't it just be fiction?" We all write, but I realize that labels are necessary sometimes.

LG: Can you tell me about your university experience?
CNA: I did it because I wanted to learn about my history and because Yale has a fabulous African collection, probably the best in the world. It just turned out not to be what I imagined. I met really lovely people and it's a good place to be and all of that, but academia wasn't for me. I felt very stifled. It made me think about that almost vexed relationship that the creative and the academic have. On the one hand you can make your career from studying somebody's fiction, but then on the other, I wasn't allowed to do a thesis that was fiction. I had wanted to and was doing all of this research on the history of education in West Africa, and I had discovered things that I thought were fascinating, but I didn't want to write a boring thesis. I said, "Look, the reason that I'm here is that I'm a writer and I write fiction, so why don't you let me do a thesis that's fiction?" They said no. I thought, wait a minute, people are actually teaching my novel in this school. So that didn't go very well, but it wasn't terrible. There were some good things about it.

LG: Have you seen change as a result of your work?
CNA: I don't know. It would be nice to think that I can actually make a difference, and I think it can. And there are times and moments of despair when reading Nigerian news on the Internet when I'm not in Nigeria, and I think it will take us one hundred years to get where I think we should be. I obviously think literature and storytelling matters. Before *Purple Hibiscus* was published in Nigeria, a lot of the fiction we had that people read and people could find was fiction published in the 1960s and 1970s. Other books had been done, but mostly self-published or vanity published books, and quite small, and I think *Purple Hibiscus* cut across region and class. I think it gave people a sense of possibility. Now I hear about lots of people who want to be writers, and I organize retreats and writing workshops every year. It's incredible how many people apply. Even more moving and amusing is how some of the people who apply—to apply you send a writing sample—send a sample that reads exactly like *Purple Hibiscus*, and it actually is. It's almost like they copy a section and they change the names, and I just think, well that's really sweet. In some ways that's encouraging.

LG: You're only thirty-one. As a young writer I'd like to say, what the hell?
CNA: I'm thirty-one going on seventy. There are some writers for whom it's easy. Well, actually, I don't know, I just like to imagine that's true to make

myself feel even worse. [*laughs*] I think that my process is always . . . I'm obsessive. I write and I rewrite and I rewrite and I rewrite.

It's very strange to talk about the writing process. I don't think I like it. And I also don't like to listen to it. Some of my writer friends love to, and I think, let's just stop. A, it can come across as . . . there's a sense that there is a certain self-indulgence about it, and then on the other hand, because the process itself is not entirely conscious, because you are struggling, and you've been there for two hours and you're staring at your laptop screen and you just hate every sentence you've written, and then something happens and you write a sentence you like, but you're not entirely conscious of it. Some people ask, why did you make that choice to do that? And I think, I don't know. For me, writing fiction is not the analytical process that some questions assume that it is. Why did you make the choice to have a character do that? And I think, the character spoke to me. I think that's what art is. Sometimes we assume that everything is deliberate and there is a reason behind it, and that's when you become a critic—you're no longer a creator. I don't like to think that way, because I don't want to ever fall into thinking like a critic. I think that's a danger for writing.

LG: You now divide your time between the US and Nigeria. Why?
CNA: I wish I knew. Well, I like America. In America you don't think about the electricity going off. And where I am depends what I'm doing. I've been spending a lot of time in the US. Because I was going to school there. I kept finding myself in institutions of higher learning for no reason. When I graduated from grad school last year I went back home to Nigeria and I was home until March, so I was home for eight months straight. This year I'm traveling for the book. And next year when I really want to get some work done, I'll stay in the US, because in Nigeria there's just too much going on with family and relatives and all the demands on my time.

LG: Will you with stick with fiction while you have the MacArthur grant?
CNA: Well I don't really have an excuse now, do I? It's no strings attached money. It's fantastic, I was thrilled and also a bit shocked. I kept waiting for them to call back and say, "You know, we've made a mistake. We didn't mean you." So that was really lovely, and it just means that I don't have to think about money. It's getting a check for doing nothing, which means I have to write.

A Conversation with Chimamanda Ngozi Adichie

Susan VanZanten / 2010

From *Image* 65 (2010): 86–99. Reprinted by permission.

Born in Nigeria in 1977, Chimamanda Ngozi Adichie grew up in the university town of Nsukka, living for a time in a house once occupied by Chinua Achebe. After briefly studying medicine and pharmacy at the University of Nigeria, Adichie moved to the United States to attend college, graduating *summa cum laude* from Eastern Connecticut State. She holds a master's degree in creative writing from Johns Hopkins and in African studies from Yale. A 2005–2006 Hodder Fellow at Princeton, Adichie has been widely heralded as one of the new global voices in African literature. Her first novel, *Purple Hibiscus* (Algonquin), won the Commonwealth Writers' Prize, and her second, *Half of a Yellow Sun* (Fourth Estate), won the Orange Prize for Fiction, one of the United Kingdom's most prestigious annual literary awards, and was a finalist for the National Book Critics Circle Award. Adichie's work has been translated into thirty languages, and her short stories have been published in journals such as the *New Yorker, Granta, Iowa Review,* and *Zoetrope.* She received the O. Henry Prize in 2003 for her short story "The American Embassy," which appears in the recent collection, *The Thing around Your Neck* (Fourth Estate). After receiving a 2008 MacArthur Foundation Fellowship, Adichie now divides her time between the United States and Nigeria.

Susan VanZanten: You've said, "I didn't choose writing, writing chose me." How did this happen? How did you discern this calling to become a writer? Would you identify it as a vocation?
Chimamanda Ngozi Adichie: I have writer friends with elaborate and exciting stories about how they came to writing, but I just don't have that.

I wrote from when I was six. Even then I knew that this was something that truly mattered to me. When I was ten, though I had a lot of friends, I remember looking forward to when I could go up to my father's study and be alone and write. It was considered something odd for me to want to do when it was sunny outside. Now, as an adult, I realize it's what I care about. It gives me a sense that this is what I am meant to be doing.

SVZ: Would you use the word vocation to talk about that?

CNA: I think so. I've often said that even if I hadn't been fortunate enough to be published, I would be writing. I love that I am published, and it was a choice that I made to try and get published. But publishing is very different from writing.

Of course, one wants to be published. Otherwise I would just write in my diary and put it in a drawer. But publishing is public, which is why I feel a sense of distance from my books after they come out. I get stupidly emotional about my own work when I am with it alone. I don't show people what I am doing until I am done, until I feel comfortable enough to let it out. The writing part is very private and gives me that marvelous high when it's going well, but when I finally send something out to my editor, that's when I have to put on my practical glasses and think about the work in a less intuitive and more pragmatic way. My editor will say, "I don't think this character would say that." And I will think, "Well, in my head she did, but all right."

SVZ: Initially you wrote poetry and plays, but you seem to have found your voice and your genre in fiction. What is it about fiction in particular that attracts you? Why are you a storyteller?

CNA: Why indeed. Because poetry's too hard to do well. Also, my process isn't an entirely conscious thing. I just do. But I will say that fiction is true. This is something my friends who write nonfiction and I argue about all the time. I feel that fiction is much more honest than nonfiction. I know from my limited experience in writing nonfiction, particularly memoir, that in the process of writing I am constantly negotiating different levels of self-censorship and self-protection, and protection of people I love, and sometimes protection of people I don't necessarily care about but I worry that the reader might have biased feelings about. When I write fiction, I don't think about any of that. Radical honesty is possible in fiction. With fictional characters, I don't have to think about protecting anybody.

SVZ: So you don't worry about people you know seeing themselves in your fiction?

CNA: They do, invariably, but no, I don't worry about that. The funny thing is that often when I do base characters on people, they don't know, and when I don't, they're convinced that I have.

SVZ: Many Western readers in a post-secular culture don't understand the pervasive role that religion plays in African life. Your fiction vividly depicts the presence and weight of religion, with its accounts of traditional Catholicism, African Pentecostalism, Islam, a more liberal Catholicism, and indigenous beliefs. What was it like to grow up as a Catholic in Nigeria in such a spiritually teeming world?

CNA: It was indeed spiritually teeming. But is America actually a post-secular society? I'm not sure. I think it's quite religious as well, but it manifests itself in a different way. It's less direct. I even think that in many ways the anti-religion movement is in itself a religion—and sometimes it is more strident than any religious movement.

What's interesting about Nigeria, and much of sub-Saharan Africa, is how there's a geographical element to religion. In Igboland where I come from, in Southeastern Nigeria, the Presbyterian missionaries came from one side and the Irish-Catholics came from another, and they reached an agreement in the late 1880s or 1890s to respect one another's turf (though I recently read that one of the Protestant ministers accused the Irish Catholics of encroaching on their territory and going to convert people). My grandfather converted to Catholicism in the 1920s, and my father was born in 1932, so he was baptized Catholic as a baby, and so was my mother. My family, like many families around us, were moderate Catholics. Everybody around me was religious. People went to church. It was something you didn't question.

When I go back to Nigeria it strikes me how on Sunday people will say, "Have you been to church?" It's expected, and they say it matter-of-factly. They're saying it because they want to make sure. They'll ask, "Will you come out to dinner with us? Have you gone to church, by the way?" Because if you haven't gone to church then you can't come to dinner because it means you're going to evening mass. The option of not going to church doesn't occur to people, and it doesn't matter what denomination.

As I was growing up, we went to church every Sunday. I was drawn to religion, but I was the kid who just wouldn't shut up. I had questions.

Everybody else went to church and came home. I wanted to go to the sacristy and talk to the priest about why he said that, I'm sure much to my father's irritation. But my parents were very, very patient people, and they continue to be. I was drawn to the drama of the Catholic Church. I would cry at Paschal Mass when we raised the candles. They would turn out all the lights and people would hold candles. When it was time to renew your vows and they would light the candles, I would burst into tears because I was so moved. I loved the smell of incense and I loved the Latin. I keep meaning to write about it. I was a happily Catholic child.

I also got into a lot of fights with Anglican friends. There was a Catholic-Protestant divide on campus, and it did affect a lot of things. Looking back now, it's hilarious. An Anglican would say, "All you Catholics worship Mary and it means you're going to hell." I was very enthusiastic about those fights. I could quote the bits of the Bible that were supposed to conform to Catholic tradition, like the letter of Saint James about confession, and of course we had been taught that bits of the Revelation were about the blessed Virgin, and I would quote that as well.

SVZ: What about indigenous religions when you were growing up? Were they a presence?

CNA: I was among people who viewed indigenous religion with disdain mostly. I became interested in traditional Igbo religion when we would go to our ancestral hometown, and I remain interested. Like most Igbo people, we would go back for Christmases and Easters. Cousins would gather. I noticed that most of my family was Catholic but a few members of the extended family weren't, and I remember my grandmother saying, "You can't eat in their home because they worship idols." Somehow the food they had was tainted. I think that's when I started to question. I come from a culture where whenever you go into somebody's home, they give you food; they don't ask you if you want any, they just give it, and you're expected to eat it. And so it was an awkward thing to go into those homes. But often those relatives didn't give us food, because they knew. I was aware of a general Christian attitude of looking down on traditional religious adherence, an assumption that it was somehow bad. The Catholic-Protestant rivalry didn't really have that element, because of course we had Jesus in common. People would fight about the blessed Virgin Mary and about the Rosary, but you didn't get a sense of disdain. With traditional religion, there was.

SVZ: Do you think Catholicism is a Western religion? How do you respond to those critics who see the growing presence of Christianity in Africa as a triumph of colonialism?

CNA: I feel ambivalent. I started to question early on, and when I got older I disliked in a visceral way the way that religion was so intertwined with Western images: Jesus had to have blue eyes and blond hair, and the blessed Virgin was a beautiful blonde. Once at school during a nativity play somebody suggested that Jesus be dark, be black, and people were horrified. I remember thinking, "Well, we actually don't know what he looked like." People have said that Africans have made of Christianity what they will, that they have Africanized Christianity, but I am not always sure. I think they have to an extent. African Christianity has an immediacy that cuts across denominations. I go to mass in the US and it seems tepid by comparison. In Africa, people are very aware of the presence of spirits. There's the idea that we coexist with other beings in a way that's very present.

Christianity includes ideas that are cultural rather than religious, and these ideas have been absorbed into African Christianity. This is changing, of course, but even the idea of singing Christian songs in local languages offends some people. I recently heard about a woman who was horrified because she didn't want Igbo carols at Christmas. Only the English ones were real Christmas carols to her. But even so, the idea of Christianity as a triumph of colonialism might be too simplistic.

SVZ: I know you recently were doing an African Studies master's at Yale, where Lamin Sanneh has done a lot with the spread of Christianity in Africa.

CNA: Yes, though I would listen to some of his lectures in disbelief, because his Africa wasn't my Africa. He's brilliant and speaks wonderfully, and his grand vision of African Christianity is wonderfully optimistic; he sees everything for the good, but I'm not so sure. In one lecture, he spoke about a Nigerian man who got sick and didn't go to the hospital but prayed, because he felt that this was the way to cure himself. For Professor Sanneh, this was proof of the active faith people had, but I think we need to talk about the state of the healthcare system. When I was growing up in the eighties, people went to church, people were religious, but you didn't see this kind of attitude. You see it a lot now. What's happened in that time? Things have become worse economically. The medical center isn't as it used to be. Before, you would go there and get free healthcare, good doctors; you'd get your malaria shot; you'd be fine. Now it doesn't happen. Now it's expensive. And so now you have a lot more people praying themselves into health. I remember pointing that out in class, and I don't think he was pleased. I don't want to discount faith, but I think that to talk about this thing honestly, we need to talk about what's happened to the healthcare system, and what's happened in general in Nigeria, where our middle class is disappearing.

SVZ: The American memoirist Mary Karr calls herself a "cafeteria Catholic," embracing some aspects of Catholicism and rejecting others. Do you still identify yourself as a Catholic? If so, would you be comfortable calling yourself a cafeteria Catholic? How do you make your choices?

CNA: It's an interesting expression. There are times when I'm happy to be a cafeteria Catholic. I'm certainly not the child I was. I used to think the pope had all the answers. It really changes, and it depends on where I am, what's happened recently in my life. I find that I am interested in the idea of faith, but I don't know if I have faith. There are times when I am certain that I will never believe in anything, and there are other times when I find this odd longing and I think there has to be something. A friend of mine who is a priest, one of my closest friends, actually, who by the way is the reason that I haven't entirely given up on the Catholic Church, said to me once that to seek was to find. He said to seek God is to find God. He said to me, "You're never going to catch God and put God in a bottle. That's what you want to do, but it's never going to happen because of the nature of God." And I thought, "Why does it have to be so complicated? Why can't I capture God in a bottle?"

I suppose to an extent I am a cafeteria Catholic. The good thing—actually, it's not a good thing—the remarkable thing about growing up Catholic is that you can never get rid of it. It's in you. Catholics will leave the church, but it's still there. I don't know that I can ever run away from it.

SVZ: Do you still go to mass?

CNA: I do go to mass sometimes, but I've also been known to get up and stalk out when I felt the priest was being ridiculous. My last heated argument with a priest was in Nigeria about a year ago. After mass I went to speak to him about what I felt was his misogyny, because his entire mass was about attacking women for what they wore. He wouldn't let you into the church if you arrived in short sleeves. "You're showing your arms. You want to tempt men," he would say. So I went to talk to him, and it wasn't pleasant. I was furious. I remember feeling that this was the problem I had with religion as a whole, that this man had been given so much power. An immense power comes with being a priest, and particularly in an area like

Nigeria, where there's an automatic hero worship of religious figures and an unwillingness to criticize them.

I remember thinking, "I'm going to speak out, and I know people will support me." I wrote a piece about it in a local newspaper, and the back-lash was incredible. The editor said they had never received as many letters about anything. It was ninety-five percent against me and five percent for me. It was, "Shut up. Just because you're a writer doesn't mean you have a right to criticize the priest. You must listen to the priest, and, yes, women tempt men." It was incredible, and really demoralizing for me. I haven't been back in that church since, and I don't know that I ever will. It was the church where I grew up. It just happens to have new management. So it's a very complicated relationship that I have with the church.

SVZ: In your first novel, *Purple Hibiscus*, the character Eugene is a strict, authoritative and domineering father who is a devout traditional Catholic. Some reviewers view him as a thoroughly evil character and the novel as a condemnation of Catholicism, but this seems overly simplistic. How do you see Eugene, and what is the importance of the kind of Catholicism lived out by his sister, Aunty Ifeoma?

CNA: I didn't intend for *Purple Hibiscus* to be an anti-Catholic book, and I think that there are alternatives to Eugene in the book. Aunty Ifeoma is the character I most admired. I am a very keen believer in the middle ground and the possibility of coexistence, and I am suspicious of extremes of either side. Eugene was not a character who I wanted to come across as a mon-ster. I disliked what he did and didn't like him, really, but I also felt that he somehow demanded our sympathy—a complicated sympathy, but still. And I had observed people like him. My father would tell me stories. In Igboland there was always the figure of the mean catechist, half-educated, again invested with the power of the church. They didn't have many priests, so the catechists did a lot. They didn't really understand this new faith, and so they would cover their ignorance with silly violence and things that are not humane. My father talked about how the catechists would beat them for being two minutes late to mass. Actually, in my hometown, at mass you still have women—mean-looking women with big sticks—walking around and hitting kids who look like they might be falling asleep.

SVZ: Just like the Puritans in the US in the seventeenth century.

CNA: Sometimes I read about earlier forms of Christianity, and I think, "Yes, exactly. This is contemporary African Christianity." And that's the problem. A lot has remained static as things were passed down. In churches in Nigeria there's a big fuss made about covering your hair. They won't let you into the church otherwise. I just think, my God, it's so irrelevant. Eugene, for me, was a character who made people suffer, but who also had suffered and who, in a strange way, thinks he's doing the right thing. I find this interesting: "I'm going to beat you, but it's for your own good. I'm going to beat goodness into you." And, of course, he had experienced that himself. His sister, on the other hand, represents the possibility of a middle ground. She is ostensibly a happy Catholic, but she still respects her culture and doesn't see it as a zero sum game. There's room for everything for her.

SVZ: I loved both the lyricism and psychological penetration of *Purple Hibiscus*, but *Half of a Yellow Sun* is an equally stunning though very different book, chronicling the Nigerian-Biafran War of 1967 to 1970. What was it like to move to writing a historical epic, Dickensian in its sprawl and detail? Did it take a lot of research? Was it difficult to manage the changes in point of view?

CNA: It nearly killed me. I don't know if I will ever go through something like that again. Though I should never say never. It was difficult technically, because I was turning research into fiction, which I had never done before, but also emotionally, because my grandfathers died in the war and I constantly thought about them as I was writing, particularly my paternal grandfather. I would read about something that had happened and start crying. Was it like that for him, I would wonder? What did he think while he was in the refugee camp? This was a proud Igbo man who for his entire adult life had provided for his family and done the right thing, and to have to flee from his home to a refugee camp, to lose his dignity before he died—all this was heartbreaking for me. And to think about my parents was heartbreaking as well, because they lost their innocence. Like many middle-class, educated Nigerians, they were full of an enthusiastic hope. Nigeria was newly independent. They were going to build this great giant of Africa. My father went to Berkeley for his PhD. He was offered a job to stay on, and he didn't consider it for a minute. "We have a country to build," he thought. He went back to Nigeria with my mother and my two sisters, and a few months later the war started. My father and many people like him really believed in the cause, believed that injustices had been done and that the way to get justice was to have an independent nation. When the war ended, for them it was a loss of innocence. They lost hope in ideas in some ways.

SVZ: After Nigeria achieved independence, a series of military coups and tribal violence prompted the predominantly Igbo Southeastern region to secede and become the Republic of Biafra. The resulting civil war lasted for three years before Nigeria was reunited. Is *Half of a Yellow Sun* a Nigerian novel or a Biafran novel, or does it make a difference?

CNA: I don't think about it like that, but if I had to say, I'd say it's Nigerian. I am Nigerian. We have a difficult and embittered history, and there are things we haven't addressed, but I'm Nigerian and I have never felt that Biafra should come back or anything of the sort.

SVZ: You've been called an African writer, a Nigerian writer, a feminist writer, and a postcolonial writer. I haven't seen any description of you as a Catholic writer, which is surprising. What do you think about these kinds of labels? I noticed that in the short story "Jumping Monkey Hill," most of the people attending the "African Writers Workshop" are ironically named only by their national and gender identity: "the Kenyan man," "the Senegalese woman." That story does a wonderful job of mocking the expectations that African writers sometimes face to write a particular kind of fiction. To what extent does your historical situatedness affect your writing?

CNA: Being called a Catholic writer raises the question: what is a Catholic writer? I think it was Graham Greene who said that he was a writer who happened to be Catholic. I went through a phase of being completely anti-labeling and saying, "I won't be called anything. I'm a writer. I tell stories." I want us to live in a world in which labels don't matter, but we don't, at least not yet. When I won the Orange Prize, for example, I actually became quite irritated with all the talk about being the "first African" to win. I thought, you people are making it seem as though I scaled this enormous hurdle when I'm not sure that's exactly true. I don't know how many Africans have been shortlisted in the past. But I got so many emails from Africans, and not just Africans but Caribbean people as well, for whom my win became something personal. A Jamaican woman who lives in London wrote to tell me how she had saved the clippings because she wanted to show them to her daughter when her daughter was older. In that case, having people see me as a black African woman was a moving moment for me, and a moment of pride.

But then other times labels can have so much baggage. It depends on the context. Sometimes someone will say "feminist writer," and you can hear a sneer in their voice. At other times someone will use the same words and you know they're describing your awareness of gender and justice, and they don't think it's necessarily a bad thing. It's the same when someone says "African writer." Sometimes you know they consider it a slightly less worthy subgenre of real literature, and then it becomes offensive. But at other times you realize they're just describing what you do.

SVZ: With the exception of "Ghosts," the stories in *The Thing around Your Neck* depict the lives of women in contemporary Nigeria and the United States, revolving around the complications of identity in today's global world. Ethnic neighborhoods have vague geographic borders as a result of immigration, education, and jet travel. What do you think are the constants, the grounding center, in such a life, either for you or for your characters?

CNA: Family. I do think I'm quite different from many of the characters I write about, that in many ways I am more fortunate. I don't see myself as an immigrant. I am Nigerian. I have a Nigerian passport, but I spend a lot of time in the US. I consider the US my second home of convenience, and it's close to my heart, but Nigeria is still home. Nigeria is where I feel most emotionally invested. The eyes with which I look at the world are Nigerian. Sometimes here in the US I see things that make me shake my head and say, "Only in America."

SVZ: How does gender affect these questions of identity? Are these questions more pressing or do they take unique forms for women?

CNA: I was asked recently why my male characters seem to react to immigration differently, about how they seem either overly enthusiastic or clueless. I don't intend for them to be. Men also struggle. But I'm primarily interested in exploring women's experiences, I think because that's what I know. It's not just my story. It's my sister's and her friends' and my cousins' and their friends.' I suppose identity is central to one's work in how it shifts depending on where one is. I have often said that I didn't know I was black until I came to the US. It had never occurred to me. I'd read *Roots* and I was very moved by Kunta Kinte, but I never thought of myself as black. I remember in Brooklyn, after I had been in the US maybe a month, an African American man referred to me as "sister," and I thought, "How offensive! I don't want it." I had watched TV and I knew that to be black was not a good thing, so I thought, "No, don't include me in your group. I am not part of you." It took reading and asking questions and understanding African American history, which I didn't have much of a sense of, to accept that identity, which I am completely happy with now.

I think that immigration into places like the US for Africans is always about shifting identities. When I go back to Nigeria, one of the things I like to joke about with my friends is that I get off the plane, and the heat is crazy, but I drop my race baggage. Race just doesn't occur to me in Nigeria. You become something else, though there are still labels. There I am an Igbo woman, and there's the stereotype of the Igbo as a penny-pinching people, so if I'm with a group of friends from different ethnic groups in Lagos and I say something like, "Oh, that's really expensive," they'll say, "Oh, you Igbo woman." And then in my hometown, I don't have that because most people around me are Igbo. So identity shifts. I'm particularly interested in how it changes when you leave home. In the US you discover race, but gender dynamics also change. I know a number of Nigerian women who have discovered that they could do things in the US that in Nigeria they didn't think they could. With your family and friends around you, you have the weight of tradition, of "how things are done." But then you move to a new place and you think, why the heck not? That affects gender, and particularly dynamics between couples.

SVZ: My favorite story in *The Thing around Your Neck* is "The Shivering," which depicts the unlikely friendship of a female Nigerian graduate student at Princeton with a less-educated Nigerian man whose visa has expired and who is facing deportation. They meet when a plane crashes in Nigeria and the man, Chinedu, comes to Ukamaka's apartment to ask her to pray with him. To what extent is this story about faith? What kind of faith does each of these characters have?
CNA: It's the most recent story in the collection, and also in some ways my favorite. I think it came from the part of me that longs to capture God in a bottle. When I lived in Princeton, once while I was away and my brother was staying in my apartment, a plane crashed in Nigeria and the Nigerian first lady died. Somebody knocked on the door, and my brother opened it. It was a strange man, a Nigerian. He said, "I've come to pray about what is happening in Nigeria." He had seen my name on the mailbox and knew someone from Nigeria lived there.

My brother said that this was a man who in Nigeria we would never be friends with. Class is very present in the way our lives work there. Even as a child, you only needed to hear the way somebody spoke English to know that they didn't go to a good school. It meant that people were divided, so you couldn't be friends with the kind of person who didn't speak English well.

My brother says that he and the man prayed, and then the man left. I asked my brother how he felt afterwards, and he said, "You know, I thought it was quite nice that he came by." We laughed about it, but I was very moved by this story. On the one hand, one could think, "How dare he invade my personal space? For all he knows, I might be a Buddhist." But on the other hand, it made me think about how being away from home makes you want these strange bonds.

That's how the story started. It's about an unlikely friendship, but also about the possibility of faith, of finding the kind of faith that works for you. The woman character grew up Catholic, very much like me, and went through the establishment religion and its routines, and I think that can be quite comforting to some people, but eventually it didn't work for her. The story becomes about how it is possible for her to find some kind of faith, a version of faith with which she can make peace.

SVZ: How strong is the Pentecostal movement in Nigeria? You make references to it frequently, and I sense that the character Chinedu was Pentecostal. **CNA:** Pentecostalism is huge in Nigeria—and in much of sub-Saharan Africa, from what I have seen and heard and read. I have to say I dislike the version of Pentecostalism that's sweeping across Nigeria. Not only because it's a strange fundamentalist brand, but also because I find it un-Christian. It's very inward-looking. I don't find it charitable. I don't find it to be a brand of Christianity that's aware of the other. I suppose it makes sense: things have become quite difficult in the past twenty years in Nigeria. As I said, people could get healthcare relatively easily in the 1980s, and they no longer can. Now you have pastors who will say, "Bring all your money to the altar, and God will give you back a Mercedes." It's no longer about being kind to the person who lives next to you; it's about God giving you the Mercedes. This kind of thinking has seeped into the social fabric. You go to a cocktail party or a dinner and someone will say very casually, "I am waiting on God. I have sowed my seeds and God will give me my something."

There's so much wrong with Pentecostalism as it is in Nigeria, though there are a few exceptions. I've been to quite a number of those churches, mostly because I'm curious. There's intense drama, people being asked to kick the devil. But I feel that it exploits poor people. The most dramatic moments in these churches are when it's time for giving money. "Sowing your seeds," they call it. The pastor has a private jet and wears designer suits, and he'll prance around in front of the congregation and tell them, "God gave me this." And I think, "Well, no, actually it's these poor people who paid for your bloody private jet."

Pentecostalism is spreading, and a lot of the ideas have influenced the more orthodox traditional denominations. In Catholic and Anglican and Methodist services, there's a lot more prosperity preaching.

Something else about Pentecostalism is that it sees everything remotely associated with traditional religion as bad in a no-holds-barred way. In my hometown, a number of Pentecostal groups have been burning shrines and cutting down trees, because they believe the devil lives in them, and harassing people who aren't Christian. This is not the way to win people to your God. You do not go and burn somebody's shrine and think that they will find your God attractive.

SVZ: You've spoken of the influence on you of Chinua Achebe, the author of *Things Fall Apart*, who is often called the father of African literature. *Purple Hibiscus* opens with an echo of that famous novel, and the final story in *The Thing around Your Neck* essentially presents an alternative feminist rendition of the final chapter of *Things Fall Apart*. What is it about Achebe that inspires you? In what ways are you attempting to build on but also to move beyond his example?

CNA: I respect and love Chinua Achebe's work, but I don't want to be a second Chinua Achebe, or a third. I just want to be Chimamanda Adichie.

Achebe is a man of immense integrity. I believe him. There are some writers whose work you read and you think, "This is a performance. I don't think you believe this." And for me, fiction should be truth. There are times when I've thought, "I'm going to write this story because I want to show that I can." But then I'll think, "No, it's a lie," and I won't, because life is short and I want to do what I care about. Chinua Achebe's work is full of integrity. He does what he believes in. Growing up an Igbo child, I was fortunate to be educated, but my education didn't teach me anything about my past. But when I read *Things Fall Apart*, it became my great-grandfather's life. It became more than literature for me. It became my story. I am quite protective of Achebe's novels in a way that I don't think I am with any other book that I love.

SVZ: Who else has been important to you? What other books or writers do you love?

CNA: I fall in love and out of love quite often. I went through an Edith Wharton phase where I wanted to read everything she'd ever done, and then at some point I thought, if I read one more thing of hers, I will die.

I like Philip Roth quite a bit, much to the annoyance of my feminist friends. I like his technique, and the way he refuses to hide. I admire a writer who has the courage—and it does take courage—to look social realities in the face. It's easy in the name of fiction to hide behind art, because you're afraid somebody will say you're a little too political, or that politics is not the job of fiction. But Roth is fearless, and I respect that.

SVZ: Is there anyone who stands on the same level as Achebe for you?

CNA: No, Chinua Achebe has the misfortune of standing alone. I grew up reading mostly English and Russian novels, and I liked them quite a bit, mostly the English ones, but until Achebe, I hadn't read a book and felt it was mine. The other book I felt that way about was *The African Child*, a very slim novel by Camara Laye. I read it when I was in grade five, about the time I first read *Things Fall Apart*, and I remember there was something magical about it. It was about his childhood in Guinea, and there were things that were quite unfamiliar. There was a level of exoticism in it, but also a level of incredible familiarity. I remember falling in love with the book, with the beautiful melancholy of it. I keep meaning to go back and read it again and see.

SVZ: What effect has the MacArthur Genius Grant had on your life? What will it allow you to do as far as writing goes? Do you have a sense of where you will head in your writing from here?

CNA: I remember being absolutely thrilled and then, later, going into slight panic because I thought, "That's it. I have no excuse." My family started teasing me, "Oh, the genius," but I loved the pride in my father's voice when I told him. I have been traveling for quite a while. I was in Nigeria, organizing creative writing workshops. I like teaching, particularly in nontraditional environments. But I haven't had silence and space in a long time, and I think that when I'm done with my book-hawking travels, we'll see whether the grant is a blessing or not.

SVZ: You mention that you teach creative writing workshops. What do you tell young, aspiring creative writers?

CNA: To read and read and read. I'm a believer in reading, to see the wide range of what's been written. I'm also a believer in reading what you dislike at least once, just to know. I often say to my students, "I'm going to have you read something I don't like." I don't like cold fiction. I don't like fiction that is an experiment. I find that often it's the boys in the class who love the fiction I don't like. I say to them, "I'll tell you why I don't like it. And, then, if you like it, I want you to tell me why." Most of all I believe in reading for what you can learn in terms of not just craft and technique but worldview. It's important to think about sentences and how one develops character and all of that, but also to think about what the story is as a big thing. Most of all, we have fun in the workshops. For me, it's important that we find reasons to laugh. And we mostly do.

Chimamanda Ngozi Adichie in Conversation with Synne Rifbjerg

Synne Rifbjerg / 2014

Interview conducted at International Authors' Stage, Copenhagen, 19 May 2014. Edited transcript reprinted by permission.

SR: Many things that are obvious to you are strange to us. I mean, if I wake up a bit tired and somebody asks me, "What is the difference between an African American and an American African?," I would think, did I hear right? Is it a word play? What is the difference?

CNA: I should say that it's half-invented—I mean, I kind of made it up in the novel. But it reflects a real difference, because "African American" is a word I would use to describe a person of African descent whose ancestors were brought forcefully to the US as slaves, and an "American African" is a person of African descent who came, or whose family came, more or less willingly—at least not on a slave ship.

SR: But this is, of course, a very important issue in your new novel.
CNA: Yes.

SR: I've heard you say somewhere that "race is America's original sin," and I thought that was fantastic. Can you say something about that?
CNA: See, I come up with fairly good lines, and then I don't know what to do with them, that's the problem. I guess what I was trying to say is that race is the major organizing principle of American history—American *life*, really—and it's also the one thing that Americans are most uncomfortable about. It's the subject that they circle around; the subject that they invent codes to talk about; it's the subject that is still very unfinished. It's the subject that many Americans prefer to think has to do with the past, but it's

very much the present. It's also the most misunderstood, the most potentially contentious social subject in America.

SR: Actually, one should study American history as an immigrant before com-
ing to America, to understand this strange code of hidden racial problems.
CNA: Yes. And if you don't, as I didn't . . . I went to America very ignorant of
all of these things. It's one thing to have watched the American television as
I did—as I think everybody in the world does—and to have read American
books, but to arrive in the US and for the first time to be called "sister" by an
African American man . . . My first thought was, "Don't call me your sister;
I don't know what this is all about." And also just to learn these very subtle
things: half the time I didn't quite understand why people got upset when
somebody [used] expressions like "tar baby," or when somebody made a joke
about watermelon or fried chicken.

SR: Yes, what's up with watermelon, you'd say?
CNA: Yes, and I would think, "Why? Why is this a problem?" And I think
[there was] also the assumption that I was supposed to be angered because I
was black. But I didn't understand why I was supposed to be angered. And so,
for me, it really took going to read and learn about American history, because
when I went to the US, I just didn't know. I had read *Roots* and seen the film . . .

SR: You thought America was *The Cosby Show*?
CNA: I thought black Americans lived like *The Cosby Show*, yes.

SR: That's kind of sweet.
CNA: It is, but you know, when you think about it, that's the one thing you
see. The portrait of black American life that I had seen, that I identified with
and liked, was *The Cosby Show*. So, you can imagine my surprise when I . . .
[*audience laughs*]

SR: Even I wanted to live with the Cosbys, so I can understand why.

[*Interview paused to allow actress and voice artist Ellen Hillingsø to read the
opening of* Americanah *in Danish*]

SR: I think this [excerpt] is the perfect introduction to Ifemelu, the main
character, who is, in a way, at the top of her American stay now, because

she has this very successful blog, and she's going to have her hair done, and so on. But in reality, she is not really happy. She feels fat and has "cement in her soul." I thought that was too much to bear for one woman. [*SR and CNA laugh*] What is the matter with Ifemelu?

CNA: She was going through a bad phase. [*audience laughs*] For me, this book is a lot about longing for home—just longing in general, but more specifically longing for home—and what home means and, I guess, whether you can go home again after you've left. For her, the "cement in her soul" is just a form of homesickness. "Homesickness" seems too easy a word to use—but [what I mean is] a kind of longing for something more, and sometimes not being sure what it is you're longing for, but still feeling a sense of longing.

SR: But she is feeling fairly sure about what it is that she is longing for, this going back to Nigeria, isn't she?

CNA: She's not entirely sure that she's made the right decision. She's trying to pep herself up and say "this is the right thing," but she has her doubts.

SR: But she does a wonderful thing: she sees signs everywhere. She connects with people that she normally wouldn't connect with and she takes things in that really are not her style.

CNA: Yes—which is, I think, the consequence of her being uncertain. So, she chooses to see signs in everything. If the sun rises, she thinks it means that "my visit home will go well."

SR: She's going to the hairdresser's. One of the many wonderful things about your book is that you take one of the smallest and most intimate female universes, the hairdresser's—especially the African hair braiding salon—and, like a small box scenery, the whole story is like an Aladdin's lamp: she gets her hair rubbed and out comes this amazing story. What made you think of putting her into this [setting]?

CNA: That's actually quite a lovely image. A lot of it came from my own experience. I have spent way too much time in African hair braiding salons over the past fifteen years. And I'm fascinated by it. It's a subculture for me. I think it says a lot, it goes beyond hair—hair is important, but it goes beyond hair: it says a lot about immigration, about what it means to be African outside of Africa. I would go to these braiding salons and take notes all the time, because often the characters were hilarious. They were mostly Francophone African women. But then, you would have all these other women come in: African Americans, Anglophone African women, the rare white woman who wanted to do a Bo Derek hairstyle . . .

SR: That is so old-fashioned!
CNA: Oh, but she wanted to show that she was "down with Africa," so she got her hair in cornrows. I would be fascinated by it. Maybe I romanticize too much, but there was always for me also a kind of beautiful sadness about watching these women who were making new lives, but were also putting on and taking off different versions of themselves. Sometimes the children would come as well, sometimes the helper, just hanging around in the hair salon, and I would watch them. Even the interplay of a certain kind of Africanness, but also a new Americanness, was always fascinating to me. So, I wanted to try and capture that in the novel. I don't think that I've seen, in literature, the African hair braiding salon deconstructed. I felt it was an important subject to . . . [*trails off*]

SR: Your hair looks fantastic, I have to say.
CNA: Thank you. This [hairstyle] was made in a hair salon in Lagos, which is an entirely different planet. Equally interesting, but . . .

SR: What's the difference?
CNA: Ha! [*audience laughs*]

SR: [*gesturing to the audience*] Somebody seems to know . . .
CNA: Yes, I think there's a Nigerian here. No, it's just that African hair braiding salons in the US are very much . . . it's a subculture of a multicultural thing. In Nigeria, it isn't. In Nigeria, hair salons are very interesting but, if anything, what you learn in Nigerian hair salons are the different levels of female imperial power, in its different manifestations.

SR: Wow.
CNA: And also, the different levels of female-to-female unkindness. Yeah. [*looks at SR, audience laughs*] I don't think this is just about Lagos though.

SR: Anyway, it's difficult not to talk about hair, not just because yours is put up in such a fantastic way, but [because] it does really play a role in the novel. There is a lot about hair that I didn't know. I mean, it's not that I don't struggle with my hair—and I did make an effort tonight—but the thing about wigs, for instance, I had no idea.
CNA: Yes, yes.

SR: And the thing about the burns and the whole hassle that it is . . . Yes, you laugh, because you *know* . . .
CNA: No, no . . .

SR: How would I know?
CNA: Exactly. I'm pleased to hear that, and I've heard that from many people. I laugh only because, really, I'm happy to hear that. Because then, how would you know? And I think even that says a lot about one of the points I wanted to make with this novel, which is that the hair of black women is so little understood and so little known that it's very easy to attach assumptions to it. It's easy for example to say that a woman doesn't "look professional" because she has her hair in a certain way. But if you understand that maybe that's the way her hair grows on her head, and that she doesn't want to have to put chemicals in it to "look professional," and that even the very definition of "professional" is something that's based on an ideal that isn't the black woman's . . . So, when people say to me, "Oh, I didn't know this," I think, well, I'm pleased, because I really do believe in the importance of cross-cultural conversations. I think that it's the way to better understanding. A friend of mine who read this book—a dear close friend, a white Englishman—said, after he read it, "I didn't know Michelle Obama's hair doesn't grow like that." [*audience laughs*]

SR: Ok, that's kind of cute. That much I knew.
CNA: But he didn't.

SR: No, he didn't.
CNA: So he assumed that she wakes up and her hair has that texture.

SR: Fantastic. There is also a part in the book that discusses Michelle Obama's hair. It seems to be a kind of wishful thinking at least, what would happen, if we talk about role models, if Michelle Obama went a bit more frizzy. [*audience laughs*]
CNA: That's funny. I wouldn't call it going a bit more frizzy, I would call it, "if she stopped the straightening," because the frizzy, it's actually her. It was something wishful. It wasn't at all . . . I mean, I really adore Michelle Obama.

SR: I know you do.
CNA: For me, she's an example of a woman—a black woman—who fits all the

definitions of mainstream "black respectability": you have to straighten your hair, and even the kids now have to straighten their hair. And I wonder, are they doing it with a relaxer, or with heat? I worry about how uncomfortable it must be for the poor kids. But for me, really, it was just a larger question: if Michelle Obama had natural hair, Barack Obama would not have won. He would not have won; it's true. I mean, it's sad and it seems shallow, but it is true, because particularly in America, there are all of these assumptions attached to natural black hair. If Michelle Obama had dreadlocks or an Afro or cornrows, she might be thought to be radical, Black Panther, difficult, . . .

SR: . . . or a jazz singer.
CNA: Yes. And that's also not . . .

SR: Not good for presidents.
CNA: No.

SR: No. It's rather shocking. I mean, we can make fun of it, but it's really sad.
CNA: I think it *is* very sad.

SR: So, you have a black president but we're not all there.
CNA: You can't be too black. When you think about it as well, even the kind of enthusiasm and joy that we had, that many people in the world had, when Barack Obama became president . . . I mean, why were we so happy?

SR: Well, obviously, because he was the first.
CNA: Right. At some point, I was one of the happy ones as well: I was in Nigeria with my friends; we stayed up late to watch it. But being objective and stepping back, why are we so happy? We're happy that he's the first, but it seemed to me that our joy sometimes clouded the larger point, which is: it's also a statement of how deeply exclusionary American society still is— that we're so excited about the black man finally being the president, three hundred years after black people have been in America. We're so excited, and I'm thinking . . . [*doubtful expression*] I just wish that our joy had been tempered by a kind of reflection about what this says about race today.

SR: The reflection came afterwards. Now they don't like him.
CNA: Yes, but it's not even about race. I mean, the reflection is more about, "We wanted you to be Jesus Christ and you're not."

SR: Yes. Well, he [Jesus Christ] wasn't black, so how could he [Barack Obama] be?
CNA: Yes, that is true.

SR: Chimamanda, Ifemelu actually wanted to vote for Hillary Clinton. How can you explain that? That's very confusing.
CNA: Why?

SR: Well, I wouldn't say it's confusing; I think it's typical of Ifemelu, who has many wonderful ways of escaping the cliché. Every time you think she goes with this, or she goes with that, aah-aah [*meaning "no"; imperfect imitation of Nigerian accent*]. As they say, "Aah-aah" [*waves finger saying no*], or how you say it . . . [*laughs*]
CNA: I'm happy that you're learning Nigerian expressions as well.

SR: I'm trying my best.
CNA: But it has to go a bit quicker, "Ah-ah."

SR: "Ah-ah." [*audience laughs*] Oh, *that* fast. My gosh. I'll speed up.
CNA: And it can express surprise; it can mean many things. It's very contextual. But . . ."Ah-ah" [*said with facial expression showing annoyance*]. [*audience laughs*] Ifemelu, it's not [confusing] though. I follow American politics; I'm very interested. And I am a deep admirer of Hillary Clinton's. Before the Democratic Primaries—and I'm not an American citizen, by choice, so I don't vote—but, I think, at the beginning, if I had been an American, if I voted, I would have been a Hillary supporter. I just admired her. I thought she was just brilliant, and wonderful—and clearly, of course, I liked that she was a woman.

SR: That's okay.
CNA: Yes. It's interesting to me that when you're black or female and if you like public figures that reflect your own identity, you're supposed to be quick to say, "Oh, it's not just because she's a woman." But if you're a man, the assumption is, "Hey, you're supposed to support men." But nobody actually thinks about, "Are you doing it because you're a man, and he's a man and . . ."

SR: But they are the norm, let's face it.
CNA: Yes, exactly. So, I suppose my point is that, increasingly, I want to be open and honest about me. I deeply admired Hillary because she was a

woman, and because she was a woman who was worthy to be president. But then I read Barack Obama's book, and I fell in love.

SR: Yes. This happens.
CNA: Yes.

SR: Actually, this happens a lot in your own book. There's a lot of literature in your literature.
CNA: Yes.

SR: It's also a book about literature, because the whole notion of America for Ifemelu, in a way, comes from Obinze's obsession with all [things] American . . . and also with literature.
CNA: Yes. I think probably all of my writing has something to do with celebrating books, because I love books. Books mean so much to me, and books have formed much of my worldview. And Ifemelu's not a reader, at least not in the beginning, which is very unlike me.

SR: Yes.
CNA: So, in some ways, I'm Obinze and Obinze is me. I didn't have that kind of obsession with America, but I had friends who did, who knew everything about American history, [who] had never come close to America itself, but who'd recite to you all the presidents, that kind of thing. [In terms of] Ifemelu, I wanted this also to be a journey of somebody who goes from not being a reader to being a reader, and how it changes her life, and how reading has real and practical consequences for her: it helps her with her homesickness, it helps her adapting to this new country—[this is] sort of a utilitarian view of literature.

SR: I wrote it down, but I tried to see how many books and references I could find. I'm sure I didn't find them all, because it was an idea that came to me this afternoon. But at least Graham Greene plays a role with *The Heart of the Matter*, because Obinze's mother loves this book.
CNA: Yes.

SR: And I think Ifemelu finds it morose? Or is that you?
CNA: [*laughs*] No, I'm not in the book. It's the characters.

SR: I know.
CNA: No, Obinze finds it . . .

SR: . . . a bit too morose.

CNA: Yes. He just doesn't understand his mother's obsession with it.

SR: No . . .

CNA: But his finding it that way is also partly a result of his America obsession, so that everything that's not American just immediately isn't good enough. And Graham Greene is the most English you can get.

SR: Yes, yes, [he's] too British. But I mean, it's a book that plays out in Africa.

CNA: It does, and it's also a book that . . . I think there are people who are surprised that I love that novel, and I do.

SR: I am surprised.

CNA: Ah.

SR: I love that novel, but I'm surprised that you do.

CNA: Ah. I do because I find it an honest novel, a novel that doesn't have malice. And I think there's a difference. I think there are many novels that have been written about "Aa-frica" that are deeply . . .

SR: The way you say "Aa-frica" . . .

CNA: . . . that are deeply ignorant and often quite malicious. Graham Greene, I think there's a beautiful sadness about that book that I really connect to. But also, the portrayal of these people's lives . . . he's very honest about the power structures of that time—colonial Sierra Leone or Liberia, we're not really sure. And I admire that. But at its heart, it's really this melancholy man, and love.

SR: Yes. Two things that you really like.

CNA: Yes.

SR: Whereas you don't like Naipaul. *A Bend in the* . . . what is it? *A Bend* . . .

CNA: *A Bend in the River.*

SR: . . . *in the River*, yes, of course. This is actually the white woman who comes to have her hair done. She's going to visit Africa. I don't remember where she's going. She's going to several places, because she wants to really "do" Africa. And she has read this amazing book, she says. You don't mention the author, but you do the title, so it's not so difficult to find out who it is. And then Ifemelu makes a review in the book. Was that not a funny day at the office? I mean, imagine getting back at Naipaul in your book, and there it is, it's not a newspaper, it doesn't go away.

CNA: Yes, but I think I should say that the novel has its merits. I mean, there are some novels I read and I think, "Why did anybody publish this?" But *A Bend in the River* is not one of them. I think it has its merits. I can understand somebody who says, "I liked it." When I first read it, I didn't really connect. I was indifferent to it. And for me, it's important to connect emotionally with a novel. But what was then very annoying was to be told by somebody—not in a hair salon—that it was the most honest book about Africa. I found it very annoying because, really, what that person was saying, and what people who think that really mean, is that a book about Africa that confirms all the negative stereotypes is somehow "true." But it's not a literary judgment; it's a political judgment. It annoyed me very much, so I thought I would throw it into the novel.

SR: *Plaf,* there it went. Well . . . this white woman in the salon, however, doesn't like Achebe, Chinua Achebe. She finds it a bit quaint.
CNA: Yes.

SR: And I think that may be one of your favorite novels, *Things Fall Apart . . .*
CNA: Yes.

SR: Because, when I was reading *Purple Hibiscus*, your first book, it's almost the first sentence. Is that not correct?
CNA: Yes, it's true.

SR: "Things started to fall apart . . ." So this is literature within literature. This is why, I mean, it can almost be difficult to make a conversation, because I have been finding thousands of sentences that I thought, "Oh, but I could also just quote this and quote that," it's really so interesting and so beautifully written. But I thought we could talk about different levels of being an immigrant in this book, because Ifemelu comes to America with a scholarship. It doesn't get her all the way; she has to make a living. Later, Obinze—who is Ifemelu's love, the love of her life; "love at first sight," because there is also a "love at first laugh," with another man, but Obinze is "the man"—he goes to London at a certain point to make his way through, but with no scholarship. He has a hard time, but they actually go through a kind of similar hard time . . .

CNA: Yes, but Obinze's experience is very much shaped by his being undocumented. His visa expires, and so he has to live as a shadow of himself; he has to live as somebody else because the only way he can work is with somebody else's papers. His story is based on a number of interviews with real people, because that's quite normal for many people. And I wonder what that does to your soul, really. I mean, people are very practical about it: I have to work; I have to send money back home. But I've wondered about what it does to you—the things that you don't let yourself dwell on, because you have to be pragmatic. Ifemelu, it's a bit easier for her because she's documented, even though, when she's done with her studies, she has to figure out how to get a job and stay on. But she doesn't live in shadow. She deals with disorientation, but at least she bears her name.

SR: That's very important.
CNA: Yes.

SR: Obinze at a certain point has to have a different name.
CNA: Yes, because he works with somebody else's papers, which means that he has to bear somebody else's name, and which means he has to remind himself every day that "This is my name," even though it really isn't.

SR: And then there's Aunty Uju, who also goes to have a career in America, which is not easy . . .
CNA: She's a doctor, and she leaves Nigeria because her relationship ended very badly. And . . . we won't give out the details.

SR: I don't know how many of you [in the audience] have already read it, but I suppose we must not put in everything; just suggest things.
CNA: So she goes to America to start over. She's a doctor, and she has a difficult time. I think that the prevailing notion of African immigration that many people in the West have is very much about the African single story: it's people who are refugees from war, people who have fled terrible poverty, people who are expected to be deeply grateful to have been allowed into a Western country. But the immigration that I know, and that the people I know [also] know, is very different. It's educated people who are middle class, who often choose to leave because they want more, because they have dreams, and who end up doing very well in the countries they go to. So Ifemelu does well; Aunty Uju, who has a hard time at the beginning adjusting, ends up being this doctor with a job, and a life, and independence, and

all of those things. But there's still a sense of longing. There are things that one loses, in addition to gaining.

SR: Immigration is one word for it, but another word which I think could apply to more of your novels and the characters in them, is the search to fit in—how do you fit in in different contexts?
CNA: Yes.

SR: And I mean, of course immigration is a very touchable thing, but there are several ways of being uncomfortable about who you are, where you are, why you are the way you are, and at a certain point Ifemelu says—I think it's with one of her lovers—"If I only could feel what I want to feel, that would be so much easier."
CNA: I think that is true, the idea of fitting in—it's the question of, "How do I fit in?," "What does it mean?," but even more, the other question of, "Should I fit in?"

SR: Yes.
CNA: And I think, for Ifemelu the answer is that one does not necessarily have to. So, I like to think of this novel as that cliché thing of "she finds herself in the end." Maybe I'll do a revised version that will be a self-help book, *How to Find Your True Authentic Self—Write a Blog*. But I do think that . . . yes, I'm very interested in what it means to be part of a group, but also in what it means to be different. If I had to have a political position, if I ran for office, my major platform would be, "Let's create room for difference," because—and I say this from a personal perspective—I am very much like Ifemelu: I'm fiercely, proudly Nigerian; fiercely, proudly African; fiercely, proudly Igbo. I think that the very little about me that is good is a result of my having grown up in Nigeria, of my having this rootedness in who I am. But at the same time, I've always felt just ever so slightly removed from things. There are things I know I'm supposed to like that I don't like, and things that I'm supposed to believe that I don't necessarily believe. And being part of a group means that sometimes you have to pretend that you believe it, even though you don't. So, in Igboland, and I think in much of sub-Saharan Africa, the idea of children, and the idea of the role of femaleness being reproduction, is central; it's not something you question: of course you must! I mean, children, . . . And while I love children, especially when they don't belong to me [*SR and audience laugh*], there isn't any room for the conversation and for the fact that there might be women

who don't in fact share this kind of idea. You can't even have the conversation; there's no room for it, because you're immediately silenced, and the kind of [response] you might get is, "It's not our culture." I sometimes find myself wondering, how many women are silenced about what they're really thinking and feeling?

SR: Not just in this respect, but in lots of things . . .
CNA: Oh yes, in general.

SR: In general.
CNA: And also, not just in Nigeria, by the way, I want to say. I mean, Nigeria is where my heart is, so I talk about it all the time, but everywhere in the world. I have to say I'm particularly interested in the experience of women, because I think that idea of silencing to be part of a [group], that idea of conforming, is something that's very gendered. It's mostly women, all over the world, who are expected to [conform].

SR: When you say a group, could we call it family? Because family means a lot in your books.
CNA: Family means a lot, yes. Family means a lot to me. Family means a lot to the people I write about. I think a lot of contemporary literary fiction assumes that there are certain things one has to be ironic about, such as family. If you're going to write about your parents, it'd better be dark and complicated. My sense of family is not really like that. My family is actually quite happy, and we actually really love one another.

SR: And there are a lot of you, so there is a lot of love.
CNA: Yes, there is a lot of love, there is a lot of laughter. I'm the fifth of six children. My parents have been married for fifty years, and they're actually good friends. They bicker very often, because you can't live with somebody for fifty years without bickering all the time, but it's very charming to watch them. Even the bickering, for me, is an act of love. So, for me, family is a warm fuzzy thing, mostly. I think it's possible to have a very positive attitude to family but still find oneself questioning certain things. In other words, the idea of, "Do I belong," "How do I belong," doesn't have to come with the baggage of negativity. At least it doesn't for me.

SR: Around the family or, perhaps, as you would say, part of the family, there are always aunts, and they are always wonderful. Is that because, even within a happy family, you need an aunt to get relief from the family sometimes? [*laughs*]

CNA: No. For me, family is actually an extended thing. My definition of family is quite broad, and so [includes] my siblings, my parents, but also my cousins—I have cousins who are as close to me as my siblings. As a child, growing up, I had aunts who played major roles in my life, simply by being present. And I've modeled . . . I mean, Aunty Uju not so much, but in *Purple Hibiscus*, I have yet another aunty character. I think that my next novel will be called *The Aunties*.

SR: [*laughs*] *The Aunties*, yes . . .

CNA: That character, in *Purple Hibiscus*, is modelled after an aunt of mine. I mean, I'm just thinking about this now, it's not something I've thought about; maybe it's also a way for me to write about female characters, but with a certain kind of distance. Because, if I wrote about mothers and sisters, it can be too close. "Aunty" is close enough, but it gives a bit of distance to do things with the character, I think.

SR: Ok, you have to be more careful with mum and dad . . .

CNA: Yes. [*laughs*]

SR: Now, Ifemelu in America is happy, and unhappy, and through her we get a fantastic description of what America is like for a woman like her, coming from Nigeria. She sees things and she says things that are not always popular. Some of the "worst" things she says about race, and how the Americans are—I mean, even the opening chapter, with the American eating ice cream—that is so mean of you, but that is so funny.

CNA: Mean?

SR: Yes, because we all think like that sometimes, and it's not good to see it in writing. Yes, it is. What I wanted to say is that she has another way of expressing herself, which is the blog.

CNA: Yes.

SR: I was wondering if you invented this blog for Ifemelu to have an even sharper say on things.

CNA: Yes, yes. I wanted to say many things about race, because I wanted this novel to also be social commentary. But I wanted to say them in ways that are different from what one is supposed to say in literary fiction. I just knew that, if I had her say them as dialogue, it wouldn't work. It just wouldn't seem right. I also wanted these things to be said in a voice that was kind of different from her real voice, because the self that is in that blog is different from the self that lives every day. So, the blog was a device, which I enjoyed very much. I've never blogged, but I would write these blogs and just stop and laugh—which in some ways was also worrying, because I thought, why am I so amused by my own humor?

SR: But it is very funny.

CNA: Yes, but you know what, I would laugh and stop and think, is this normal? You know, should I be worried? But I had so much fun writing it. But also, I wanted to say things that I do think are important to be said, and the blog just seemed the perfect device—the immediacy of the blog, the way that the language could be very different, and the way that it just allowed certain things to be said.

SR: The blog is a fiction, but of course it stands out almost like something out of nonfiction, because it's based on, apparently, facts. I mean, literature is really confusing, because you think that you're in a novel, and suddenly you are in a blog, and what is what?

CNA: And you have things where she says, "For all the Zipped-Up Negroes out there, this is your safe space." I've never actually seen that in a blog, but I would like to. I think the idea of the "Zipped-Up Negro"—which I found hilarious when I came up with it—says something about American life. I mean, in some ways, Barack Obama is a Zipped-Up Negro. The poor guy has to be.

SR: Of course.

CNA: Yes.

SR: How can we unzip him? [*SR and CNA laugh*] But . . . she gets a lot of followers for this blog. I mean, apparently there really is a need for a blogger of her kind.

CNA: Well, so I imagined, for the novel.

SR: I mean, you had me thinking that that would be very nice. This blog is then discussed often between the friends that she is with, with her different boyfriends—because in spite of Obinze being the great first love of her life, and love of her life also eventually, there are other men in her life.

CNA: As there should be.

SR: As there should be. But I understand that in Nigeria, this was not a popular issue. That's a worry with Ifemelu, is that not right?

CNA: It wasn't about the other men in her life, it was more that many Nigerian women who read this book—and I must say I'm very happy that Nigerians actually are reading it; it's doing very well in Nigeria—but many of the women are very upset about what they call Ifemelu being a "husband snatcher," and Ifemelu breaking a marriage, and that kind of discourse. It doesn't surprise me, that Ifemelu is not necessarily popular. Ifemelu isn't a female character who shies away from sexuality; she's a female character who is not reactive, who's proactive. She's in a good relationship with a man, but she cheats on him anyway. And these are not things that we expect of women.

SR: Those are things we do not forgive easily.

CNA: Yes, we don't forgive women easily, because we forgive men. I think if Ifemelu had been a man, and everything was the same, Nigerian women wouldn't have a complaint. They would say, "Well, men will be men." But that is important to me, really, the idea of a woman not being apologetic for her sexuality—just even the subject of sex itself not being something that's used to shame a woman. I like that Ifemelu is deeply flawed. I wanted her to be, because I think that's what it means to be human.

SR: There is a lot of good sex in your book. I mean, actually this could be a problem, because while they have amazing sex in your books, it's . . .

CNA: Not all the time!

SR: Not all the time, not all the time . . . actually, that's one reason why Ifemelu has a funny thing, a feature, which is also something a lot of people have in your books: it's boredom. She's quite easily bored. Actually, she cheats on one of her boyfriends because she's bored.

CNA: And kind of curious as well.

SR: Yes, I had put those words together: curious and boredom.

CNA: I think people are. People do. But I also think that, when her friend says to her, "How could you have done it?," she's supposed to have a reason that's very deep; she's supposed to say, "I felt abandoned" by the boyfriend, but she's really just bored. Because he's wonderful: he's good to her, he's kind. Sometimes, she finds him annoying, but fundamentally he's a very good partner. But she still destroys it, and . . .

SR: And he's white.

CNA: He's white, yes, but that's not why. [*audience laughs*] That's not why. Actually, if anything, it's less his whiteness and more his Americanness. He's a particular kind of American—she would look at him sometimes and just think, "Why are you so optimistic and sunny and happy?"

SR: He's too little melancholy for her, actually. Poor Curt. His name isn't even [melancholy], Curt. He's actually a very sympathetic character, I must say. You can mock him a little, but I know you like him.

CNA: Very much, yes.

SR: He is sunny side up.

CNA: Yes. I mean, it's a generalization about America, but I think it's largely true. It's also a class thing. There's a certain kind of middle-class, upper-middle-class American enthusiastic optimism.

SR: [*imitates American accent*] Excited?

CNA: Yeah. [*imitates American accent*] Oh my God, I'm so excited! [*audience laugh*] It can sometimes seem like a kind of naïve innocence, in some ways. It can be very charming, but it's easy to lose patience with it sometimes.

SR: I can see you as the strict teacher in some contexts, here.

CNA: Hehehe. [*mock sneering*]

SR: But it's true. What do they say, in America, about *Americanah*? Are they happy with your book? I know the reviews have been raving; I'm not talking about this. I mean, what we are doing here tonight, you've done in several places in America. Do they accept this? Because it is a satire of their country, and you do come from abroad. So, what do they say?

CNA: They say, "Shut up and be grateful we let you in." No, that's not true. That's actually not true. But I was prepared to have it be battered by reviewers and by readers. I wrote it because it's a book that I wanted to write, and also because I still get royalty checks from *Half of a Yellow Sun*, so I can still actually buy diesel for my generator in Nigeria and eat and go shopping, even if nobody buys this book. So I wrote the book I wanted to write. What has made me so happy is that I've actually been very surprised by people, who have embraced it. When I do these events, I often have a big academic turnout, and this is a book that makes fun of academia in America.

SR: Oh yes. Even on the first page, I mean . . .

CNA: But, you know, it's my American family. So, it's kind of self-mockery. I mean, these are people I know, and I'm kind of like them in some ways, right? So it's also looking in the mirror and saying, "Ha ha ha ha ha, we're really very silly sometimes." Many academics have said to me, "Thank you for writing the sort of thing that often isn't written about in serious fiction." Many of them are using this in their classes, because they say it starts a conversation about race. And of course, this is America, where there are certain things one is not supposed to say about race. An African American woman, at an event in Cambridge, said to me—and this remains the best compliment in my opinion that I've received about this book—she said: "Thank you, you've written everything we think but we don't say." And then she said, "And please know that you're never going to win any more prizes."

SR: [*laughs*]

CNA: And for me that was such a compliment. I said to her, "It's fine, I've won a few, so I'm kind of happy not to." But I think, really, what she was saying is, "There's something truthful and raw about this that might make people so uncomfortable that they will not reward you in the conventional way." I was very grateful to her for saying that. But she was wrong.

SR: Yes. Which makes it easier to be happy—double happy.

CNA: Yes. So really, I've been very grateful and very pleasantly surprised by the Americans.

SR: And I think you also really do love America because you cannot make fun of somebody that you don't also love.

CNA: Yes. Yes, I do. I mean, I feel very grateful for America, and to America. America is my rich uncle. [*audience laughs*]

SR: You're so naughty.

CNA: . . . or my rich aunty. Well, no, rich uncle—rich uncle who gives me pocket money but doesn't remember my name. [*audience laughs*] That's what America is. So you're very affectionate towards that uncle. But you're right, [in] this book, there's a lot of affection for America.

SR: There really is. I read George Eliot's *Middlemarch* not so long ago, and I thought it has the same [quality]. I mean, *Middlemarch* is tough on its people, but there's a lot of love there too.

CNA: Yes, I adore that novel.

SR: [*turns to Ellen Hillingsø, who read the opening of* Americanah *in Danish*] I think we should perhaps hear from you again, Ellen. This is an extract from the end of the book. I will say two words about it. This is a scene that I chose because to me it's heartbreaking and scary, and we've touched upon what it is about because it's the result of Ifemelu's being a "husband snatcher." This is Obinze leaving the wife that he has married while she [Ifemelu] was in America and actually left him, so there's nothing to be hurt about, but she comes back, and things happen, and he's now telling his wife the consequences. Let's hear it.

[*Reading in Danish by Ellen Hillingsø*]

CNA: You have to tell me why you chose that.

SR: Well, for many reasons—because this is a novel about race and hair and love, and I think that, of all the things that appeal to me, for several reasons, this is where love and obligation meet. And isn't that an eternal problem with any love? That, or boredom and curiosity, and the way you handle things. I think it's a brave scene, because you say that it's important to talk about things that are difficult to talk about. Race is of course difficult to talk about, but it's an issue that you will be able to discuss . . . But this is very difficult, because it's pure emotion, and a lot of moral on top of it. So why did you write it, I might ask? [*SR and CNA laugh*]
CNA: I don't know. Just to go back . . .

SR: You see, it's even more difficult to talk about than race.
CNA: The thinking about the "why" is quite difficult, because I'm not even sure I know the "why"; I'm not sure I know the "whys" of much of my fiction-writing. But what we said earlier about many, particularly Nigerian . . . actually, not just Nigerian, also African readers, and African American, who have labelled Ifemelu such things as "husband-snatcher," "destroyer of a marriage" . . . I think maybe I wrote that scene because it rings true. I remember a story about a man who wanted to leave his wife in Lagos; she knew he was seeing somebody else and had been seeing somebody else for a long time. The usual thing is to pretend that it's not happening, as long as the marriage remains a marriage of sorts. But this man was a little unusual, as is Obinze in the novel, because this is not the norm. The norm

for a Nigerian man is not to say, "I want to leave because I'm in love." The norm is to have the wife and then have . . .

SR: . . . the mistress.
CNA: Yes. And I remember this story of this woman getting down on her knees as a response to the man wanting to leave her. It stayed with me for a long time, because it made me sad. And, as is the case with gender for me, all the time, I like to switch things, so I thought, the reverse would never happen—that the woman says to a man in Nigeria, "I want to leave you," and the man [gets on his knees]. He might get violent or he might say, "Get out." The idea that a reasonable response, instead of anger, hurt, or other complex things, is to beg, and not even to beg with dignity—to beg with that kind of absolute humiliation . . . I wanted to write that. But Kosi is actually not a character that I'm very sympathetic to, so it was also quite interesting. I mean, I'm sympathetic to the position she occupies in the world, but to the character itself? I find her quite annoying. She's the kind of woman who is very interested in performing gender. So, it's not really about what she thinks; she says what she thinks she should say. She pretends to be deeply upset when Obinze's mother won't ask her to clean up, because she says, "I'm here to help," and that sort of thing. Inside her she might actually be quite irritated about helping, but she won't show it, because she has to be the "good wife." I wanted to write about that idea of never holding men responsible: this happens in this marriage but many of my female readers think Ifemelu "snatched husband," as though somehow the husband is this inanimate subject that you can pick up when you want to.

SR: [*laughs*]
CNA: But in the larger sense, one of the things I'm interested in [in] gender is not just male-female, but also female-female. It's the way that women are very quick to be . . .

SR: Judgmental?
CNA: . . . to judge other women, very quick to condemn other women. So, Obinze is immediately innocent; Ifemelu is the problem, and I find that very interesting, because if it's a question of being a problem, they both are problems.

SR: I thought, why would he marry her in the first place? My own answer was that she's very pretty.

CNA: She *is* very pretty but also, he cares about her, and she's a good wife, and he's at a point in his life where he felt very uncertain about things. He'd suddenly become very wealthy, and just wasn't sure . . . He felt unsteady.

SR: I like the way you defend Obinze—look at you! You just said you didn't really like the wife, but Obinze, he has all the reasons in the world to marry her . . . [*laughs*]
CNA: All right, all right. A friend of mine said, "It's so annoying; Obinze's the only character you're just blinded by." And ever since she said that, I think it's tr . . .

SR: You are in love with Obinze.
CNA: I think that is a fair comment. [*audience laughs*]

SR: But he is also a very sweet man.
CNA: He's a romanticized version of what I think all men should be.

SR: Yes, so that's kind of a clue. Now all the male listeners will read your book and just . . . [*pretends to read the novel frantically*]
CNA: But you know, he's kind and he's thoughtful, and he is intelligent, and he listens.

SR: But I must say, if I may say so, actually most of the men that Ifemelu deals with are kind.
CNA: Yes.

SR: And intelligent.
CNA: Yes, that's true.

SR: And helpful and . . .
CNA: Yes.

SR: . . . cook for her, and take her to Paris and . . . [*audience laughs*]
CNA: Yes. I mean, for me, what's interesting [is] I think there are female readers who have disliked Ifemelu because of that.

SR: Really?
CNA: Yes, they've said, why isn't she grateful? She has all of these good men

and she doesn't really deserve them. But it's true, the men are good men. I mean, I think the world is full of good men. But I also wanted this book to be a certain kind of love story, the sort of traditional, ridiculously romantic love story, which is why she leaves these ostensibly good men, because there is the idea of the great love. I don't know how true this is, but I like the idea of it.

SR: You like a happy ending.
CNA: I actually usually don't. I was very worried that I wouldn't be able to do the happy ending, because it's hard for me. I'm a little suspicious of a certain kind of excessive happiness. I like to say that this novel was written in the grand tradition of the romance novels I read when I was a teenager, but hopefully that this is a much better version of them.

SR: What were they? Can you mention one?
CNA: Yes, there's a series of [them], it was called the Mills & Boon. [*one person laughs in the audience*] Aha! [*looks at audience*] I think every teenage girl in Nigeria—and boy—read Mills & Boon novels. I mean, I could actually write one in a week, because it's very formulaic. And of course, as [in] most romance books at the time, they would hate each other when they first meet, and then the man would be forceful, maybe he would pull her to him and then she would melt. You see, that sort of thing.

SR: That sounds great.
CNA: Well . . . The assumption, somehow, in those books, was there was no female agency. You waited until the man [acted]; the woman didn't act.

SR: So actually, you're striking back with Ifemelu, because she doesn't wait.
CNA: Yes. Female agency is very important to me, yes. At the same time, I think love is very important. I think love is the most important human emotion, and I wanted to celebrate love in this book, and different kinds of love. So Ifemelu adores her cousin. That love was very much based on my own adoration of my nephew—I just deeply adore that child; he is twenty-one and he can do no wrong in my eyes. I think it's vaguely dangerous to love somebody too much. But I wanted to celebrate that love [and] also romantic love, which is why, when I was getting to the end of it—and I never quite know how my books will end—I started to worry that I might not be able to pull off the romantic ending. Because there's a part of me that just is drawn to the dark, so I thought, maybe somebody will die?

SR: You had me worried, actually.
CNA: Did I? [*laughs*]

SR: Yes.
CNA: But you know, in the end, it's a triumph of love. And I quite like the ending. Many of my serious literary friends don't like the ending.

SR: Really?
CNA: Yes. Which is a good sign, I think.

SR: Yes. [*laughs*] It's funny because, what we talked about before—that there's so much literature within the literature, and writing is so important . . . when Obinze comes to actually beg Ifemelu to take him on, he has written the whole explanation down. Is it easier to write things than to say them?
CNA: For me? Yes. Well, maybe not easier, but I think writing can . . . Sometimes, if I have friends who are going through difficult, deeply emotional uncertainties, I say to them, "Write." I think it can be helpful. I mean, it sounds a bit clichéd, but in Obinze's case of course, again, it was part of this book being a celebration of words: the reading of words, the writing of them. Because when she and Obinze reconnect, it's a relationship that's also based on words because they're writing to each other, and they haven't spoken. They write about what's happened to them in the times that they haven't been in touch, and I think that even the writing itself becomes some sort of symbol of reconnection or something.

SR: Even now, here, in the extract we heard, when he's most desperate, he turns around and takes out a book.
CNA: Yes.

SR: So, there is this notion of a kind of salvation within the written and read word.
CNA: Yes. Yes. I like that reading. I'm going to say that the next time I do an interview.

SR: You're a sentence-snatcher! [*SR and CNA laugh*]
CNA: I am.

SR: Good for you. We're going to end this conversation by having you read a small part from the book, because you should always have the last word.

But I was just wondering, while we find the place [in the book], if this love for Obinze is not just the character he is, but somehow . . . I felt while I was reading it, that he was also a reminder of *Half of a Yellow Sun*. Somehow he takes some of *Half of a Yellow Sun* [into *Americanah*]; there's a connection between those two books. I don't know if this is completely spooky thinking, but I felt that he was like a character who could have been there too. A ghost from *Half of a Yellow Sun* . . .

CNA: That's very interesting. No, I mean, of course it wasn't conscious, but I think that's a . . . maybe I'll say that again. I'll say that in my next [interview]. [*audience laughs*] Actually, I say the same things over and over; then I get so bored with myself, so I have think about something else to say. So I'll just steal your sentences.

SR: You prick up your curiosity. I was so afraid you were going to be too bored tonight.
CNA: No, not with you, Synne, not with you. Not with you.

SR: So, we will end this conversation. I will say thank you to Ellen for reading . . .
CNA: Yes, thank you. [*claps*]

SR: Can you find it [the passage]? Because I think I marked it with my taxi receipt. Here, this is it. [*audience laughs*] I thought we might have this problem. [*hands her copy of* Americanah *over to CNA*]
CNA: Ok. [*reads the end of chapter 29*]

Exclusive Interview:
Chimamanda Ngozi Adichie

Mazi Nwonwu / 2015

From *Olisa.tv*, 12 and 13 March 2015. Reprinted by permission.

Years ago, before I ever met her, I wrote an intro, in my mind, for my imaginary interview with Chimamanda Ngozi Adichie. Now, I finally get the chance to write that intro, to gush about Chimamanda the person and Chimamanda the world-famous author, and I can't find my qualifiers. When you get through this interview, perhaps you will understand why. Chimamanda takes us on a very personal journey, and it does make sense to just let her speak.

Mazi Nwonwu: I have been requesting this interview for about a year now, and you finally agreed to it. Thank you.
Chimamanda Ngozi Adichie: I decided I wanted to address certain things, and you were the one person I wanted to talk to. So thank YOU.

MW: A few weeks ago, the UK *Guardian* published an article online that you wrote about depression. Then a day later the article was removed. Many people were confused about this. There was much speculation. Some people even suggested that you might not have been the author of the article. I'd like for you to talk about depression and the story surrounding that article; why was it removed?
CNA: I was certainly the author. I have actually always been quite open about having depression. By depression, I don't mean being sad. I mean a health condition that comes from time to time and has different symptoms and is very debilitating. I've mentioned it publicly in the past, but I have always wanted to write about it. I was meeting many people who I could tell were also depressive, and I was noticing how hush-hush it all was, how

there was often a veil of silence over it, and I think the terrible consequence of silence is shame. Depression is difficult. It is difficult to experience, difficult to write about, difficult to be open about. But I wanted to do it. For myself, in a way, because it forced me to tell myself my own story, which can be helpful. But also for other possible sufferers, especially fellow Africans, because there is something very powerful about knowing that you are not alone, and that what happens to you also happens to other people.

Depression is something I have recognized since I was a child. It is something I have accepted. It is something I will have to find ways to manage for the rest of my life. Many creative people have depression. I wonder if I would be so drawn to storytelling if I were not also a person who suffers from depression. But I am very interested in demystifying it. Young creative people, especially on our continent, have enough to deal with without thinking—as I did for so long—that something is fundamentally wrong with feeling this strange thing from time to time. Our African societies are not very knowledgeable or open or supportive about depression. People who don't have depression have a lot of difficulty understanding it, but people who have it are also often befuddled by it. I wanted to make sure I was emotionally ready to write the piece. I don't usually write about myself and certainly not very personally. I wanted it to be honest and true. The only way to write about a subject like that is to be honest.

Last year, a major magazine that I admire asked me to write a personal piece for them. I decided to use that as a prodding to finally write about depression. They liked the piece and were keen to publish it. They suggested some edits, and at some point, I began to feel that the article was being made to follow a script, and that its integrity was being compromised. So I withdrew the piece. This was the most personal thing I have ever written, and I felt it had to be in the form that felt most true. My agent then said that the UK *Guardian* was launching a new section that was supposed to publish long, serious pieces. She sent it to them and they were interested. But I had already begun to rethink the piece itself. I was no longer sure I was ready for it to be published. I thought about changing the structure. To make it two essays, one about women's premenstrual issues and one about depression, so as to be more effective as a kind of advocacy memoir. Most of all, I decided I was not emotionally ready to have the piece out in the world. I wanted first to finish the new writing and research I was doing. So a day after my agent told me that the UK *Guardian* wanted it, I told her to please withdraw the piece completely. That I no longer wanted it to be published. The *Guardian* told her they were sorry I was withdrawing, but they understood. I didn't think about it after that. My plan was—put it away, go back to it in a year, and see how I feel and revise and edit it.

This happened in September 2014. Then a few weeks ago, I was traveling, and I get off a plane, turn on my phone, and see messages from acquaintances telling me how "brave" I was. I was astonished. I had just written a piece for the *New York Times* about my issues with light in Lagos and so I thought "*haba*, since when is writing about light brave?"

MW: I read that article about light in the *New York Times* and loved how you wrote about something all of us Nigerians can identify with and all of us complain about but you turned it into a poem and a political statement at the same time.

CNA: Thank you. A friend of mine was teasing me about how diesel is a Big Man Problem, and how she deals only with petrol for her generator. Which I thought was funny, and true. But also interesting is how the light situation stunts everyone, how the privileged—except maybe for diesel importers—are not immune. Anyway, I soon realized that the messages I was getting were not about the article on light. Somebody specifically mentioned the *Guardian*. So I immediately went to the *Guardian* website.

MW: Do you remember what your first reaction was when you saw that an article you decided not to publish had suddenly appeared in public?

CNA: I felt violated. It felt like a horrible violation. This was the most personal piece I had written and the only person who deserved to decide when it would be read publicly was me. Even their choice of words felt like a violation. They wrote that it was about my "struggling" with depression. I would never have agreed to that caption. I do not think of the article as being about my "struggle" with depression, but about my journey to accepting something I have had since I was born, and my choosing to "come out" about it. I also hated that the sentence they highlighted from the whole piece was about how "the nights are dark . . ." etc. It felt sensationalizing and cheap. I was angry with the *Guardian*. Especially as their first apology was "we are obviously sorry." Any apology that contains the word "obviously" is not an apology. They took it down and replaced it with an explanation about a "technical error," which even a child would have reason to doubt. It's probably naïve of me but I had expected that they would be quick to admit their fault and make amends. There is something predatory about Big Journalism. Big Journalism doesn't care about the humanity of it subjects. Big Journalism cares about "good copy" and about not being sued. It took longer than it should have, but at least they subsequently published a proper explanation and apology, with the prodding of lawyers.

MW: What did you make of the *Guardian*'s explanation that they had produced a "mock-up" of the piece and then forgot to delete it in their system after you withdrew it and then it was automatically launched on their site? Also, after it was taken down, many websites had already copied it and posted it, especially here in Nigeria.

CNA: I don't understand how something stays on the website of a major, widely read newspaper for a whole day, something you have no right to publish, and nobody in your organization notices. As for the Nigerian websites, I think any website that puts it up is using what does not belong to them, which is called stealing. But this is the Internet age and of course I can't really control any of that.

MW: Well, I know for a fact that that article has been very widely read and the consensus was that you were brave to write it and many people praised you. So I think it had a positive impact.

CNA: I really hope other people who have depression found strength in it. My agent got many moving emails from people who were grateful that I had written about depression because they too had trouble even accepting that they had depression. I got responses from some distant friends and most were thoughtful and full of empathy and I was struck by how many said the piece made them feel better about acknowledging their own depression.

I also got a few responses that troubled me. Because I was generally quite upset by the *Guardian*, those responses further upset me. William Styron, who wrote the great novel *Sophie's Choice*, also wrote a memoir of depression, *Darkness Visible*, where he writes about being enraged by people patronizing him and simplifying his depression to platitudes. I got a patronizing email, for example, from an acquaintance which was full of passive-aggressive comments and then ended with "you are loved." And I thought: but that is obvious from the piece. I have a small solid circle of family and friends and I feel very loved and very grateful. But the piece is about the paradox of depression, that it is often a kind of sorrow without a cause. That being depressed makes even the sufferer feel bad and guilty because you are thinking of all these people you love and who love you and who you now feel strangely disconnected from. Another patronizing person told me "don't worry, I won't judge you." Which infuriated me beyond belief. Judge me? I didn't know judgement was an option. Shame is not an option for me and never will be. Writing this piece was a choice I made. Being open about my vulnerability was a choice I made, and I don't regret making it. There was also the usual Nigerian response of "just pray about it." I realized that many people who contacted my manager had either not understood the piece or had just read the *Guardian*'s choice caption of "nights are dark and I cry often" and then decided to send me solutions ranging from Bible quotes to various churches.

MW: Did any of the responses really affect you?

CNA: I feel strongly, on principle, about the right to tell my own story. By publishing something I was not ready to publish, the *Guardian* violated that right, and I was very much affected by that. One particular response really saddened me. Someone asked my manager whether this was just a publicity stunt. I thought—have we become so soullessly cynical? Somebody actually thinks that if I wanted to pull a publicity stunt, I would write the most personal essay I have ever written about my own life?

MW: Well, if you were looking for publicity, I would say you have the best source—Beyoncé. One of the most famous pop musicians in the world used a part of your speech "We Should All Be Feminists" in her song "Flawless." Many people say that you helped her shore up (or even create) her feminist credentials. What are your thoughts about that and on having given permission for Beyoncé to sample your TED Talk?

CNA: I think Beyoncé is a cultural force for good, in general. It's a shame that we live in a world so blindly obsessed by celebrity—an actor or musician talking about a social issue should not be a reason for the press to pay attention to that issue, because they should pay attention to it anyway—but sadly it is what it is. Ours is an age in which celebrities have enormous influence. Beyoncé could easily have chosen to embrace something easy and vanilla like "world peace." Or she could have embraced nothing at all because she is, after all, immensely successful and talented and she can actually sing—we all know that not all famous musicians can sing. Feminism is not a subject that will win you universal admiration as an entertainer and to make the choice she did is admirable. I was happy to give my permission.

MW: But people have questioned her right to identify as feminist because of the sexual nature of some of her performances?

CNA: This is actually the question I kept being asked, and I found it tedious. There is a moralistic and troubling strain of feminism that equates all forms of female sexuality with shame. What matters is that Beyoncé controls her own image. Female sexuality is a feminist issue only when there is a power imbalance. Actually, Beyoncé's brand of sexuality is mainstream-conservative, with the whole idea of "put a ring on it" and the title of "Mrs" as an honorific and so on. It seems to me that people who criticize her for being sexual should also acknowledge that underlying her version of sexuality is quite an old-fashioned wholesomeness. If the fear of a subversive depiction of female sexuality is the problem, then they really should leave her alone.

MW: You seem to be more in the camp of subversion.

CNA: I am indeed. I do not believe that female sexuality needs to be clothed in "respectability." Male sexuality certainly doesn't need "respectability" to be valid and the same should be true of female sexuality.

MW: A friend of mine said I should ask you why you are "falling her hand." She said you are too humble about this Beyoncé thing. She said if she were you, she would be giving interviews about Beyoncé every day and putting things on Instagram about your collaboration. She said she felt very proud to hear your voice at the VMA awards but that you didn't even give any interview about it. Her words were "Chimamanda has never made noise about this Beyoncé thing." I hear you turned down every interview that wanted to focus on Beyoncé.

CNA: Yes, when the song came out I turned down all interview requests. I was also a bit taken aback because I had expected some interest, but I was startled that even the so-called serious news sources wanted to talk about it and in a kind of frenzied and goading sort of way. It all just seemed like too much noise. I realized it was something I would not be able to speak about with any nuance because whatever I said would be reduced to one line and become yet another source of noise. So I turned everything down. I was also working on some writing and wanted to be able to focus.

Later, when I was on book tour, there were people who wanted to talk about Beyoncé and when I responded by saying I was happy to give her my permission and happy that so many young people would now become aware of gender issues and happy that my nieces and nephews now thought Aunty was cool—which was how I truly felt—people kept pushing and prodding as though they wanted me to say something I was not saying. Or people who were eager to tell me how excited they were about Beyoncé using my speech, but oh, they hadn't read my book. A serious literary person introduced me as "Beyoncé's favorite writer," even though my novel had just won a well-respected prize. Another person said to me, "Tell me how excited and honored you were when she called you!"—and I thought: "What an inane question and what a limited choice of options." I very quickly became tired of such questions. The point is that I am a writer. I gave a talk about a subject I feel passionate about. When I gave the talk, I had no idea that anybody would even be really interested in it. It ended up that a music star watched it and was inspired by it and wanted to use it. I was happy to give my permission. But I refuse to have that define me in any way. If I am doing an interview, I should be talking about my work, not being asked to speculate on the authenticity of somebody else's feminist motivation. By the way, please tell your friend to forgive me for "falling her hand"!

MW: So do you think the Beyoncé song increased the sales of your novel *Americanah*?

CNA: I'm not sure, but I doubt it. Mostly because many people who were excited about Beyoncé having used my talk in her song didn't go off to buy my novel, but instead watched the TED Talk that she had sampled—which I was quite happy about. What actually happened is that at around the same time as the "Flawless" song release, *Americanah* was chosen as one of the Ten Best Books of the Year by the *New York Times* and won the US National Book Critics Circle Award. Those certainly had a major impact on the sales, especially the former.

MW: This is a good way to switch to literature. The general rule is that books that are well reviewed do not sell and that books that sell are not well reviewed. Very few writers have both. I can think of Ian McEwan for example. *Americanah* was a *New York Times* bestseller and I hear it is still a bestseller in many independent bookshops in America. It has just been published in France and is a bestseller there. It has also done well in Germany, Sweden and other countries. It is a bestseller here in Nigeria. What is it like to have both critical and commercial success?

CNA: Even if I did not have the good fortune of being widely read, I would still be somewhere writing, because writing is my life's passion. When you write a book, you just never know if it will do well or not. And so I feel this immense gratitude to be widely read and I haven't lost my sense of wonder—each time I hear about what the book means to somebody, I am newly moved. In the case of *Americanah* in particular, a novel in which I broke with a certain kind of convention and a certain kind of sense of duty, it is a feeling of double pleasure and double gratitude because I honestly didn't think it would do too well.

MW: With your novels published in more than thirty languages all over the world, you seem to travel a lot on book tours. I was asking your manager about your travel schedule and he said you are really cutting down now. I was not too surprised to learn that you receive requests from all over the world; what was astonishing was learning that you accept only about ten percent of them. Why ten percent? Why not more?

CNA: When I was first published, I was thrilled by the idea of a book tour. I thought—somebody is really going to buy me a flight ticket, put me up in a hotel, have people take care of me, go and read and sign books somewhere? It felt like a wonderful dream. But after the novelty wore off, it became tedium. It's a very good problem to have, but it doesn't make it less wearying. Increasingly I like to do a few events, because I quite enjoy them, and I get to meet interesting people, and I find that I learn from people who have read my work, but long tours exhaust me mentally. I am also a slow writer, and I really like silence and space, and travel gets in the way. So even though many of the invitations are interesting, I now reluctantly turn many down.

MW: Are there any recent events that have stood out for you?

CNA: Last year I was a keynote speaker at an Anambra State Government event in Awka. When I was done speaking, a large group of women in the audience burst into song. They sang "Nwanyi bu ife," which translates to "women are now something." It was so moving to me. Another one that stands out is Nairobi. I spoke in this huge hall full of Kenyans. I know it's a bit sentimental but I felt myself welling up with emotion, standing there. I felt this wonderful pan-African thing, and also an odd sense of duty that was beautiful. And I had an event in Oslo recently that was very special.

MW: What about "the fans"?

CNA: I think I have some of the loveliest fans in the world. The greatest compliment to me is to have my work read carefully and thoughtfully. The best moments are from ordinary people who take ownership and who disagree or agree with specific things because it means that they have really engaged with the book. A character must be real to you before you can like or dislike them.

One of my favorite stories happened some years ago at Yellow Chilli restaurant here in Lagos. A woman anonymously sent a waiter to me with a serviette. On it she had written: "I don't mean to interrupt your dinner but I just wanted you to know that you gave me a history that I may never have come to know, and for that I and my generation will always be thankful." I have that serviette framed and hanging on my study wall. (By the way, if that lovely woman reads this interview, I just want to say thank you. I owe you a hug.)

MW: You must receive many such letters. Why did that one matter so much to you?
CNA: It seemed so genuine and real and utterly lacking in both affectation and entitlement. I appreciated that very much.

MW: Do you notice affectation or entitlement in fans?
CNA: Sometimes. There are people who are loath to say a simple kind word without some preface or some sort of self-styled edge to show you how cool they think themselves to be, as though there is, for them, a competition even in the act of paying you a compliment. This mostly comes from people who think themselves intellectuals or who imagine themselves to be very good writers if only the wicked world would publish them.

MW: I can imagine that interaction with fans of all kinds is something celebrities have to become used to . . .
CNA: I don't really think of myself as a celebrity.

MW: But you are. You have transcended just being a writer. You have an impact on the culture. People respond to what you say, whether for good or for bad. Even the interest in your personal life is a sign of your celebrity. I know of young women who are inspired by you and not just by your books.
CNA: The word celebrity feels alien to me. It makes me think of people who are more visually public figures, if that makes sense, like actors and musicians. I have a lot of sympathy for them because it must be very hard to have a career whose main requirement is placating strangers. So I mean that I don't see myself as a celebrity in that way. But of course I am very much aware that I have become a public person.

A woman once got nasty when she asked to take a picture with me and I said no, because I was exhausted and I looked terrible. Another person once said to me—"You must always smile no matter what." I thought: "How absurd. Do YOU always smile?" I'm actually quite the smiler but I certainly will not smile if I am upset about something. Everyone has good days and bad days and I treasure my human right to have good days and bad days. I think the idea of celebrity is that you are supposed always to be "on," always in performance mode. And I certainly can't and won't do that. I do not gauge what I say or do based on how somebody will respond. I gauge it based on what I truly think and feel. My only responsibility is to speak truthfully. I never set out to offend anybody, but I also never censor myself because of the fear of causing offense. I like to be honest and open with people and I like them to be the same with me. I am not sure real celebrities have that choice. I have a great amount of sympathy for famous people who have to live a certain kind of pretend-life because they are afraid of the consequences hurting their career—that maybe somebody won't go and see their film or won't buy their album. You become trapped in a performance of your own life. I could never live like that. And I think it's become worse in recent years, with celebrities expected to make their choices based on what other people think and what other people want. I realize some celebrities might be happy with that kind of life but my sense is that many talented people find it constraining. Talib Kweli wrote a fantastic piece about Lauryn Hill that challenged this idea of a celebrity as a person owned by fans.

MW: I read that article, loved how he captured that thing that we more often than not miss: celebrities are human and suffer from human frailties. However, I think it would be apt to ask what your relationship to fame is?
CNA: Interesting question. There are some wonderful benefits—strangers secretly paying for my dinner at restaurants for example, ha! But seriously, I think I have a conflicted relationship with it. There are things it has made happen in my life for which I am grateful and appreciative but there are also times when I deeply resent being a public person, when I don't want to be.

MW: You have celebrity friends like Kerry Washington and Thandie Newton. Tell me about the friendship, and what it means to know these black women who have also made a mark in their own professions—Thandie Newton is the top-ranked black British actress today and Kerry Washington is the first black woman to star in an American prime time show since the 1970s.
CNA: They are both intelligent, thoughtful and beautiful inside and out.

MW: I can see you don't want to talk about your friends. I heard Will Smith is a fan of yours. If you won't talk about your friends, at least you have talked about this one before. Just try for me.
CNA: Some years ago his people called and said he wanted to set up a call. So we had a nice chat. He said he just wanted to let me know that he had been following my writing and my speaking and loved what I was doing and wanted to encourage me. He spoke in specifics. It meant a lot to me because it wasn't just an empty "well done!" but there was a kind of thoughtfulness

that I really appreciated. And of course, I made sure I told him how much I loved *Fresh Prince of Bel-Air* when I was growing up in Nsukka. I love his humour and I loved his remarkable transformation in the movie *Ali*.

MW: You are well known in Nigeria and I would say that you first became famous in Nigeria after your first novel *Purple Hibiscus* was shortlisted for the Orange Prize in 2004 and then won the Commonwealth Writers' Prize the next year. There was the generation of Achebe and Soyinka that made names for themselves internationally, and the generation after them did not quite achieve that level of international success. There were some successes, but no writer achieved the resonance that you did with *Purple Hibiscus*. I think it was because it was a novel that spoke to a new generation of Nigerians and had a contemporary setting. *Purple Hibiscus* is now on the WAEC syllabus and you have gone on to have so many other recognitions. Let's talk about your youth. You started very early with these recognitions, getting the best results in your secondary school, University Secondary School, Nsukka, in both the JSCE and SSCE.
CNA: Yes, I did. I never liked mathematics, but I was determined to do well. I ended up with an A2, not an A1, and I was a bit upset with myself. I was one of those annoying people who got upset when they scored ninety-six percent in a test.

MW: Which is why you were expected to study medicine at university.
CNA: Yes. And so I did. I always knew deep down that I really didn't want to study medicine. I liked chemistry, but biology bored me and I am quite squeamish, so laboratory dissections made me sick. The only thing I liked about medicine was psychiatry. I have a certain intuition about people; I am actually an amateur psychologist otherwise known as "winch." I did one year of medicine at Nsukka then switched to pharmacy before leaving for the US. The real reason I wanted to go to America was to escape the sciences.

MW: The world of literature gained from that decision. I was researching your awards. Very impressive. Fellowships from Harvard and Princeton. Shortlisted three times for the Orange Prize (now called the Baileys Women's Prize) and won once, Commonwealth Writers' Prize, the US National Book Critics Circle Award, the *New York Times* Top Ten Best Books of the Year, the *Chicago Tribune* Heartland Prize, the MacArthur Foundation "Genius" Award, the Global Ambassador Achievement Award from the Nigerian government and many others. What do these prizes and recognitions mean to you? Do any of the prizes stand out or have a particular meaning?

CNA: It's always lovely to have your work recognized. Prizes are nice, but they are not the reason I write. I would still be somewhere writing even if I had never won a single award. I like and respect the Orange Prize—sorry, Baileys Prize—because I think the shortlist is always strong, and I like the worldview of the Prize, if that makes sense. I was particularly thrilled about the National Book Critics Circle Award because I wasn't expecting it. I was on a shortlist of writers I respect, and it really is such a cool prize, judged by a group of fiction critics, people who actually read a lot of books. The recognition of *Americanah* as a *New York Times* Top Ten book made me squeal in surprised pleasure. The *New York Times* has a "100 notable books" list every year, which is quite nice to be on. But the top ten books of the year? I never knew that would happen. So when my editor sent me an email telling me, I actually said "No way!" aloud. It made me very happy. And the next thing I did was what I do when anything good happens—I tell my parents. The pride in my father's eyes is one of my life's greatest sources of joy.

MW: You speak about your father often. He seems to be a great inspiration to you.

CNA: He is more than an inspiration. He is the loveliest, kindest, wisest, funniest, sweetest man in the world. I am an unabashed Daddy's Girl. I have wonderful parents. I adore my mother. My father just turned 83, and you realize how important it is to cherish time spent together. We have these long precious meandering conversations where he tells me about our family history and I find myself wishing I could pause each moment, make it stay still, savor it for longer. He reads everything I write and he tells me exactly what he thinks, which I deeply appreciate. If he thinks something isn't very good, he says so, and if he thinks it's good, he says so.

MW: Before your first novel was published, you were shortlisted for the Caine Prize for a short story in 2002. How instrumental was the Caine Prize in your career? Did it help you get published?

CNA: The honest answer is no. By time I was shortlisted for the Caine Prize, I already had an agent and a finished novel, *Purple Hibiscus*. Let me give you a bit of the background story. My first publication was a poem written when I was fifteen and published in Nigeria. Then I wrote a terrible book of poems published by a vanity press. Then at the age of seventeen, I wrote a play that was published in Nigeria. I don't really think of them as real publications, mostly because prose is my true love. When I got to the US, I did some research and learned that, if you wanted to get published, you needed an agent who would then find you a publisher—if you were lucky. I finished my novel and started sending it out to agents. I got many, many rejections. Some of the agents told me that they liked my writing but because I was writing about Nigeria, they would not be able to sell my work to a publisher. Others told me they had nobody to compare me to. One agent told me nicely, "If you were Indian, it would be easier." There was no contemporary Nigerian writer who was well known in the US. And nobody really cared about Nigeria as subject matter for fiction. At the time, in American publishing, "African writing" was something students read in a college course.

So it was extremely difficult. But I kept at it. I wrote and rewrote stories and kept sending them out to agents. I went to the library and spent hours researching publishing journals. I was a student and I had a job, so every night I stayed up until 3 a.m. working on my fiction. It was my real passion. Finally, an agent told me she was "willing to take a chance on me." Those were her words. Willing to take a chance. She was very honest. She told me my chances were low since I was completely unknown and I came from a part of the world that nobody cared about. She said it might also be a problem that I used bits of what she called "an African dialect" in my novel. I told her that Igbo, like English, was not a dialect but a language with many dialects. (I have never understood why people say that Europeans speak "languages" but what comes out of African mouths is described as "dialect" or "tongue." Even some Africans themselves use this distinction and I find it profoundly annoying.) I made the case that it was important for me to have the Igbo bits in the book because I wanted to try and capture the reality of characters who were constantly straddling two languages. I had read books written in English where bits of French or bits of Italian were thrown in, because the writers wanted to create the texture of their characters' lives. I didn't see why it should be different for an African language.

MW: It was at your writing workshop that I first heard you tell the story of how you got published. You were very generous and told us all the details and it was good to hear because it made us realize that this Successful Chimamanda did not just fall from the sky like that and it came with a lot of hard work. So after the agent took a chance on you, she then sent the manuscript out to publishers?

CNA: Yes. Not long afterwards, a publisher told her they were interested. A small but very good publisher based in North Carolina. I was really happy that they took me on. They had a small budget. They didn't have much money for publicity and marketing. But what was lovely was that they really believed in the novel. I did a small book tour and I remember one event somewhere in the American Midwest to which only two people came! Because there was just very little publicity around the book.

The book itself became popular with booksellers, and independent booksellers are simply the best and most committed readers of literature. Even without much publicity, the booksellers were hand-selling the novel: people would come into their shop and the bookseller would personally recommend the novel to them. I think even my publishers were surprised when the novel very soon became an independent bookshops bestseller. It didn't mean much money because actual sales numbers were relatively small, but it did mean a certain grassroots legitimacy that quite frankly is priceless.

My British editor heard about the book from another editor in New York. She read it, loved it and knew right away that she wanted to publish it in the UK. So the Caine Prize didn't play a role. Actually, I remember that at the Caine Prize, which was attended by some agents, I excused myself from meeting agents because I already had an American agent.

MW: Is there anything in particular you would say was your "big break"?
CNA: Being shortlisted for the Orange Prize definitely. I was the only first-time author on the shortlist and I think I was also the youngest author to be shortlisted and so that brought large-scale attention to my work. I was on the shortlist with the great Shirley Hazzard and it was such an honor. I will always be grateful to that agent who took me on as a complete unknown. And I will always be grateful to the Orange Prize.

MW: You have called for the West to respect us as equal citizens of the world in the past (I read and loved your piece on real heroes in the war against Ebola). In the light of that, what do you think of Binyavanga Wainaina's call, in a recent interview, for us to develop our existing literary platforms and stop overly legitimizing the Caine Prize?
CNA: It is true that the Caine Prize benefits African writers, but the benefits go both ways. The Caine Prize also gains legitimacy from African writers. Some people think that the response to any kind of "foreign help" should be an unquestioning, near-servile gratitude. It shouldn't be.

Prizes matter because they bring recognition to writers. But what is even more important for us here in Nigeria is to start at the root of the problem. Our education system is a disaster. Our graduates are barely literate. You often hear Nigerians bemoaning this and blaming the young people. But it is not the young people's fault. If you are in a system that has failed you, there is little that the majority of people can do to overcome a poor foundation. I sometimes see how much money is spent in Nigeria on things like music, and indeed how much money exists in Nigeria albeit in severely limited hands, and I realize there is so much more we can do for literature. I would like Nigerian corporate sponsorship to fund programs in universities. Fund a journalism program, which would mean the students have access to visiting professors from all over the world, the proper computer hardware and software, access to the latest scholarly research. Fund an English program. Fund a library. Provide books and demand some kind of accountability from the institution. Fund a program like "Teach For America" that organizes short-term training for graduates who can then go to all parts of Nigeria and be paid well for teaching. The current practice of sending Youth Corpers to schools is not useful because many of the corpers don't know the first thing about teaching. Make writing and reading a fundamental part of the curriculum in primary and secondary schools. We still have an attitude that a "story book" is not as much real study as maths. Actually, both are equally important.

MW: Before Binya's declaration, there was another big controversy surrounding the Caine Prize and your statement about it not being the true representation of African writing. One of your workshop attendees who insiders say you gave a lot of support was in the middle of the Caine Prize uproar. You've never talked about this; I am sure people want to know what you think about that incident.

CNA: I remember I was at home when a friend came by and saw me having dinner with family and friends and he said, "Ah, you are here laughing and eating while they are talking about you online." I remember later being amused because I thought: "So now I'm not supposed to eat?" I asked him what was going on and he told me that this person who had been at my workshop the year before had written a misogynistic, insulting piece about me because he was angry that I had referred to him as "one of my boys at the workshop" in an interview. I was very surprised.

First, I have to give some background: this person applied to my workshop and was accepted. I was interested in one of the early pieces he wrote at the workshop, which was about homosexuality and was progressive in tone. He was from the North and I have always particularly wanted to support writers from the North because I think we don't have as many stories coming from Northern Nigeria as we do from Southern Nigeria, and if we are going to make any sense of Nigeria as a nation, we need more stories. More human stories, not just check-the-box journalism. Especially from the minorities in the North, because it is easy to think of the North as one huge monolith.

So it was the major reason I chose to support him. I remember telling him at the workshop that a lot of his work was about provoking for the sake of provoking, which I thought was hollow. He seemed more focused on the response he could elicit than on the integrity of the story he was telling. I also remember that he often acted very superior to the other workshop participants in a way that was unpleasant. As far as I was concerned, if you choose to apply to a workshop that I am teaching, then you are a student like everyone else. And all the students are there because they have talent, you can learn from anyone and you really should save your superiority until you have actually published something worthwhile.

Anyway, after the workshop, another workshop alum sent me a story that this person had written, which the alum thought I should see because it was good. I also thought it was good. So I took my time, read it and sent this person an email saying he needed to make some edits but that I thought he should get it published. Time passed. He wrote me from time to time. I did not always reply because I am often overwhelmed and am quite terrible with emails. But I wrote back a few times, to send him my good wishes, to encourage him to keep writing, that sort of thing. His emails were always very polite. Mine were always warm and encouraging. He sent me a collection of stories that he had finished writing. I then decided to introduce him to my agent.

MW: That is some serious compliment, if I may say so.
CNA: I certainly don't do it often. And by the way, I don't do it anymore. I asked my agent to please contact him and to look at his collection. She read his stories and thought he still needed to do some more work on them. The idea was that if he revised them or wrote something else, he would send to her. He now had the possibility of being represented by one of the best literary agents in the world. For this story to continue making sense, we have to go back to another story about natural hair.

MW: Are they related? I mean, does the natural hair controversy have any bearing on the "one of my boys at the workshop" controversy . . .

CNA: Well, yes, because it was the last communication I had with this person before he turned into an attack dog. After somebody put out that headline about weaves and low self-esteem, I was told that people were tweeting this quote that I had never said, and that this person had tweeted it as well. So I wrote to him and told him I expected better from him, that I was disappointed he would join a bandwagon in repeating what I never said. I expected that somebody like him would be astute enough to go and read the actual interview. He wrote back and was very apologetic, effusively apologetic, and said he had not actually been referring to me and that his tweets had been misunderstood. I believed him. That was the last communication I had with him. Which is why I was astonished to hear, later, that he had written this attack piece about how I had called him "boy" in an interview. He knew that there was no way I meant "boy" in a demeaning way. It was a playful and affectionate way of saying that he was a protégé of sorts. Which at the time he was. This was somebody I had been helpful to and supportive of. This is somebody who once knelt down in front of me as a greeting, in public, to show how grateful he was for my support. He didn't have to write a public attack piece; he could have written me himself if he genuinely minded the "boy." I don't often use the word immoral, but I think what he did was immoral. What he wrote was apparently so full of ugly innuendo that people said to me that there must be some "back story." There was of course no "back story."

Some of my friends told me that I should release all the emails I had ever exchanged with him. Because to anyone who saw those emails, seeing that he had spent months being (in hindsight) falsely extra-nice and borderline sycophantic, it would be obvious that his "outrage" about being called "boy" was a cynical attempt to grab attention for himself. But I decided against it. It just wasn't worth the emotional energy. I also didn't want to feel that I had to "open" my private space because of this person's cynical action.

I cannot blame the public for their response. To be honest, if I were an observer, I think I too would have taken on that outrage of "how dare she call him boy." I used to automatically think that there was virtue in the non-famous person and vice in the famous person. If you read the interview in which I referred to him as "one of my boys" in its proper context and with an open mind, it is clear that I am being very pro-Nigerian nationalist and also mocking Nigerian nationalism at the same time. But I can easily see how people would take on an outrage. We live in an age of easy shallow outrage. It's a case of "what is the twitter outrage of the day?" Many people don't even read the original article that is being referenced before they join the outrage bandwagon. And remember, the source of outrage was not my actual referring to him as "one of my boys" but his own piece about it. I am sure many people read his piece, and so I can't blame them at all for then attacking me. I am told he referred to me as a cocoyam of some sort. An unfortunate choice of metaphors, by the way. I had hoped he might have learned better at my workshop.

MW: You have a way with sarcasm that can be bitingly funny.
CNA: I am the proud granddaughter of Nwabuodu of Umunnachi, and my grandmother had the most deliciously cutting tongue. Her sarcasm was an absolute art form, and I aspire to that. I admire a certain kind of female sarcasm, which has a wonderful tradition, with such people as Jane Austen and Rebecca West and Dorothy Parker. So yes, I am often sarcastic. Happily so.

MW: I want to go back to the natural hair controversy. There was social media uproar about a statement you had allegedly made about natural hair. It was reported that you said in an interview with a UK newspaper that Nigerian women who wear weaves have low self-esteem. I kind of feel, and I said it at that time, that there is this "waiting for Chimamanda to take a wrong step" thing existing within the Nigerian intellectual class. I read the interview and saw that you clearly never said that.
CNA: No, I never did. By the way, to be clear, if that is what I thought, I would absolutely say so. But it is just such a simplistic and sophomoric idea. You can't even remotely believe that if you have a sister like my wonderful sister Uche, one of the most self-confident women in the world and a keen fan of straight long weaves. I also said in that interview that while I prefer natural hair, I would buy straight hair wigs for my nieces if that was what they wanted, because life is short.

Anyway, I understand that somebody deliberately put out the headline "Chimamanda said women who wear weaves have low self-esteem" and it was repeated over and over until it felt true. At first I could not understand all the noise, since the original interview was there for anybody to read and see that it was not what I said. But I soon realized that many people WANTED it to be what I said. Because it would be an easy way to form a Society of the Outraged, and nobody would actually have to think about what I did say. I was told about an ardent member of the Society of the Outraged who was asked to point out exactly where in the interview I had said what she was so outraged about. She then replied, "Read the interview again slowly!" as if there was some magical clue to be unravelled by reading it slowly.

I don't mind at all when people disagree with my opinion as long as it is truly my opinion. There are many people whose opinions I disagree with and I expect mine to be disagreed with as well. I actually quite like a good argument, but it is frustrating when people say you've said something that you haven't said.

MW: True. I find it interesting that there is this link between the natural hair controversy and the controversy about your referring to a former participant in your workshop as "one of my boys." So the last contact you had with this former workshop participant was because he had reportedly joined in retweeting the false quote about natural hair, and you heard about it, and contacted him to tell him you expected better from him. The quote itself came from a question about the Caine Prize and I would like to ask what your views are on the Caine Prize.

CNA: I want to say very clearly that I do not much care for the Caine Prize. When I was shortlisted for the prize years ago, I had a horrible personal experience with the first administrator of the prize, on which I based my short story "Jumping Monkey Hill." He was sexist and lecherous. I still sometimes blame myself for not handling things better. I think women who have had similar experiences will recognize that sense of self-blame, when someone says something disgusting and offensive to you and instead of telling them off, you find yourself laughing along, because you are uncomfortable, and because a part of you still has this reluctant respect for an "older" man.

He did not like the few times I challenged him (I wish I had done so more often but I was really young . . .), and he certainly did not like that I already had an agent in America, because it meant I didn't really need anything from him. He then later told all kinds of petty lies, which are presently still being told and retold in the Caine Prize network, and when I first heard of them, I thought: my goodness, there are some things that a man his age should be above doing. He is no longer with the Caine Prize, but I think there is a kind of self-righteous entitlement in the very DNA of the Caine Prize administration. So, while I think any writer who wants to enter should certainly do so, I am categorically not an enthusiast.

MW: I must ask, how did you feel—personally—about the whole fallout from that "boy" controversy?

CNA: I was hurt at first, mostly because what started it was shocking in its utter falseness. And also because once you put out an ugly falsehood, it is very hard to undo the damage. I heard different versions of the story—somebody told my aunt that I was shortlisted for a prize and because I did not win, I then insulted the winner by calling him "boy!" I found that very funny in a dark sort of way. It shows how easily untrue stories, when they are told and retold, can change and become even more untrue.

As I said earlier, there were people who genuinely bought into this person's attention-seeking action and I don't blame such people for attacking me. But I also think some of the attacks had nothing to do with the "boy." It was an opportunity for people who already had preexisting issues. There are people for whom another person's success is like an itchy skin rash. Your success bothers them, and so they want to manage it for you. If you don't wear your success in a way that keeps them comfortable, they respond with a vicious hostility. There are also people who dislike you because you do not dislike yourself. And so the "boy" thing was an opportunity for such people.

MW: What is your reaction to that kind of hostility? How do you deal with it?
CNA: When I'm not in a good mood, it just upsets me. When I'm in a good mood, I laugh about how many unhappy and unfulfilled people there are in the world who channel their misery outward. Someone will say, for example, that you are successful because you don't have too many pimples on your face or because you went to America or because the sky is blue, which may all well be true. But they always conveniently forget another possible reason, that maybe you are successful because you wrote a book that people actually want to read. But, you know, negative talk comes with the territory. I would actually be worried if it didn't happen to me. It happens to all public figures. Actually, I think it happens to everyone, whether public figures or not. The difference is one of degree. Think of it like this: most people have at least one or two coworkers who don't wish them well. It might be a coworker who wants to prevent your next promotion, or a coworker who is envious of your car or your flat or who resents the fact that the boss likes you. In my case, these coworkers are people I don't actually know but would most likely dislike if I knew them. And I have to say that, in general, there are far more nonhostile responses than not. The world is really full of good people. It's worth remembering that.

MW: I read a response by James Eze that suggested that the journalist who conducted the interview in which you said "one of my boys" also bears some responsibility for the fallout.
CNA: The only person who bears responsibility is the person who wrote an ugly public piece knowing fully well that he was deliberately distorting

things. But I think the journalist could have done more. The interview was long and so he edited it. The reason I said the Caine Prize was overprivileged was because he had talked for quite a bit about how he and his academic friends followed it and read each story and discussed it and what not, and my response was to challenge that kind of overprivileging of the prize. Which is a position I completely stand by. Because he edited out the part where he talks about all the attention he and his cohorts were giving the Caine Prize, it read as though I had just said the Caine Prize was overprivileged, without the proper context. I don't think there was any malice in his editing. But I do think he could have responded when it became such an obsession for people. He could have released the whole interview. He could have clarified that I had not meant "boy" in a demeaning way, because he could certainly tell from the tone and context.

Also the bit in the interview where I said that I look in my email inbox for new African writing, which I'm told a number of people were quite exercised by, would have been clearer in context. Because I had told the interviewer that he and his group were overprivileging the Caine Prize, he then asked—"Well, where do you go to find new African writing?" His subtext seemed to be a kind of smug "if you don't look at the exalted Caine Prize, which you really should, then where do you look?" To be fair, it might not actually have been his subtext because I was also really tired and unrested and in the middle of something like a fourteen-city book tour. But anyway I gave that grumpy reply. Of course I don't literally depend on my inbox to find new writing, but it was an irritable way of saying "I look anywhere but at the Caine Prize." Which is true. I think people read that response to mean that I think I am the final arbiter of African literature. I definitely don't think that. I don't even WANT to be the final arbiter. I do in fact get sent all kinds of stories and manuscripts and things. I actually don't want people sending these to me.

MW: Why do you think the interviewer didn't take the initiative and clarify or release the full interview?

CNA: I guess because there was nothing to lose in doing nothing. Often when dealing with somebody who is a public figure, the journalistic ego is front and center. Being unfairly critical is often conflated with being objective. So if you are unkind to a famous person, then you are more likely to be considered "objective." And if you are kind, then you might come under suspicion. An interview with a journalist is invariably going to be edited. What the journalist chooses to include or exclude is much more about the journalist than it is about the subject. And so it becomes an exercise in a certain kind of power. There is a wonderful book about journalism by Janet Malcolm that is worth reading.

I suppose for him, the interviewer, it was a question not of what was ethically correct, because it is obvious that releasing the full interview was the right thing to do since his editing had led to a furore and possible misunderstanding (I say "possible" because I am sure some die-hard members of the Society of the Outraged would still not think it made a difference). But for him it must have been: "if I say nothing, I lose nothing, but if I go out of my way to clarify, then people might say I am 'biased' or 'caving in to a famous person' and my virtuous ego will be compromised."

MW: One question comes to my mind now, and that is why didn't you address it then with all these details? I am sure some people will still believe what they want, but there are others who would really have appreciated hearing your side of the story. Those of us who have had the privilege of attending your workshop, and thus got to know you on a one-on-one basis, pushed back at the media distortions because we knew what this person wrote was not true. But you remained silent.

CNA: I did consider addressing it then. But I decided not to. I have always disliked the idea of somebody else setting my agenda. This person certainly got the attention he was seeking, and my silence made it even easier for him, but I was just not going to allow him to dictate what I would do. I did not want to disrupt what I was doing in my life in order to give interviews just because somebody had thrown a childish, misogynistic tantrum. I thought: I will talk about it only when I am ready to.

It also pushed me off a pedestal and I was grateful for that. A pedestal is a very difficult and suffocating thing. I do not want to be on one. I kept silent also because I am quite an old-fashioned believer in what my people call "iji ofo." I can't translate that well. It means something like karma. If somebody has shown deliberate ill-will to you, just hold on to your own lack of ill-will. But the whole "boy" thing also gave me something to laugh about. You have to laugh at life sometimes. Since then, each year at the workshop I announce the special Boys and Girls Club of Chimamanda and ask interested participants to sign up and I tell them that space is limited!

MW: The word I heard used most often to refer to you when this controversy was going on was "arrogant." Some people said that if you were a male writer with all the accomplishments that you have, being the best-known and most widely read contemporary Nigerian writer, in fact contemporary African writer, who has organized the most important Nigerian writing workshop in recent years, who has gone out of her way to nurture talent and support new writers, that there would not have been the kind of outrage there was about your calling somebody you were a mentor to "one of my boys at the workshop."

CNA: If you are female and you stand your ground and challenge and push back and boldly speak your mind, you are labeled arrogant. Difficult. Bossy. If you are male and have the same qualities, you are considered in a more positive light: Tough. Strong. A good leader. A lot of the outrage from both men and women was definitely shaped by my being female. But "arrogant" is not a word that scares me. "Arrogant" is not a word that will ever silence me. I have heard it many times.

MW: It has been two years since the whole "boy" controversy happened. Would you say that it has left a lasting impression on you?

CNA: Well, it's not something I think about a lot, but it was clarifying for me, in the way that hurtful things can be clarifying. It taught me that when you are a public person, only a few remarkable people will say in public the same things they say to you in private. Most people become double-faced. Even with some friends, your status as a public person comes in the way. They suddenly see you not just as their friend, but also as this commodity, and they have to gauge their own value as it relates to the commodity. Being a commodity also means that people assume that you have somehow given up on your humanness, and they think of you on the basis of how "useful" you can be.

I also learned that being a public person means that there will always be value in your slander. People are going to lie about you because there are potential benefits for them in doing so. Obviously it has made me wary. The wonderful Shonda Rhimes, when asked about this person she had helped who ended up being unreasonably ungracious to her, said that her philosophy after that was: No More Assholes. That sounds just about perfect to me.

MW: I want to go back to something you said earlier in reference to the *Guardian* publishing your article without your permission. You said that Big Journalism will use you, as a public person. I want to ask about your experiences with Nigerian journalism.

CNA: When I was younger, I used to believe everything I read about public figures. Now I know better. I have been misquoted so often and so many times by journalists and I see now why many public figures complain about being misrepresented. These days, I read stories about famous people with a lot of scepticism.

By the way, it is not just print journalism. There is a Nigerian news website known for political sensationalism. Some years ago, they asked my publisher for an interview with me, as part of my book tour. I said yes. Because my schedule was so tight, the interview could only be fit in after one of my book-signing events. Before the interview started, I went to say hello and I sat around joking with them. They said, "We have been asking to interview you for years and you keep saying no, but you say yes to BBC and CNN, so is it because we are not international that you keep turning us down?" And I said, "Okay o, if you don't want to interview me again, I am going." And I got up and pretended to walk away. We were all laughing. You know, it was the kind of joking around that you do when you are with "your own people." There was lots of nice camaraderie. I remember the camera person was from Zimbabwe and we talked about Zimbabwe and it was all pan-African bliss.

I did not know they were filming all this. The interview had not yet begun. And so when the former participant at my workshop wrote the attack piece about me, and when the social media noise started, this Nigerian news website took that footage, edited it, mixed it up, created an entirely different context and put it up online as some sort of supposed comedy video about me being "arrogant" and "difficult." And they did NOT make it clear that they had manipulated the footage. This is a website that often crows about accountability from the government and yet they were unable to be ethically accountable in their work. Anyway, I shrugged it off. Some things are not worth wasting emotional energy on.

MW: Could their excuse be that it was comedy? It was a comedy show, as I recall.
CNA: I actually thought it was kind of funny. But you can't just use a person's image like that without making it clear that you have manipulated the footage and that things didn't in fact happen that way. I don't mind good humor at all. I don't mind being made fun of. I have three brothers, so it is something I grew up with, endless teasing and mockery. And I quite like that. I'm also very good at mocking and teasing. But this is different. This is an ostensible news organization. It is a question of intent. Do your viewers know you have manipulated this? No. Therefore it is a deception of your viewers and a defamation of the subject.

MW: It seems clear that this website did it deliberately. Do you think all the other instances of your being misquoted have been deliberate on the part of the journalists?

CNA: No, not at all. Many of the instances of Nigerian misquotes are actually just a result of incompetence or carelessness. Actually, the one example of deliberateness happened with a serious British newspaper, not a Nigerian one. It was during the height of the "Chibok girls" news coverage. I was being asked by various news outlets to give comments or write about Boko Haram and what not and I said no, because I had nothing to say and honestly I felt that there was a lot even we Nigerians didn't really know about Boko Haram. This particular newspaper had asked for an interview that I turned down. And so they sent a journalist to a public event I did in Wales, and he asked me a question as though he was just a normal member of the audience. He then twisted my words out of shape, added something I never said, and created a headline. I was shocked. For some stupid reason, I would not have been as shocked if this had happened in Nigeria. I kept thinking: "but how can you just make up something that I never said?" They took it down but the whole experience was jarring.

Journalism is a sacred and beautiful art when done well. But there is a lot about contemporary journalism that is disturbing. Sometimes journalists will goad you in the name of interviewing. And many of them implicitly believe that good news is not interesting. Scepticism is essential, but there is a kind of cynicism in some contemporary journalism that is stomach-churning.

MW: You can also look at all this as a sign of great interest in your opinion on issues. It can be seen as a compliment, in a way, because the words don't matter on their own, but they matter because they are attributed to you.

CNA: Well, it would be nice if they used my actual words. You know, I often say that I have enough opinions that depart from the mainstream. Anybody who is keen to find something to disagree with just needs to look hard enough and they will certainly find it. They don't need to make things up. Or distort what I have said.

MW: What about cases where people have disagreed with what you actually said, without any distortions or inventions?

CNA: Probably the most vociferous responses to any opinion I have publicly shared came from the article I wrote after the so-called antigay law was passed. There were quite a number of people who said I had made them think differently. But by far many more were extremely hostile. People even called my family members. Tell her to shut up! Abomination! She used to be my role model, but I will never buy her books again! She is writing this non-sense because white people give her prizes! That sort of thing. Even some of my family members were uncomfortable. The sense I got was they would just rather I keep quiet about gay issues. But I would say exactly the same thing if I had to do it again. If my voice can get just one person to think dif-ferently then it is worth it, because it means there is one person who is likely to stand up for the justice of her fellow citizens.

Why do we respond with antagonism to what we do not entirely under-stand? Why can't we say, "Okay, this person loves in a way that is different from how I love and I may not entirely understand it, but I do not believe it is a crime?" It's really that simple. And it's very sad when people use "Afri-can culture" to justify antigay discrimination. Many African cultures are traditionally tolerant. In fact I think it's the fundamental tolerance in the cultures of Africa that made colonialism so successful. We need to live and let live. We need to make space to accommodate what is different. Diversity is human. Throughout our history as human beings, there has never been a time when we were all the same.

MW: What about criticism of your books? How do you deal with that?
CNA: I don't read reviews. Just because it's important to preserve a certain kind of head space. The good reviews can be just as distracting as the bad. I also don't read articles about myself, because there is a certain kind of self-consciousness I want to try and avoid. I have a beloved small circle of family and very close friends who sometimes read certain things written about me, just so that we know, as my people say, "ndi anyi ga na-eze eze."

I quite like hearing directly from readers at my events. I love stories of how people "found themselves" in my work. In general, I like to hear what people really think, rather than what they think I want to hear. Some criticism can be very interesting. One reader told me she had trouble with *Americanah* because she felt that the ending betrayed the entire premise and voice of the novel, which is that the ending was about wish-fulfilment in a novel that was really about tearing down fantasies. I thought it was very thoughtful and fair criticism. But some criticism I don't find interesting. Like a woman telling me that Ifemelu should have been grateful to have a man who loved her and Ifemelu should not have had all the success she had. That told me more about the reader than about the book.

It also often depends on the tone of the criticism. So much depends on tone and context. You can say the same thing in two different tones and get two entirely different reactions from me. For example, somebody told me that *Americanah* was not as good as *Half of a Yellow Sun*, which I could tell was obviously coming from a sincere place. I told her I respected her opinion, and that my own feeling was that it was like comparing a bicycle and a mango, but I was interested in her thoughts. Another person said the same thing to me in a spiteful tone, and my response was: well, guess who wrote *Half of a Yellow Sun*?

MW: This anecdote has just reminded me of an article in which you were described as being essentially without guile. You have also often been described as "fearless." I believe these descriptions refer to your tendency to speak your mind without fear or favor.

CNA: My family and friends always tell me that my emotions are unusually obvious, which is not something I am conscious of. So, apparently, when I like, it is obvious that I like, and when I dislike, it is obvious that I dislike. My friend Michelle told me I have a kind of autism. I found that very funny, but it perhaps also has a ring of truth.

In general, I think it's a waste of precious life to pretend. I don't talk behind people. I say what I want to say in front of people. I don't have patience for people who do not wish other people well. I dislike falseness. If we don't care about each other, why bother fake-smiling with each other? When you are about to die, are you going to be thinking about how many frenemies you accumulated throughout your life or are you going to be thinking of how much in your life was truly meaningful?

MW: I know you have been asked this often but how much of *Americanah* is you?

CNA: A woman once asked me how I had dealt with my weight issues and at first I was puzzled and then I realized she had conflated me with Ifemelu. I have actually never had weight issues. I'm always amused when people meet me and say they are surprised by how tiny I am! I have not been bigger than a US size eight most of my adult life. But I do feel strongly about the way the global idea of female beauty is so narrow. "Fat" should never be used as a pejorative. Women should not be made to feel that they have to overfocus on their weight. If anything, both men and women should focus on being healthy, so that the question should be: whether you are fat or thin, can you comfortably run up a flight of stairs? I know slim people who cannot and overweight people who can.

Actually, I have a lot of Blaine's annoying healthy-food enthusiasms, which my family and friends endlessly tease me about. It was easy for me to write about Blaine eating quinoa because I am a quinoa eater, while Ifemelu finds that sort of thing ridiculous. I can spend the rest of my life happily eating my own healthy-ish *moimoi* recipe and lentils and salads. I spend time online looking for pastry recipes that use almond flour instead of regular flour. It's terrible. I'm not a "foodie" but I've always been a picky eater and I'm very interested in what Americans call "wellness." I am very keen on healthy, simple, nutritious foods. I am also a huge chocolate connoisseur and one of the latest ways that I have been wasting my writing time is by researching different cocoa beans online.

MW: In *Americanah*, Ifemelu says that having an American passport means that she has the choice to always go back to America. Do you feel the same way?

CNA: I don't have an American passport. I have only a Nigerian passport, and it is a choice I made. I love America; I think it's the best country in which to be an immigrant. I also really admire that it is one country that holds on to its sense of its foundation as an idea. It is a second home to me. But for a long time, I didn't even apply for a green card. I had this foolish self-righteous idea of "I want to suffer like my fellow Nigerians so that I can write truthfully about how humiliating it is to apply for a visa on a Nigerian passport." Until one day my friend who I thought was my fellow Freedom Fighter—ha!—told me he was going for his green card interview. I didn't even know he had applied. He said—"it's a travel document that makes life easier." Which is true. So I brought my head out of my foolish cloud and went and applied for a green card, and got it in this interesting category called Immigrant of Extraordinary Ability. Very American. The sort of thing that sets America apart from other countries in the world really.

I still apply for visas, but I don't deal with as much bullshit as I used to before I had a green card. There is something very wrong about a world where a certain kind of value you are given as a human being depends on the passport you carry. I still haven't decided if I want to get American citizenship.

MW: Somebody who read your *New York Times* article about light commented that it sounded as if you had really moved back to Lagos and settled down but that you were not "visible" on the social scene.

CNA: I spend much more of my time in Nigeria now. In Lagos. Sometimes

I go to my hometown in Anambra but not so much since my beloved Uncle passed away, although I usually go home at Christmas. But my ideal dream house has not been built. It will be in Enugu, and I will have a huge frangipani tree in the back, and a riotous garden of roses and hibiscus in the front.

I am very much a stay home person. So I guess that's why people think that I live just in the US and don't realize that I live in Nigeria much of the time. I'm one of those people who, when I do go out, I have a lovely time. And I like to entertain friends from time to time, but in general I am a stay-at-home person. If the world were divided into people who need to go out and people who don't need to go out, I am firmly in the latter group. I think that by the time I am sixty, if I live to be sixty, I will be a slightly right-wing recluse reading Muriel Spark and muttering to myself in my dark study in Enugu. A vision I find quite appealing.

MW: I'd like to ask you about another controversy, and I have to say that calling it a "controversy" is again because you are a celebrity, or a "public person" as you say. It was not a controversy in actual fact. You gave an interview to a Nigerian newspaper where you told the journalist not to call you by the title of Mrs.

CNA: Yes, a Nigerian journalist decided to give me a name because he felt it SHOULD be my name. How can I tell you what my name is, and then you unilaterally decide what my name should be? Whether or not I am married, I have told you that my name is Ms Chimamanda Adichie. You then decide to create a name for me, and not only do you call me Mrs but you give me another surname and you use that as my name in a newspaper article. Your newspaper article spreads far and wide. Before I know it, other people are calling me by that name.

MW: This journalist who gave you a new name, as you put it, did so after discovering that you have been married for some years. He found out your husband's name and then created the new name for you. I have noticed that you don't talk publicly about your personal life. There is really nothing out there that can be directly attributed to you about your husband or marriage. Is there a reason for this?

CNA: I choose not to talk publicly about my personal life.

MW: I recall that the newspaper subsequently issued a retraction and an apology.

CNA: My manager made a formal complaint to the editor of the newspaper, as well as to the journalist. The next thing I know, the journalist wrote another article that completely garbled what I said, so the headline became "Chimamanda wants to be called Miss." I remember that I even spelled Ms out to him, because some Nigerians pronounce it as the two separate letters but I pronounce it as "Miz" and so I made a clear distinction for him. My basic point was that every adult woman should have the freedom to choose to be called Ms or Mrs. I actually think it just makes more sense for every adult woman, whether married or not, to be called Ms just as every adult man is called Mr, as a starting point, and a woman who wants to change that can do so.

To be fair, quite a few people apparently responded to the so-called controversy by saying that even here in Nigeria there are many examples of women who chose to keep their own names, especially those who have become successful using that name. For me, it is not at all about being successful. I like my name. I am attached to my name. It is part of my identity. I have always known I would keep my name, whether or not I was successful. The title Mrs should simply be a choice that women can make or not make.

I have never seen the title Mrs as a source of pride. I do not understand why it should be a source of pride as it apparently is to many women. Marriage can be a lovely thing, or it can be an unlovely thing, but it is not an accomplishment. Birthing a child is an accomplishment. Birthing an idea is an accomplishment. Building something or creating something or raising a good human being or contributing to making the world better in some way is an accomplishment. But marriage is not. Sadly, it is women who are raised to view marriage as an accomplishment. Men are not raised that way, and that already sets up a terrible imbalance.

The journalist's action was disrespectful and an act of provocation. The sad thing is that he really didn't get what was so wrong about his decision to give me a new name. He was even trying to explain to me why my name should be Mrs something. He kept saying it was our "African culture" and that it was what we have been doing "since time immemorial."

MW: I have observed that this idea of "African culture" is something you are very interested in challenging. There is a memorable line from your TED talk: "Culture does not make people. People make culture."
CNA: It is true that conventionally most Nigerian women take their husband's surnames—and it puzzles me that more people don't question that

act of erasure, of giving up a name you have had your entire life. But it is not an ancient African practice at all (and by the way, there are parts of the world where women do NOT take their husband's surnames as norm). A lot of what we call ancient African cultural practices are really Victorian Christian practices. Christianity and colonialism created a lot of what we now call "authentic culture." Take this example of surnames. Igbo people didn't even have surnames until the 1910s. As in many other societies, people just had one name. Many surnames were invented as a response to colonialism. So people just took the name of their father or grandfather or even the title of somebody in their family.

Nwafor and Nwoye are very common names where I come from. Before Christianity, Igbo culture was polygamous. And often, in a polygamous household with many children, a child would be distinguished by the mother and not the father, since there was just one father and various possible mothers. I know a person in my grandfather's generation called Nwoye Nwamgba, and Nwamgba was his mother. Because in the same household, there might be a Nwoye Mgbafor, Mgbafor being another wife. Some of those people are still alive and even though they now have legal surnames, they are still referred to with their mothers' names.

Here's another example. In my part of Igboland, women were traditionally buried in the homes where they were born and not in the homes of the men they married. My great-grandmother—the last person in my family before our conversion to Christianity—was from Ifite-Ukpo but married a man from Abba. When she died, she was taken back to Ifite-Ukpo and buried there. The traditional Igbo view is that a wife is a temporary gift to the man's family, and she is there primarily to have children. But her birth home is where she really belongs and where she has a real say. Of course this is far from perfect—for example, children were solely part of the man's family and a woman had little rights to her own children. Igbo culture was terribly patriarchal but it was more complex and less rigid than it is now with Christianity. This idea that a woman should become completely submerged in her husband is actually NOT a traditional idea of Igbo people. It is instead a traditional British idea. Igbo women and Yoruba women in 1850 actually had more social and political rights than English women. My point is that since cultures evolve and since what we do today in the name of culture is not at all what happened a hundred years ago, then everything is open for negotiation. Everything is changeable. The basis for the change should then be: how do we evolve in a way to ensure the least discrimination and the most dignity for everyone?

I love the language, the folklore, the wisdom, the myths of Igbo culture. There is so much I love. But there are many things I don't love. "Just accept it as the way it is" is not an acceptable answer to me. The answer is to work towards changing it from within.

MW: Do you have any concrete ideas about how to achieve this cultural change from within?

CNA: Education. The problem is that we know very little of our precolonial history. False popular images and the religion-induced demonization of our past have taken over our imagination. So we think our history is what we see in Nollywood's so-called historical films. I wish Nollywood would actually do some proper research and portray precolonial life as it was, because Nollywood can be a powerful teaching tool. It shouldn't just be about drawing chalk designs on people's bodies and having medicine men turn people into snakes. I wish somebody would make a film about the female king of Nsukka and the female co-king of Onitsha called the *omu*. They all existed. History is about the stories that were selected and told and retold. But there are other stories. We need to find them and tell them.

MW: Your creative writing workshop is in its tenth year and has seen some of the most notable writers of what many are calling the social media generation happy to state that they are Farafina Workshop Alumni in their resumes. What does the future look like?

CNA: I'm very pleased and very proud of the workshop. I want to do more. I have been thinking of a nonfiction and journalism workshop. I think we are doing very well now with writing our own fiction, but nonfiction has a long way to go.

MW: Your passion for education is well known, and this goes beyond your creative writing workshops. You have said in the past that you have no interest in a political position but I am wondering if something could change your mind. For instance, if you were asked to become Minister of Education, is it something you would consider?

CNA: I never say never. But it is very unlikely. Nigeria is a really tough place to be in a position of political leadership and to make the slightest difference you have to be able to give three hundred percent. And you have to be able to compromise on things you don't believe in, which would be very hard for me to do. Because I am primarily a writer, because my greatest loves are to read and write, because I value silence and solitude, I don't think I would do my best as a political person. There are many people who would do it much better than I could. But I would love to be an adviser of some sort, because I do care deeply about education.

MW: I read somewhere that you turned down a merit award from the Nigerian government, and you also turned down an MBE honor from the British government.

CNA: There are some things you turn down and you don't do it publicly because that isn't the point. So I really don't want to talk about the things that I have turned down.

MW: I want to ask you about style. You were featured in the recent style issue of *New York Magazine* alongside the designer Carolina Herrera. Something you said in the interview is that your rule is "Never admire quietly."

CNA: Yes. I was being asked what people most compliment me about and I said I give more compliments than I get. Which is true. I never admire quietly. If I admire something about somebody, I always make a point of telling them so.

MW: You are now considered a style icon. You wrote an essay titled "Why Can't a Smart Woman Love Fashion?," which has been widely republished. Your headwrap for a long time was your style statement. What is it like to be a writer who is also known for her style? Do you have what is called a "stylist"?

CNA: Stylist *kwa*? No, I make all my choices myself. I've always been interested in style. I like buying fabric in the market. The other day I went to Balogun with a friend to buy fabric and a woman said to me, "You look like Chimamanda," and I said "Yes, people tell me that." Ha! I like to design my own clothes. I do these really atrocious sketches in a notebook, and I even color them with crayons. I find it quite calming. By the way, I love headwraps, but I really wear them mostly when my hair is a disaster and when I don't have the energy to do anything about my hair.

Anyway, I wrote that piece because it was a response to the idea that in the West a woman who wants to be taken seriously cannot be perceived as being interested in her appearance. I thought this was such an unfeminist idea. But I'm really not unusual. There are many contemporary women writers who write well and dress well. Like Zadie Smith and Elif Shafak and Yvonne Owuor and Chika Unigwe and Tayari Jones and Kiran Desai and Ahdaf Soueif and many others. Two older-generation writers I love, Flora Nwapa and Mary McCarthy, had great style.

MW: Are there other female public figures who are not writers but whose style you like?

CNA: I think the actress Aïssa Maïga and the singer Adele are great beauties. I admire the style of women like Aisha Oyebode, Solange Knowles, Marion Cotillard, Olivia Palermo, and Michelle Obama.

MW: Since you have become an internationally recognized voice for feminism, are there women who inspire you as a feminist?

CNA: Of course. There are many women I know who are not public figures but who have taught me much more about feminism than any book could. My sister from another mother, Uju Egonu, and my cousin Nneka Adichie Okeke are huge inspiration sources. I admire Jessye Norman and Viola Davis and Toni Morrison, because they occupy their space in the world without apology. I admire Josephine Anenih. I once heard her speak about gender, and for a Nigerian woman of her generation, she was so unusually blunt and progressive that her words lifted my spirit. I admire Gloria Steinem and Alice Walker and Hillary Clinton. There are many Nigerian women who inspire me, not because I know them personally, but because of the space they occupy in the world, like Joe Odumakin and Ayo Obe. So many friends inspire me with their strength and their ability to live the life they want and not the life they are supposed to want, like Jackie Kay, Bose Afolabi and Yewande Sadiku. There are so many others. I am generally admiring of women who like themselves and who wish other women well and who do their part in working for a more just world.

MW: What about men?

CNA: Most of the men I admire and am inspired by are not public figures. But there are many and they belie the idea that to be feminist is to believe that there are no good men in the world. There certainly are many good men in the world. I greatly admire the late Thomas Sankara who as president of Burkina Faso spoke out about gender equality.

MW: What are you reading now? Do you have any reading rituals while writing?

CNA: I read a number of books at the same time, depending on my mood. I'm reading Professor Kenneth Dike's remarkable book called *Trade and Politics in the Niger Delta*. The title doesn't capture how fascinating it is, and it makes you realize how academia has changed. Academics of his time were not so jargon-drenched and "specialized." He is one of the many Nigerian heroes we should better celebrate. I'm reading a biography called *Sons of Wichita* by Daniel Schulman, which is a biography of the extremely wealthy Koch brothers and their influence on American politics. I'm also reading two lovely novels, *A Month in the Country* by J. L. Carr and *Final Payments* by Mary Gordon. I usually read poetry when I am writing fiction. I dip in and out. I don't much care for the kind of poetry as "puzzle to be decoded," I'm much more drawn to a sort of lush dense poetry and I read it as language to be relished, to have wash over me. Derek Walcott is a long-time favorite. I have just fallen in love with the poetry of Eamon Grennan.

MW: Let's go back to the subject of hair. Your novel *Americanah* is often described as being about hair, among other things. It was of course during an interview while promoting *Americanah* that you were misquoted as saying that Nigerian women who wear weaves lack self-esteem.
CNA: *Americanah* is really not as much about hair as people who haven't read it think it is. Anyway, I think hair is an important subject that goes beyond aesthetics and I wanted to start a conversation about black women's hair. But it was never about blaming individual women. It was about challenging our society's narrow definition of mainstream beauty. Our society gives women limited options. I think there are many women who would like to wear their hair in a short afro or in cornrows with no attachments or in twists, but they can't because there are social consequences. Their boss at work will say they don't look professional. Or their mother will say they look "rough." Or somebody will say that men won't find them attractive.

MW: You said you wanted to start a conversation about black women's hair. Why black women in particular?
CNA: Actually, I am interested in women's hair in general. White women's hair is also politicized, and when a white woman starts to go grey and chooses not to color her hair, for example, there are assumptions made because she is not the mainstream norm—and she would probably never get a job as a television news anchor. Asian and Hispanic women also have issues of hair choices going beyond the mere aesthetic. But why do I focus on black women in particular? Because I am a black woman. Because black women are the only women on the planet who permanently change their hair into something that looks as far removed as possible from what God put on their heads. Because black women are the only women on the planet who actively acquire the hair of women from other parts of the world. Because

black women are the only women for whom it requires some form of an "effort" to consider their natural hair as equal an option to anything else.

People get tied up in semantic knots about "what is natural?" For me, the answer is simple: it is a question of texture. It is not about whether you add attachments or not. It is a question of texture. What kind of texture gets value? What kind of texture does not get value? I think we are generally raised to devalue our natural hair. We say it's rough, ugly, that sort of thing. We laugh at our hair when normal relaxers can't straighten it. All these are value judgments about texture.

MW: What, if anything, is the ultimate goal of this conversation that you wanted to start—and have indeed started—about black women's hair?
CNA: My goal is a dream. The dream is that natural kinky black hair—and the various associated styles—will have the same value as any other kind of hair. I'm inspired by photographs from the 1960s. There is a particular photograph of my mother and her friends, three university women, at a cocktail party in Nsukka. One of them was wearing a big glamorous wig, one had her hair threaded in *isi owu,* and one had her hair in a short afro. That is the world I dream about—where these different styles are seen as equal choices.

When I recently threaded my hair in *isi owu,* I was told that I was "making a statement." Actually I wasn't. I did it because I think *isi owu* is architectural and beautiful. Sadly, it is very difficult to find anyone who can thread hair well. The few people who can are generally contemptuous of it. Only forty years ago, *isi owu* was a Nigerian hairstyle that could be worn to a cocktail party and NOT as costume. My question is: what happened?

MW: What do you think is responsible for this shift?
CNA: Globalization, maybe. And globalization is a function of power, so that a small and powerful section of the world determines what the rest of the world considers aspirational.

MW: Since you were deliberately misquoted on the subject of weaves, I want to ask exactly what your position or thoughts are on that subject. I am not an expert but I assume that "weaves" means extensions that are sewn into women's hair.
CNA: I admire certain weaves when they are done well. I like Michelle Obama's weave choices, for example. I also admire textured weaves that mimic black women's hair. I do not find silky, shiny, overlong weaves

attractive at all. Especially a certain kind that reminds me of American reality shows. Which also happens to be the kind that is popular in Nigeria.

I used to wear only silky straight-hair weaves when I was younger, and I used to put a lot of energy into overstraightening the front bits of my hair to get it to blend with the weave—and to this day, those front bits of my hair don't grow properly. There are things you do because everybody is doing them and then one day you start questioning and you discover how completely your aesthetics can change, and how something you once admired is now uninteresting to you. I have no interest in such things as "Brazilian" and "Malaysian" and "Peruvian" hair. I actually find it odd that there is such a lack of irony in the way Nigerians casually talk of buying the hair of women from other parts of the world. Hair can be a source of stress, and sometimes women want a break from having to deal with their hair, which is completely understandable. But kinky-textured weave sales are miniscule compared to silky hair weave sales. Again, it is a question of texture.

In general, women wearing their own hair in whatever form—short, long, natural, relaxed—is more attractive to me. It's much easier to fail with a weave than with your own hair. A disaster that grows on your head will always look better than a disaster that is stuck to your head. And trust me, I speak from experience, having had a number of weaves in the past that made me look like *mmonwu*.

MW: I came across some comments about women with natural hair feeling superior to women who do not have natural hair. What do you think of that?
CNA: It is true that some women are quite righteous about having natural hair, but those women make up a tiny minority of a minority. More importantly, natural hair does not have the power of mainstream social acceptance. So it is like a poor person feeling superior in an extremely capitalist society. For many of the women, their superior attitude is really protective armor. It's their cover for having to deal with annoying comments at the hair salon or aunties harassing them to go and "do something" about their hair or the gateman at work calling their dreads "dada" or a friend saying they are "brave" to want to wear their own hair for their wedding or a stranger saying "natural hair is not for everybody but it fits you" as though natural hair is some kind of exotic choice rather than what God put on our heads.

I used to be quite defensive, I sometimes still am, because even in my family I don't get much enthusiastic support for my hair choices: my refusal to use a relaxer, my lack of interest in long weaves. Even in my village—just in case we assume this to be an urban thing—I am often asked when I will "do my hair well." For them, "do my hair well" means to "fix hair," which means a weave. A recent comment I got at a Lagos salon was, "Aunty, how can you be doing your hair like secondary school girl." This is because I increasingly like to get cornrows with no attachments. (I like kinky attachments but sometimes they make me hot and irritated and wearing just my hair feels so light and refreshing and it is blissful to have full access to my scalp, especially when I am working out.)

When I take out my cornrows and wear my hair free, somebody will invariably say—"imagine how fine it will be when you perm it," as though the possibility of real beauty comes only with a relaxer. Or someone will overpraise my hair in a way that doth protest too much, as though my hair is some kind of quaint costume. So it can be exhausting to have to constantly be on guard, to make yourself not seem terribly abnormal. Because the truth is that you very much want to be normal and you want your hair to be seen as normal and if someone tells you "I like your hair," you want to feel that it is the same "I like your hair" that they would tell a person with a long weave, and not the "I like your hair" that is reserved for some sort of dancer in one of those costumey cultural dance troupes. I think that the natural-haired women who are self-righteous about hair are coming from that place. I am not trying to excuse their attitude, I am merely trying to put it in context. (A lot of the extreme Naturalistas terrify me, by the way, the sort of women who wash their hair with special clay and never comb it and harass other women for wearing afro wigs.)

So my goal with the hair conversation is this: to bring natural hair to the table as an equal partner. Maybe I should ask the lovely Beyoncé to please wear *isi owu* on her next major concert. That might suddenly make *isi owu* attractive to some of our people. My point is that what is desirable, what is given aesthetic value, never falls from the sky. We remake and make these things. Remember that just forty years ago, stylish university women in Nigeria wore *isi owu* to cocktail parties and it was considered as equal an option as a wig.

MW: I know of women who have "gone natural" or are encouraged to "go natural" because of you.
CNA: That's nice to know. I have to say that the idea of natural hair as inherently inferior is changing, very slowly, but it is changing. Natural hair is becoming an option, but I wish it didn't have the stereotype of "returnee hairstyle." Or the stereotype of being "alternative" or "artsy." I would love to see mainstream banks, for example, let their female staff know that it is

okay to wear their hair the way God made it. In many hair salons in Nigeria, the hairdressers know what to do with weaves but have no idea how to take proper care of real hair, whether natural or relaxed. I hope that starts to change too. So we can have fewer bald temples in the country.

MW: The Nigeria Centenary Facebook page recently polled young people on International Youth Day and you were voted as the favorite role model for Nigerian youths. What words of advice would you share with young Nigerians if you were asked to?

CNA: Ask questions. Never pretend to know what you don't know, otherwise you will never learn. Read books. Do things properly. Do not write formal emails in text language where "you" is one letter of the alphabet. Don't be fake. You are more interesting as you truly are. Don't measure yourself using another person's yardstick. Be curious about the world. Be kind. Don't be quick to judge, think carefully about things before you pass judgment. Try and learn something new every day. Don't decide not to try something because you are afraid you will fail. Every successful person has failed at something. Think of it like this: you might fall down, but if you fall down you can stand up and try again.

MW: You're very specific when you say, "Do not write formal emails in text language where 'you' is one letter of the alphabet." Is that something you have personally observed?

CNA: Yes. There is a general acceptance of mediocrity in Nigerian life today. An "anyhow" attitude. A fashion designer, for example, will say I am "difficult" because I insist that the tailoring on a dress not be crooked. It is not talent we lack. Nigerians are the most intelligent and most enterprising people I know. But there is a general attention to detail, a sedulousness, that we now lack culturally. I know this sounds like a leap, but I think the wave of religiosity in the 1980s contributed to it. We now have a culture of everything being explained by the "spiritual." So you don't study and you pass your exams because you prayed. It reduces the ethic of serious and sustained hard work, the ethic of critical thinking and the ethic of delayed gratification.

"Show don't tell" is a classic rule of fiction writing and I think it should equally apply to Nigerian religiosity. Imagine a Two Week Challenge where people do not say the word "God" but they show "God" through their actions. If you viciously gossip about other people, forget that your driver is human, cheat at business, steal, plot somebody's downfall and then turn around and say "We Thank God," then no, you are not showing, you are merely telling.

MW: I understand you kept away from the process of adapting *Half of a Yellow Sun* into a movie. I read somewhere you described it as "not wanting to be there when your baby is cut up." Are you going to be there when the *Americanah* baby is cut up? I understand that Lupita Nyong'o and David Oyelowo will star in the film and that Brad Pitt is one of the producers.
CNA: Yes, I think I might be closer this time, hovering around the cutting-up table.

MW: What are your thoughts on the adaptation of books to films? Do you watch films?
CNA: I generally prefer books to films. But yes, I watch films. I just saw *Boyhood*, which I liked very much. I adored *Selma*; it made me cry. More generally I am drawn to European films. Not art house films o. Two films I watched recently that I loved: *Flame and Citron*, which is Danish, and a German film called *Barbara* with Nina Hoss.

Some of my favorite films are *The Lives of Others, City of God, The Secret in Their Eyes, Babette's Feast, The Battle of Algiers*. I think I'm drawn to similar things in film and fiction: the ability to tell a real human story in a specific political context. I have some strange likes. I'm drawn to European films about the Holocaust, for example. So the standing joke in my family is that when I say "let's watch a movie," nobody wants to. Because I will invariably choose something subtitled and dark. I also like British television shows like *Broadchurch* and *Downton Abbey*.

MW: Do you have a life philosophy? Do you have a guiding principle that you try to live by?
CNA: It's a common cliché. Life is short. I really do try to live by this. I don't mean short in the Hobbesian and brutish sense, but short in the sense that it is precious and fragile, and none of us know how long we are here for. So it's important to make choices in your life keeping that in mind.

MW: Do you have a favorite quote?
CNA: My favorite quotes change often, but lately it has been this from a Phillip Larkin poem: "What will survive of us is love."

"Talking to Chimamanda Ngozi Adichie, the Beauty Brand Ambassador We All Need Right Now"

2016 / Cheryl Wischhover

From *Racked*, 22 November 2016. [Cheryl Wischhover / Vox.com]

Feminist author and newly minted No.7 brand ambassador Chimamanda Ngozi Adichie loves makeup. She certainly never expected to be tapped as the face of a beauty brand, however. "I have no idea how they found me and I really don't know what the hell they were thinking asking me," she laughs about getting the call from Boots, the UK-based company that owns No.7 and that is now a part of Walgreens. "My only hope is that the sales don't fall. This is a very genuine hope."

It's highly unlikely. No.7 hired her for its new "Ready" campaign, a platform that recognizes that women wear makeup to be ready for something, to show up or make an impact. Adichie notes that this is consistent with her own beliefs. (She's also delighting in the free makeup coming her way, including her new favorite lipstick, the No.7 Moisture Drench in Cranberry Kiss.)

I had the pleasure of chatting with her on the phone for thirty minutes about makeup, how she wishes beauty standards for little girls were different, and her thoughts about the online sport of picking apart women like Alicia Keys and Hillary Clinton for their makeup decisions.

Cheryl Wischhover: How did Boots find you and approach you for this campaign and what was your initial response to that?

Chimamanda Ngozi Adichie: They talked to my management and my initial response was that it just seemed so strange and out there, so I thought, *No.* But I thought about it a little more and I realized there was a good possibility of being sent a lot of free makeup. [*laughs*] I like the aesthetic of the brand, that it's relatable but the idea is that every woman can wear makeup of good quality that's also affordable.

It's not at all something that I thought I would ever do. And I also want to be honest and say there have been moments since I've done the shoot that I've felt quite vulnerable in a way that isn't comfortable. But I think in the larger sense I wanted to be part of the message that women who like makeup also have important and serious things that they're doing in their lives. And that those can coexist, that women are a multiplicity of things. I think it's time to really stop that ridiculous idea that somehow if you're a serious woman you can't and should not care about how you look.

CW: Have you always felt that way?

CNA: When I moved to the US and I was publishing my first novel, I had quickly realized that for a woman to be taken seriously and to be seen as a "serious intellectual person" she couldn't possibly look as though she cared a lot about her appearance. My mother raised us to think of our appearance as a mark of courtesy to other people. So she would often say, "If you're going to see somebody or someone is going to visit us, we owe it to them to at least have showered and put a bit of moisturizer on our faces so we don't look ashy."

I think there are some women who genuinely don't much care about those things. I have friends who don't care about makeup and I actually like that about them. But there are women who do and I'm one of those women. I think that for a while I just thought that I couldn't possibly wear the lipstick I wanted to wear because I felt that I would be judged. I think that changed just with getting older, getting more comfortable in my own skin, and realizing that life is so damn short. There is just no point in living life based on what you imagine people expect.

CW: What do you think is the deeper significance of Boots using a writer instead of a model or an actress for a beauty campaign?

CNA: I think that there are many women in the world today who are more inspired by "ordinary" women, women who are not actresses or models. One of the things I liked about what No.7 wanted to do was the idea that so many women are doing so many important things. And they put on makeup and go off and do those things. I felt that it was something I could identify with. On the days when I think my cat eye is good, it just makes me happy.

CW: Who are some of those women who are inspirational in that way to you?

CNA: Michelle Obama is a woman whom I deeply admire. I just love her from head to toe. I love what she represents, love what she speaks about. I think that there are many women like that who look fantastic but in addition to that are doing fantastic things.

CW: What are some of your earliest makeup memories that have shaped how you view makeup now?

CNA: When I was a little girl, my mother had a dressing table and she had her makeup lined up there. I remember being quite young and putting on her lip gloss. It was a particularly sticky lip gloss that was quite popular in Nigeria in the early 1980s and it was extremely shiny. My mother was quite amused by it. She was laughing and she said, "You look like you just ate a hot plate of *jollof* rice and you did not wipe your lips afterwards." *Jollof* rice is the staple Nigerian rice dish and it's quite oily. It's actually a warm memory for me. Throughout my teenage years, I wore horrible frosty lipstick and there was a period where my friends and I would only wear lipstick on the lower lip and it was a bit of a frosty bronze, which when I think about it now was an absolute disaster, but at the time we felt we were very cool.

CW: How would you change beauty standards for young girls now if you could?

CNA: One of the things that makes me sad is when I read stories about a dark-skinned girl saying "Oh, I'm finally at peace with my looks." There's something about that that's really sad because she shouldn't even have to go through a journey where she comes to be "at peace" with her looks. It should be something that she takes for granted from the beginning.

CW: Do you think it can change?

CNA: I think it's changeable. I think it's easy for us to have these conversations and bemoan the narrowness of the figures that are considered aspirational in the beauty world. The people who are in charge can change it. It would be nice if they saw women of different sizes. It would be nice if they saw women of different skin colors. It would be nice to see a black woman with really kinky hair. It would be nice to see a white woman with very red hair. I think that's important because the reality of our world is that it's an incredibly diverse place. I don't believe that there's an objective beauty standard that falls from the sky. I think that we as a society create what we aspire to. I've been studying a bit of precolonial history in West Africa and there are regions there where in the 1860s very, very dark skin was valued. People would actually darken their skin. And now, fast forward a hundred years later and it's the opposite. But the point is we create what is considered beautiful, so we can recreate it.

CW: What do you think about when women, like Alicia Keys and Hillary Clinton, to name some recent examples, are analyzed for their makeup choices?
CNA: This is a conversation that I wish we didn't have to have, but I understand that we have to have it because it's what's happening. I just think it's so weird that women make individual choices and then absolute strangers think they can have all kinds of opinions about them. It's largely something that happens to women and their appearance. I think Al Gore, after he lost [the presidential election], grew a beard. And there was a lot of gushing and, "Ooh, look how interesting." I just feel like there's just way too much judgment on women and their choices about their appearance and I wish there would be less. As a person who deeply supports and admires Hillary Clinton, I just wish instead of talking about her hair and her makeup we would talk about the misogyny that was really at the core of the way her public image was created.

As for Alicia Keys, I really respect her and her choice. For her, I think makeup has always been some sort of mask and she felt she was hiding behind it, and for her it was almost a liberation. That's my hope and my prayer for women, that women are allowed to be whatever version makes them feel truly like themselves. For some women it's exactly what she's done, which is that she took the mask off. For other women it's the opposite. I remember actually not wearing makeup and feeling false because I wanted to wear lipstick.

CW: One thing my colleagues and I have struggled with is how to cover fashion and beauty meaningfully after the election when so many people are worried about other things. Do you have thoughts?
CNA: I think America is at a strange place now. But I think women still need to know what damn moisturizer works in the winter! As I mourn, and for me the election result is a case for mourning, I still want to know what moisturizer will keep my winter skin from being too dry. One of the things that I think is important is that we shouldn't moralize makeup. I find that in many cultures there's almost a moral thing around makeup and appearance for women. I think we just need to get away from it. And also the idea that for men the things that are considered traditionally masculine are not things that our culture dismisses as frivolous. I wish I had a real answer

but I don't. I don't think men who write about sports—and I'm using an example that our culture considers traditionally masculine—would necessarily be worried about appearing frivolous. Things that are traditionally masculine sort of have this patina of seriousness, even when they're not, in a way that makeup and fashion don't. And I find myself questioning that more and more.

There are different forms of resistance. Sometimes just the fact that one continues to do what one is doing is also a way of speaking out for something.

Chimamanda Ngozi Adichie: Bold and Unflappable

Belinda Otas / 2017

From *New African Woman* 42 (April-May 2017): 10–17. © *New African Woman* 2017,
reproduced with permission of IC Publications Ltd.

Interview by Belinda Otas, additional reporting by reGina Jane Jere.

Chimamanda Ngozi Adichie: It is a name many can't hear enough of. But aside from her "unapologetic feminist" persona, the prolific author is also a wife, mother, and a global African, who cannot be fitted into one box— "feminist." After some recent back-to-back media interviews and photoshoots, *New African Woman* caught up with her and in this exclusive interview she opens up on all things feminism, her new book, media sexualization of women, ideal beauty, depression, supporting Hillary Clinton and raising her young daughter in Donald Trump's America.

It's an unseasonably pleasant March day in London, and there is a flurry of activity in the lobby of the hotel where Chimamanda Ngozi Adichie is staying. A photoshoot is taking place with a London weekly in the hotel's basement media room. They are overrunning their allocated time and one of Adichie's spokespersons respectfully apologizes to our team as we patiently await our slot in—more than an hour has passed since our allocated time.

But this is Adichie—everyone wants a piece of her, and we don't mind waiting. We are not the only ones. A group of six Middle Eastern women are crouching in a corner near the reception area. One of them approaches our editor, asking excitedly: "Are you with Chimamanda Ngozi?" She says she and her friends, refugees from Afghanistan, are fans and had heard she was at the hotel. "We just want her to sign our books and have a photograph, is it possible?" she asks. Our editor explains that she is not part of the famous author's team. "We hope to get a chance for an autograph," the woman adds.

Later, after our slot, our art director fishes out a copy of *Dear Ijeawele* from her bag, and approaches Adichie. "Excuse me, if you do not mind, my friend is from India and a huge fan or yours," she says. "She is based in Palestine where she works with women on gender equality. She asked if you could sign the book for her, and I will send it to her." Adichie has by this time—as we learn from her PR—not slept in forty-eight hours due to press interviews from both sides of the Atlantic. Nevertheless, she obliges and signs the book with a beaming smile, whispering words of encouragement.

As she is rushed off to the next media slot, she still shows no sign of tiredness and her pleasantness is infectious. She stops to pose for photos with those waiting outside the hotel's media room. No doubt she will give the Afghan refugee women waiting in the lobby their chance.

Adichie indeed transcends borders. Her award-winning books and stories, delivered with the intellect, wisdom and wit of a matriarch resonate and are endearing to women (and some men) across the world. This would be attested to later that evening when a full auditorium of people (men and women of all colors) packed into London's Southbank Centre to listen to her in conversation with journalist Ellah Wakatama Allfrey on the topic: "What does it mean to be a woman, to be a feminist?" It is part of the center's Women of the World (WOW) annual festival that celebrates the global achievements of women while putting a spotlight on gender inequality.

Adichie's new book, *Dear Ijeawele, or A Feminist Manifesto in Fifteen Suggestions*, started off as a viral Facebook post in 2016, in which she was giving advice to a friend on how to raise a feminist daughter. It explores what it means to be a woman in a world that is still packed to the rim with the patriarchy, sexism, misogyny and toxic masculinity that contributes to the systemic oppression and holding back of women at all levels—issues that she discusses in this exclusive interview.

Belinda Otas: There are so many voices on women's issues and sometimes it can be confusing to decide which one to follow. How can the women's movement strengthen its voice in numbers with one clear goal where there is no right or wrong voice?

Chimamanda Ngozi Adichie: I understand that. One thing that I would say is that maybe we shouldn't expect [that] . . . We can't all be one united voice, and this is why I talk about thinking about feminism as "feminisms." Which is to say that as long as we start off with that basic premise of full equality, people can have different opinions. Lately, I have been thinking about how

Christianity works and is such a force on the continent of Africa. I actually believe that it's possible to forge a feminist platform around Christianity. Now, I am not the person to have this conversation. It has to be someone who is very involved with Pentecostal Christianity. My point is that there are people who are feminists and see religion as part of the problem, which I think is also true; but I also think that within religion, we can in fact create a platform that is feminist.

I have often said that I wish Africans would read the history of the Bible because you can use the Bible to justify anything. I mean let's not even get started on the Old Testament. Let's just look at the life of this man called Jesus Christ; if he lived today, we would say he is a crazy left-wing hippie. But Jesus Christ was a person of love, and he clearly believed that men and women were equally worthy. So if we can start from there, we don't have to have one single voice. We just have to have the same basic premise. And that's partly why I started the book by talking about the two feminists' tools because people have different experiences and interpretations. In the end, as long as what we are talking about is not diminishing women.

BO: You share your time between the US and Nigeria. Given the political direction under Donald Trump, how do you feel about raising your daughter in this environment and has it made you extra protective of her?
CNA: Yes, in a way, America has become less aspirational to me, but at the same time I would like to think of Donald Trump's administration as a temporary setback. I don't know if it's because I am being naïve, but it's almost impossible for me to accept that this will now be the new America. And my daughter, I am lucky that I can have both worlds and she is going to have both worlds. I worry obviously; I have a friend who teaches in elementary school and she was telling me that after Trump won, the children in her class—I mean, these are children who are six years old—were telling the Hispanic children, go home, go back to where you came from.

I thought that was the most horrible thing and that they are so young. Obviously it's concerning, but again, it's this thing where it's a temporary setback, as bad as it is.

BO: We can only all hope this will come to pass soon. But in the meantime, it seems that the election of Donald Trump has spurred more women into action—the Global Women's marches for instance. However, on the other hand, a lot of white women voted for Donald Trump despite everything he stood for during the campaign. How do you feel about that?

CNA: I know, I know. It's incredible to me. Honestly, I am still digesting it. I mean, Gloria Steinem in her memoir wrote what I thought was actually quite interesting. She wrote about talking to many of the white women who did not like or support Hillary Clinton. She said she was struck by how for many of them, it was very personal—they resented her because she seemed to be equal with her husband and did not hold back from chasing her own dreams. Somehow, they resented her for this, and I found it very interesting because I hadn't really thought of it that way, and there's probably some truth to that.

I also think that Donald Trump appealed to race in a certain way, and his campaign was very coded about race. While white women are women, they are also white, and I can see how some of those appeals to race resonated with them. The idea of "America first" and sending immigrants home and all of that, I can see how all of that can also appeal to them.

BO: Hillary Clinton was heavily criticized for some of her policies in Africa when she was Secretary of State. How were you able to reconcile that with supporting her? Did you ever question her legacy in Africa when she was in that powerful position?

CNA: You are talking about her intervention in Libya, for example. I don't expect American policy to think of Africa's wellbeing as a primary thing. Let's be realistic, America's policy will be about America and protecting America. Personally, I thought that the whole Libya thing was a complete disaster and was ill-conceived, but I just refuse to hold Hillary Clinton personally responsible for it. It's a larger part of a long history of American policy and so I don't take it as a personal failing of Hillary Clinton. If anything, I think of it as a failure of American foreign policy.

BO: Trump's misogyny and sexism is indisputable, but sexualization of women in images, music videos, lyrics and other media platforms has continued unabated for centuries and is getting worse. What's your take and what can be done to halt this once and for all?

CNA: I don't know. Honestly, I don't know. I don't even watch music videos. Is there a new way? Maybe not. Changing the status quo is never easy and is never going to be something that happens when you say it a few times. Sometimes, you need to say it a few thousand times.

It's similar to the representation of women in magazines and media. I am a person who likes fashion and I read fashion magazines, and I often talk about how I wish there was a wider range of women's images because I think those are aspirational. Magazines for young girls teach them to think what they see is the ideal beauty. And when editors say to me, how can we change that, it is as though somehow, it is something very difficult to do! I say we can change it by just stopping it. I mean, people have power. It's not as if these things fall from the sky. So during your editorial meetings, decide you are not going to have twenty pages of thin white women. Have two pages of thin white women, two pages of white women who are not thin, two pages of black women and two pages of Asian women, you know, it's actually not that difficult.

People often have commercial concerns and they think if we change it, it's not going to do well commercially, but I don't think that is true at all. People are hungry for images that reflect the real world, and I really believe that. The people who have made changes have seen it work. In some ways it's similar to saying that films with black people will not do well, but they do. I don't think any of these things will stop or end overnight or that it will be easy. But I also just don't think it's a reason to stop trying or stop talking about it.

BO: The last time we spoke to you was four years ago, when we published the article "Africa Needs Feminism," which was very well received. Does that statement still ring true and do you think the need is more urgent today than it was then, given the antagonism and hostility the word "feminism" elicits?
CNA: I think it still rings true. I don't think it's any more or less urgent. It has always been urgent and still is. I see a lot of young women from the continent starting to talk about these things and the fact that this conversation is being had, is a good thing. I see younger women being more willing to question things and that is probably what is very important, the ability and the willingness to question.

The hostility and antagonism is something I think one should expect. For me, I try to focus less on the hostile pushback, and it's not so much, it's just that it's almost an automatic response from many people. You say the word feminist and there is automatic hostility and it closes the door to debate. It's also important to say that a lot of this hostility is primarily coming from men. There are some women who are hostile to feminism, but it's primarily from men and in a certain sense, it's not that surprising because all attempts to correct injustice are met with hostility and antagonism. It comes with the territory.

I guess my point is that it's not a reason to stop or lose hope, because for every one hundred loud voices of hostility, there are also those who are quieter and more reflective, and for me that's progress.

BO: There is a lot of feminist conversation on social media. May I draw your attention specifically to the Nigerian context of the issue, which by and large reduces the subject to cooking. Is this not a distraction from the core issues of gender and equality that feminism wants to address?

CNA: I don't necessarily think it's a distraction that cooking is part of the discourse. I think it's important because it symbolizes this idea that a woman's place is domestic and only domestic, and it suggest that a woman's worth is measured by how good she is in domestic things. It's also important because it's actually a central part of the conversation about whether a woman can have it all. When we talk about women having it all, we really are talking about domestic work, and obviously, cooking to me symbolizes domestic work in general. So I actually don't think it is a distraction at all. It's a conversation that should be had particularly because it seems to matter to a lot of people, which is to say that men who are hostile to the idea of equality should relinquish the notion that cooking should be gender based. I mean they have a really visceral rage about it.

So it's important to talk about it. I think it's also important to acknowledge that we live in a culture across the entire continent and, in fact, the world, that somehow continues to insist and to teach girls that cooking is part of what makes them worthy. It's like a central part of their worth. To challenge that, we need to talk about it.

BO: Do you believe that intersectional feminism is necessary for uncomfortable conversations that enable better collaboration?

CNA: I have talked endlessly about how race shapes the way women experience gender, class and sexism. To be a black woman who has taken on that feminist label, in some ways, it is automatically intersectional. Western feminism focused on white women in the past and so the idea of intersectionality was a response to that and a means of being more inclusive.

BO: In your new book, *Dear Ijeawele, or A Feminist Manifesto in Fifteen Suggestions*, you write about women learning to know that they matter. How can women coming into the feminist and equality conversation at an older age begin to unlearn ingrained biases about women and gender?

CNA: It's difficult because, as I said at the Southbank conversation with Ellah, half joking, I think it might be too late for older women. It's very difficult if you have lived with something for thirty or forty years, but at the same time, I think it's necessary and better if we are to achieve a more just world. And more people in general will be happier when more women reach their potentials. It's a difficult thing but at the end of the day, women who have absorbed many of these ideas want things to be different and I say this knowing it's very difficult. So for me, it's about trying.

BO: Talking about trying, Hillary Clinton did just that in the last US elections. As a part US resident, you were a vocal supporter. How does her defeat affect women's confidence in vying for political office?
CNA: I actually think that it's going to make more women want to get out there and try.

It's tough and it's not just the psychological impact on these women. I remember wondering often how Hillary Clinton coped because I just thought my god, to have to endure all of these things.

For many young women in America it's sad, partly because Hillary lost and also partly because Donald Trump represents that idea of casual disrespect and disregard of women. But I see many are getting much more politically active in response to all that. So I am actually not concerned. I am hopeful.

BO: Let me touch on another subject that affects many, but is rarely discussed. Depression. You wrote an article in 2014 about your experience with depression. How would you like to see the conversation around this illness progress to a place where people, more so Africans, are not ashamed to talk about it?
CNA: I really think [the article] has added to the conversation. The reason I was so upset with the *Guardian* is that I wanted to write it and then go out and talk about it. Even that requires a type of mental energy, so I wanted to be ready to do that. And then the *Guardian* just sort of put it out there and I was very upset by that. It was sort of like you are planning to go out and you want to dress up and like the way you look, and then somebody pushes you outside when you are still naked or just in your underwear and you are not ready.

At some point, I still plan to write about it properly and publish it because I want to take the stigma out of it. I meet so many young people and I can tell depression is something they live with. It's important to know that one is not alone. It's also to let them know that it's okay, it's not a bad thing or something to be ashamed of. It's just what it is. You have these moments, a terrible darkness and you can't control it, you didn't make it and it's not your fault. It's something one has to learn to manage.

So I am happy that the article started a conversation and I plan to talk about depression some more, particularly for us in Africa. I think it's important for us to not be dismissive about depression. People will often just say, what's your problem? Cheer up or go and pray. And I feel as though those approaches kind of blame the person and I feel we just need a bit more kindness and a bit more knowledge. Part of it is not that people are mean, it's that people are ignorant and they don't understand.

BO: In *Dear Ijeawele, or A Feminist Manifesto in Fifteen Suggestions*, you write: "Make sure she doesn't inherit shame from you, you have to free yourself of your own inherited shame." Is shame a weapon of oppression, deeply ingrained in African societies?

CNA: The first step is to recognize how very difficult it is. It's being alert, it's being yourself over and over and being aware that this shame is there and in some ways, it's like giving yourself therapy every day, and it's hard. This is why I keep saying, unlearning gender and stereotypes is very difficult but we have to try. It's being aware, talking to yourself. It's what they say about talking to yourself the way you would talk to a dear friend or a family member or someone you love.

BO: Finally, do you remain hopeful for young African women, who are out there making change happen?

CNA: Yes, that's the most exciting thing for me and I see it more and more. Anytime I meet a young African woman who talks about what she is doing, it gives me hope. That's what I was talking about, being hopeful despite all of the hostility. Even in Nigeria, there are young women interested in information technology and web design. They are not all going the more traditional route of being a lawyer, which is fine, it's that they are saying I want to code, I want to start a web magazine, I want to start a fashion business and I want to sell affordable clothes.

You have young women starting their own businesses and they have a can-do-ness. It is gratifying to see this can-do-ness because they are doing things that are not necessarily expected. I think that's fantastic.

Interview with Chimamanda Ngozi Adichie

Tom Hall / 2017

From *Midday*, WYPR, broadcast on 18 April 2017. Used by permission of WYPR Radio, Baltimore, MD, USA.

Tom Hall: Good afternoon, welcome to *Midday*, everybody. I'm Tom Hall, on this very beautiful spring day. I hope it is as beautiful where you are, as it is here at WYPR. Thanks for joining us today. My guest is going to be the Nigerian author, essayist, and activist Chimamanda Ngozi Adichie. She splits her time between Nigeria and the United States, where she has a home in Columbia, Maryland. She has won several prestigious awards, including the Orange Broadband Prize for Fiction, and a MacArthur Foundation Fellowship, often referred to as a "Genius Grant." She will be headlining the 2017 Baltimore City Lit Festival later this month. That takes place on Saturday 29 April; it's an annual affair. It's going to take place at the University of Baltimore. It's a terrific event, has lots of authors, panels of folks in the book business—it's great for writers, it's great for readers, it's great for folks who love literature and who love reading. There will be a number of authors speaking at that event, and Chimamanda Ngozi Adichie will be one of them. I'm very glad to have been asked to moderate a conversation with Ms. Adichie at that event. The event, by the way, with Ms. Adichie, is sold out, but they have started a list of people who get on it, like a waiting list, to be in an alternate room and have a live video feed. So if you go to our website, wypr.org/midday, you get information about how to find a ticket to that event. So again, it's an annual event; Chimamanda Ngozi Adichie is just one of several terrific authors who will be appearing, and we hope you can join us on Saturday the 29th—that's a week from Saturday.

Ms. Adichie writes with tremendous power and grace. Her prose is unshakably grounded on a fundament of authority, compassion, and an unquenchable sense of wonder. She has recently become one of my favorite authors, and I'm sad to say that I'm new to her work. I read *Americanah* just a few months ago, and I read a few of her essays since. It's just terrific stuff, so if you haven't checked it out, you should definitely do so. She's the author of three novels, *Purple Hibiscus*, *Half of a Yellow Sun*, and *Americanah*. She published a short story collection in 2009, called *The Thing around Your Neck*; and a TED talk, which she gave in December 2012, was published as a book called *We Should All Be Feminists*. Her latest book was published last month; it takes up similar issues. It's called *Dear Ijeawele, or A Feminist Manifesto in Fifteen Suggestions*. Chimamanda Ngozi Adichie, I am delighted to meet you. Welcome.

Chimamanda Ngozi Adichie: Thank you. Thanks very much.

TH: It's great to have you here.

CNA: It's nice to be here.

TH: I was so taken with this novel, *Americanah*, and I can't wait to read the other ones. You've also written essays, including *We Should All Be Feminists* that has really just taken off. You really have sort of become, whether you wanted to or not, a spokesperson for the feminist movement in large measure. But I wonder: when you set out to write an essay, you have an idea, you have some points you want to make, you decide the arc of the essay, and you do it within the confines of that. You write this book, *Americanah*, which is sweeping, it's this grand novel, it's got tons of characters; it takes place in Baltimore, in New Jersey, in New York, in London, in Lagos, in New Haven, and all over the place; [it's got] people from different generations. And you make many of the same points in *Americanah* that you're making in the essays that you're writing about feminism and other subjects. Do you set out, at the beginning of the novel-writing process, to do that in the same kind of way that you set out to do it in the essay-writing process?

CNA: No. No. But I think that's a very good question because, even for the creative process, it's a relevant question. I occupy two very different creative spaces when I do both. So, when I write essays, I'm much more deliberate, I know what I'm doing—well, I like to think I know what I'm doing . . . [*laughs*]

TH: Don't we all! [*TH and CNA laugh*]

CNA: And I know what I want to say. Of course, the question is whether or not I have in fact said it the best way possible, but I know what I'm doing in general. With fiction, it's a lot more intuitive. I like to say it's much more magical for me. Characters take on a life of their own. Sometimes I want a character to do something; the character doesn't. And of course, when I tell this story to people who don't write fiction, they look at me as though I'm crazy. So, in some ways I think that my nonfiction is about my worldview, and my fiction is about that much more magical, difficult-to-pin-down, thing about the world. Because the world is messy, and the thing that's interesting about being a creative person—and that's what I like to think of myself primarily as—is that the world doesn't always align with your ideology. So, in my essays, it's really about how I want the world to be, but my fiction, I think, is about how the world is.

TH: I have a daughter who is a playwright, and she's talked about how she is surprised, often, at the end of the process of writing a play. I wonder: were you surprised at the end of your novels about what happened? I mean, you start with a general idea, but then, what kinds of things surprised you about, say, *Americanah* or *Purple Hibiscus*?

CNA: In *Americanah*, for example, I remember the ending. I remember wanting to impose myself on the ending, and the characters resisted.

TH: So you wrote different endings?

CNA: No. It's that I had what I imagined would happen in my head, but that's not what happened when I was writing.

TH: Ah.

CNA: When I started to write it, something else happened. So, it's like the spirits calling you, and you have no choice but to answer.

TH: So the muse is a real thing?

CNA: I think so. On the other hand, I don't want to make it too mystical and overromanticize it, because it's also about hard work; it's also the craft of it.

TH: You gotta sit down and write . . .

CNA: You have to. There are times when I have wanted to write, and I'm sitting in front of my laptop, and nothing is happening. Then there are other times when I have other things to do, and a story just won't leave me alone.

TH: Explain the term "Americanah" for folks?

CNA: "Americanah" is a word used in Nigeria, and it's a playful word. It's a word used for people who have become Americanized—people who've been to the US and come back. But also, often it's used for people who affect Americanization, people who, having spent some time in the US, go back to Nigeria and suddenly pretend that they no longer understand Igbo or Yoruba or any other Nigerian languages, and put on a very affected American accent. They then become "Americanah."

TH: I have a friend who has spent much of his career in France. He's an American, he's from Brooklyn, and he does the same thing all the time. When I visit him in Paris, he'll say, "Oh, what's the word in English?" I mean, he spoke English for twenty-five years before he lived in Paris. So I don' know . . .

In this book [*Americanah*], you talk about the dynamics of the workplace, the dynamics of the family institution, the dynamics of different neighborhoods in different cities, and you capture it all so beautifully. I want you to tell us a little bit about Ifemelu and Obinze, who are the two protagonists in *Americanah*, only because I really want people to read this book, and so I want you to whet their appetite a little bit.

CNA: I like to think of *Americanah* as, among other things, an old-fashioned love story. So they meet when they're teenagers in Nigeria, and then they leave Nigeria for different reasons. Ifemelu comes to the US, Obinze goes to England. They go through many, many things, and the relationship unravels. Years pass, and things have changed in their lives; they have grown, I think in more ways than they would have, had they not left Nigeria. Then Obinze moves back to Nigeria, or rather, Obinze is deported from the UK. Ifemelu later moves back [to Nigeria], and . . .

TH: . . . stuff happens.

CNA: Yes.

TH: Chaos ensues. I'm not a literary critic; I have no credentials in this notion, but I have to say it reminded me a lot of *A Hundred Years of Solitude* because of the breadth of it. I mean, it wasn't a hundred years, but it was a long time in the lives of the people . . . And *War and Peace*, to tell you the truth. There are so many different characters, so many people; their grandparents and fathers and mothers; and they're sagacious, and they're nasty, and they're charming, and they're villainous, and they're . . . I mean, you cook up all these different people. [Then there's also] Ifemelu's job, which is to write a blog about race. That's a very convenient thing for a person—it's an ingenious solution for a novelist and a fiction writer who wants to make some statements, and very important statements, about race. So, what can you say through Ifemelu's voice? Is there stuff you can say through Ifemelu's voice that you can't say through your own?

CNA: I suppose I have said quite a few things in my own voice, but you're right that the blog is a tool. It was a convenient tool for me, because I wanted Ifemelu, the character, to say all of these things, many of which I agree with. In the form of a novel, it can seem like hectoring, but then to do it in a blog . . . I wanted the blog to be funny. I hoped it would be funny and I wanted Ifemelu to say important things, but also to hopefully make people laugh. I think race is America's original sin; I also think that there's so much about it that is absurd that it becomes quite darkly funny. I agree with maybe ninety percent of what Ifemelu says, and I think I'm generally the person who says what I think.

TH: Yes, indeed, indeed, your reputation precedes you on that score.

CNA: One of the things I learned when I came to this country—and I'm a person who grew up in Nigeria during military dictatorships . . . But only when I came to the US did I start to internalize that idea of "what you cannot say." You learn, in a subtle way, self-censorship in this country. Never mind that you're immersed in the discourse of free speech, but there's a lot of, "you *can't* say that, you *can't* say that," and I learned that quite well, I think. But I find ways to push back.

TH: Yes, that's fascinating: in the context of free speech and our obsession with free speech, there are all sorts of things you can't say.

CNA: It's incredible.

TH: There is company you can't keep . . .

CNA: Yes.

TH: You write about race so beautifully in this book. What's really great for a reader like me—a sort of standard-ish white guy—is to discern the peculiarities, the complexities of folks you call "NABs" (Non-American Blacks) vs. Americans of African descent here (African Americans), and the tension that's often between those two communities, to say nothing of the tension that's between the communities of color in general and white communities. With the increased scrutiny—because people now have cellphones that they can record incidents of police misconduct and brutality on—that has been brought to the fore in a way in these last few years that it never was heretofore. Have you seen the dynamic of race change, including between

these two communities of Non-Americans Blacks and American Blacks, as well as in the larger culture? Have you seen it evolve and change? We have this putative conversation about race—has the conversation changed much given what's happened since the Black Lives Matter movement, essentially?
CNA: That's a good question. I want to say, yes and no. I mean, what I've been struck by is how, even with the videos that we've been seeing—and I just find them horrendous—there's still a lot of commentary that seems to in some ways justify that kind of unnecessary violence of the state. There are still people who will say, "Well, why didn't so-and-so just, I don't know, raise his hands, come out of the . . . ?"—you know?

TH: Sometimes they do and get shot anyway.
CNA: Right, even when they do. Somebody says, "Well, why didn't they raise their . . . feet?" I mean, it just becomes absurd. It's very troubling to me because, just looking at it—and in some ways I still consider myself an outsider in this country—I sometimes think, surely there must be fundamental human things that everybody can agree on? But I think that the history of this country is one in which, because black people have been so dehumanized, people have inherited that thinking, and so it's almost automatic to try and find ways to justify the violence done against them. For black immigrants in this country, I think it has changed in a way, because of course when the policeman stops you, he's not asking you whether you're Ghanaian or whether you're originally from Baltimore; he's seeing a black man, and all of the assumptions that come with that apply. Part of the problem, really, has been that the most recent movement of black people to this country— people like me who came in the 1990s, people who came in the late 1980s—it was a different migration. My father was in the US in the 1960s, and it was a period where African Americans and Africans worked together in anti-colonial movement, in the civil rights movement. More recently, I think that my generation of immigrants don't really know African American history, so that's really part of the tension. You come here and you absorb all the negative stereotypes, and so sometimes, you find black immigrants saying things that remind you of the movies about 1930s Alabama. But I do think that Black Lives Matter is an impressive thing that has forced conversations—and I don't like that word, "conversation," when it comes to race, I just feel like, "Oh, we've had too many bloody conversations, maybe it's time to . . ."

TH: Quit talking! Do something!
CNA: Yes. [*laughs*]

[Commercial break and announcements]

TH: Let's talk a little bit about the new book. There's one of your friends, Ijeawele, and you've written her a letter, which is "a feminist manifesto in fifteen suggestions." Tell us a little bit about this lady you're writing to.
CNA: I grew up with this really lovely woman. She lives in Nigeria. She had a baby two years ago, and she wrote to me and said, "I want to raise her feminist, so how do I do that?" I remember thinking, "How the hell am I supposed to know?" But because I had given the speech that became sort of widely known, "We Should All Be Feminists," . . .

TH: There was a TED talk, and then that turned into a book that you released.
CNA: Yes. So, I think in the minds of many people, I became their person to go to on the subject of feminism, which in itself continues to trouble me, because I don't consider myself an expert. So, what I did was to write her an email. I decided that I wanted to be honest and practical, and sort of straightforward. But also, for me, it was a way to map out my own feminist thinking. I had never, in fact, sat down to write about the things I would do if I were to raise a child. At the time, I did not have a child. I now have a child. My daughter is almost eighteen months. I went back to revise this book after I had my child, when I decided to turn it into a book because, really, it was a personal email to a friend. It made me think about how easy it is to dispense advice when you don't have to, in fact, use it yourself . . .

TH: Yes, living other people's lives is so much easier than living our own.
CNA: I love it—I love telling people what to do. It's harder to tell myself what to do.

TH: Well, that's good, because it's a good thing for a fiction writer—you just tell anybody you want, to do what *you* want them to do.
CNA: Playing God, it's just fun. But really, it made me also think that I want to *try*, that this is also a book that I want to follow for myself.

TH: Would you raise a son any different than you would suggest raising Ijeawele's daughter, or your own daughter?
CNA: Slightly differently. There are things in the book; there are fifteen suggestions. I actually use the word "manifesto" playfully, because it's such a big word that's very off-putting, and I thought, "Let's throw it in there and see what happens." I would raise a boy slightly differently. There are things

I would do in the same way, which is just fundamentally that I would not think too much about gender, that I would see the child as an individual. But I would raise a boy, if I did have a boy, to accept vulnerability as a beautiful thing, not to be ashamed of fear. I think we raise boys in a way that's quite unfair, where we cage them up. You know, the little boy falls down, and he's crying, and somebody is saying to him, "Oh, don't cry, get up you, be a man." The girl falls down, and we comfort her. Sometimes I wonder, "Well, do we wonder, then, that many men have issues with emotion?" It's because they've been raised in a way that I think is really inhumane. And so, for me, raising a boy would be about making many of these things that I think are really universal human traits, things that boys aspire to—so, that whole idea of the macho man . . . I just wouldn't. I would not tolerate that in my house.

TH: Chimamanda Ngozi Adichie is my guest this afternoon. It's Midday. Our phone number, 410–662–8780; our email, midday@wypr.org; if you want to drop us a Tweet, we're @middaytomhall. Here is an email from Suheila, who says, "I'm a big fan and, as a mixed-race immigrant, can relate to your observations about America from the inside-outside perspective, the messiness of diaspora and cultural mixing and multi-locality. In *Americanah*, you partly explore what it means to be black and Americanized. I wonder if you could talk about your observations a bit. How are you experiencing this mixing?" Because you are now regularly splitting your time between Nigeria and here in the US, right?

CNA: I guess the thing to say is that once I get off the plane in Lagos, I don't really think about race, because I don't really need to think about race. Nigeria is, obviously, majority black. When I'm in the US, having learnt the language and the nuances of race, I'm very alert to race. I know when I walk into a restaurant and I'm the only black person; I immediately know that. In Nigeria, I get off the plane, I forget race—there are so many other things to think about, by the way, because Nigeria is the place where I'm happiest, but it's also the place where I'm most frustrated. I think that living in both places makes me an outsider in both places. Not that I much mind, because I think that to be creative, being an outsider is a good thing, because it helps you see, in a way. I feel very fortunate that I can have both, because I love both places, but I also wouldn't be happy living the entire year in either place. So, I feel very fortunate that I can be in both. I'm two different people, I think. Or rather, actually, my little theory about human beings is that we are in fact a multiplicity of selves, and those selves emerge depending on where we are. A friend of mine, who's Kenyan and came to visit me in Lagos once—and he had only seen me in the US—said to me, "You're so different," and I said, "Why?" He said, "You're so loud!"

TH: Oh, that's fascinating. Just because everybody in Lagos is loud? It's a loud, bustling, crazy city?
CNA: Yes. I hadn't thought of myself as loud in that sense. But when he said it, I thought, "I'm sure I am," because Nigeria brings it out in you. If you want to be heard, you'd better bloody be loud! [*TH and CNA laugh*]

TH: Well, that is a nice little theory about the human condition—that's terrific. I mean, the observations you bring to the immigrant experience in *Americanah* are very powerful and, of course, very timely, now where we have a discussion about immigration from a president of the United States whose rhetoric about it was deplorable, just absolutely, unforgivably hideous. But this notion of being an expat, anywhere—locality, as our emailer suggests, is very important to one's identity. Where do you think the immigration debate here, in this country, is headed, given who's been elected president?
CNA: [*sighs*] I really don't know.

TH: Let me ask you, then, a better question. Where should it be headed? What is the proper immigration policy? As long as we have the laws that are on the books that we have, anything that ICE [United States Immigration and Customs Enforcement] is doing, anything that anybody else is doing, is legally permissible. It may not be morally justifiable, but it's legally permissible. What should the immigration policy of the United States of America be?
CNA: Oh [*sighs*], how much time do we have? No, I'm kidding.

TH: [*laughs*] All day! Take a sit. Take a crack.
CNA: I think I want to probably start by saying: I respect the right that any country has about protecting its borders. I do not think that that idea of all borders being completely open is even practical, because we've sort of agreed that the nation-state is the construction that we live in. That said, I think that, for me really, it's two things: it's that there are people in this country who have been here for many years, whose lives are here, whose loves are here, who it just doesn't even make sense to talk about deporting. And I don't even mean it in terms of how it's unfair and inhumane; it just doesn't even make practical sense. Why would you decide to alienate, humiliate, remove people who love this country, who have people in

this country who they love, who contribute to this country? It really doesn't make sense to me. I think the policy should focus on the people who are here. And I really do believe that they should have a path—a very clear and, quite frankly, an easy path to citizenship. That whole idea of, "Get into line and do it the right way," if you know what the "getting into line and doing it the right way" requires, it's no surprise that people don't. Right?

TH: Yes, it is tough.

CNA: It *is*. And so I think that needs to be reconsidered, redone. And for high and low. So Canada, for example, has this thing where they focus a lot on skills, and usually it's people who have two degrees [who get in]. While that is good, of course, I think every economy needs both. We need the people with the two degrees, we need the people who don't have the degrees, the people who will do the . . . you know, strawberries need to be picked. So, I think that it has to be a policy that, while focusing on doing things legally . . . that legal route has to be a doable and a humane route.

TH: Let's go to the phones. Melanie, in Baltimore. Welcome to Midday with Chimamanda Ngozi Adichie.

Melanie: Hi. I had to call in. *Americanah* is my favorite novel in recent memory. Last December, I bought a copy for every person on my staff at work because it was such an amazing book. Ifemelu is my favorite character in all of literature. I read the book last summer, which was a very interesting summer to be an African American woman, with all that was going on with the past election. And while reading the book, I kept finding myself in conversations with my friends, saying, "Oh, I have this friend who says . . ." and I'd realize—wait, that wasn't a friend of mine, that was something Ifemelu said in her blog. In talking with other women, especially other black women, about those blog pieces—which I felt were a fantastic literary device—other women who I know brought up Awesomely Luvvie, and we were wondering, many of us, if Ifemelu's blog was mainly modeled after Awesomely Luvvie, as Luvvie is an African woman who is commenting on the African American experience, as someone who is not an American-born black person.

TH: [*to CNA*] So you're familiar with this character, Awesomely Luvvie?

CNA: Yes, I've recently come to know of her blog, and some of her writing; she is actually really incredible, very insightful, very sharp. But no, because when I was writing *Americanah*, I didn't know about this blog. I don't know how long the blog's been on, but . . . So, it wasn't so much based on any particular blog. It was something I invented to give Ifemelu an opportunity to say what I wanted her to say. I had actually started off, in earlier drafts, having her write a newspaper column, but it didn't work very well because there's something dated about [a newspaper column]. I wanted it to be immediate. There's an immediacy that blogs have, and the voice I wanted to use—the sort of slightly throwaway-ish, slightly . . . you know, serious but not that serious—I felt wouldn't work for a newspaper column. So, I thought the blog would work.

TH: It's an excellent tool and also, she could pop off a blog any time you wanted her to.
CNA: Yes, yes.

TH: She didn't have to wait until Tuesday, when her deadline was set.
CNA: Yes, exactly. And there also wouldn't be an editorial presence hovering over her. I felt that blogs gave it more of an authenticity.

TH: What's also wonderful about this writing, to me, is that the intersection between feminism, race, immigration (the immigrant experience), gender; all of these things are so beautifully interpolated. You wrote about Michelle Obama in the *New York Times*, last October, as part of a series of essays about the first lady, as the Obama administration is coming to a close. You begin that essay by saying, "She had rhythm, a flow and swerve, hands slicing air, body weight moving from foot to foot, a beautiful rhythm. In anything else but a black American body, it would have been contrived." I think that's brilliant, because it brings in so many dimensions. Michelle Obama represents for so many the epitome of grace and sophistication and guts and intelligence. That one lead sentence just epitomizes so much of how so many people feel about her.

When it comes to feminism, you got in a bit of trouble, recently, when folks called you out for comments you made about the transgender community and transgender women. Let me ask you to explain what you said, and perhaps characterize some of the blowback you got after what you said.
CNA: So, what I had said was, I think that there is a difference in the way that trans women and women born female experience gender. And I was kind of taken aback by the [reactions] . . . The reason I knew there was a lot of blowback is that I got many, many emails from friends who were sympathizing with me—and I felt like I had been bereaved or something—but also from

kind people, many of whom were trans women, who were saying, you know, "We get what you're saying." So, on the one hand, because that difference is the source of so much violence and oppression, because trans women in particular experience terrible violence, I think there is a wish on certain . . .

TH: [*interrupts*] Eight trans women [were] killed in just this area alone, in the last few months.

CNA: Yes. Yes. Actually, I was watching the news two weeks ago, and there was a black trans woman who was just shot. And because of that, there is this wish to pretend that the difference isn't there, because if we do that, then we can wish away the violence. But I think, if we don't acknowledge the differences, then we're not able to address the particular things that affect particular groups of people. I also think that some people thought I meant that, therefore, they're somehow not part of feminism, which I didn't mean, and which I don't think, right? I also had said that the experience of gender is different because trans women have lived in the world as men, and so have the kind of privileges that men have, or at least are familiar with those privileges. I think some people also saw that to mean that I was suggesting that their lives are easy, but of course their lives are not easy. It's simply that privilege is always relative. In other words, when you're growing up a girl, when you're ten and your period starts—or even before your period starts— you've already been socialized to think of your body as a shameful thing. I have [heard] so many girls who talk about what their mothers told them about the sanitary pads, like "What are you doing with the pad? Don't let your brother see the pad," and you start to feel there's something shameful about what's happening to your body. So, it's things like that. To experience that, in many ways, is not to have male privilege. To not experience that is a certain kind of male privilege. It's things like that that I meant. Of course, also, [I'm] acknowledging that to be trans is very difficult because what's going on is that you've been born in a body that is not yours. But the world is seeing that body; the world is treating you based on that body that they see. So that's really what the point was, and I think that there were people who didn't want to hear what I wanted to say and just wanted me to use exactly the kind of language that they wanted. I resisted that because I think there's becoming a kind of language orthodoxy where, if you don't say something with the particular words, you're ostracized; you're censored. I don't think it's good for continuing to learn, and sort of cross-learn. Also, to think that these are people who are members of my tribe, right? We are all on the same side. That was the thing that I was taken aback by.

TH: It's a complicated thing. We're going to post, by the way, your original comments as well as your clarifying comments that you put on your Facebook page. We'll have a link to that page, so people can look at that and see some of the comments you got on your Facebook page from some of your readers. But I did want to bring it up, make sure we mentioned it at least this afternoon.

[*Commercial break and announcements*]

TH: One of the many things I liked about *Americanah* and like about your writing on feminism is your embrace of those things that are traditionally feminine. You are the pitch-person for a makeup company in the UK; you're doing TV commercials; you're incredibly stylish; you have an Instagram account, which I guess is curated by your nieces, is that right?
CNA: Yes.

TH: And it's pictures of you in these terrific outfits. I mean, you're this fashionista, you know . . .
CNA: All of which are made in Nigeria, I need to point out.

TH: Yes, there you go . . . Now, so what does that mean? That you won't take Instagram photos of yourself with beautiful outfits on in America? What's that about? [*TH and CNA laugh*]
CNA: No, it's really that I was going to do a number of events for the new book and I thought—because the Nigerian currency has recently tumbled, and now there's sort of this thing in Nigeria where people say, "Buy Nigerian to grow the economy" . . . The president actually recently said that two days a week have to be, "Wear only Nigerian-made clothes in Nigeria." So, I thought that would be a really cool thing.

TH: Well that was stocked up, huh? [*TH and CNA laugh*]
CNA: And my nieces said to me, "Aunty, you really need to get a bit more modern. You need to do Instagram." And I said, "But I have a Facebook page." They're like, "Aunty, it's people who are sixty and above who do Facebook." I really find a lot of social media . . . it's not my thing, really. I'm enjoying having pictures taken for it, but it's really not my thing. So, the agreement was that I would make sure pictures are taken, I would send the pictures to them, and then they would make the selection and put them up. It works out really well.

TH: Never in my life have I read so much about, or considered, or thought about, hair, as when I read your novel. It's amazing, because the first scene in the book is, you're going . . . the character, Ifemelu, is getting her hair braided. First of all, it takes hours! I had no idea. I mean, it's like four hours to get your hair done.

CNA: Oh, longer.

TH: That's crazy. That's a commitment. But you know, you talk about this— I was put in mind of a Joni Mitchell song, which I love, called "The Boho Dance," where she's talking about the bohemian life versus the stylish, Parisian . . . you know, beautiful dresses and silk stockings. And she says, at the end, "Nothing is capsulized in me / On either side of town / The streets were never really mine / Not mine these glamour gowns." I mean, that tension between the rough life of the artiste and the life of the sophisticate, do you experience that personally? And how does that inform our notion of what being a woman is, what being a feminist is?

CNA: Do I experience that? No, not really, because the whole "bohemian aesthetic" has never been mine. In many ways, it's about the way that I grew up. I grew up the child of middle-class Nigerians who raised me in a particular way: you were supposed to care about your appearance; every Sunday at church, your socks were supposed to be perfectly white; the lacy ruffles were supposed to be just so; my mother put the ribbons that matched in my hair . . . I grew up in that way, and there's a part of me that's still very much that middle-class Igbo child. Actually, when I came to the US, I remember realizing that, in some ways, to be seen as a serious writer meant that you couldn't appear to care too much about your appearance. You had to have a certain look that meant you were too busy thinking about writing and books to brush your hair. And I remember thinking, "I've always thought about writing and books, but I've also always brushed my hair."

TH: But the thing is, you're allowed to be both, right?

CNA: But you know, you would be surprised at how . . . that is my position, and it's one of the reasons I wanted to do these things publicly, which is to say that feminism and femininity are not mutually exclusive, and to think about the younger women who, I know, care about these things *and* also care about ideas and books and writing but feel that they shouldn't. So, my choosing to, in some ways, come out publicly and stop hiding my high heels was simply to say, "This is who I am." It doesn't make me any less of anything, and I don't feel the need to justify it. I don't feel the need, also, to intellectualize it. I don't feel the need to say that my love of dresses is really a manifestation of something. It just is a love of dresses.

TH: You talk about feminism in the plural, "feminisms." There are social critics, public intellectuals—and you among them—who have talked about the feminism of Beyoncé or Rihanna as being not necessarily related to the feminism of others. But it is a very mixed bag. Is there such thing as a universal feminism, the one tent under which every single person fits?

CNA: Yes, I think that there is such a thing. The universal idea is the premise, which is that men and women are fundamentally, completely equal; we're not negotiating that. But then how we go about manifesting it [is different]. Because I think it's important to have a multiplicity and to have diversity within that world of feminism, also because there are other things: you know, I think race affects gender, class affects gender, religion affects [gender] . . . region—the region of the world in which you live—they're things that are not the same for people, but the premise is the same. So, this is why I often say to people that for me, feminism is always contextual, that there are certain things in certain parts of the world that somebody would say, "Oh, that doesn't really seem feminist to me," but in another part of the world, actually is. It's not to say that everything goes. Right? It's to say that, if we start off with the fundamental premise, which has to be the same for everyone, then I think that there are variations in the practice of that premise.

TH: One of the suggestions you make to your friend Ijeawele is to be careful not to turn oppressed people into saints. I mean, we have to look at this clear-eyed. You say saintliness is not a prerequisite for dignity. You don't need saintliness . . .

CNA: No.

TH: . . . to be deserving of dignity. Do you think there is an impulse—what happened with the Women's March, the day after the inauguration in January, where there was clearly a tension between white feminists and feminists of color; people who were in the pro-life movement, where women wanted to be part of it and they were disallowed. There were all across the political spectrum some difficult conversations that were not resolved. In terms of the left, the political left, is there an impulse to elevate everybody in an uncritical way? Do you worry about that?

CNA: Yes, very much. Not to unduly go back to the trans debate, but I think it's also part of it. There's that need to say that "We're all the same." "We're all the same," and to say that I think is to silence. It's a silencing tool. I think it's dishonest, and I don't think it's very helpful. It's also a way of avoiding discomfort, because if you say that we're all the same, then you don't have to talk about things that are potentially uncomfortable. With the Women's March, the one place I might take a bit of exception to is women who insist on the pro-life agenda for everybody. Now, I think that . . .

TH: Again, it's the "we're all the same" argument.

CNA: Right, right. I have a problem with that. I think it's a perfectly valid position, to be personally opposed to abortion, and I completely respect that. I grew up in a Catholic household. But I also think it's just deeply wrong to impose it on everyone, because you don't know what people's stories are.

TH: So much of the argument about feminism, or race, or gender, is about power, and it's about who's allowed to either be at the table, and then if at the table, to speak.

CNA: Yes.

TH: Who gets to be heard.

CNA: Yes.

TH: And it's difficult. I mean, you write, "If a woman has power, why do we need to disguise that she has power?" That's a danger too.

CNA: Yes. It is, absolutely. I mean, really, all of this is about power. In the end, that's what it's about. It's whose voice is heard, whose voice is given a certain kind of [prominence], you know, whose voice is *the* voice. When we talk about power and women, I find it fascinating, particularly in this country. I was telling a friend that it seems to me that women and power in this country is something that makes people even more uncomfortable than it does in Nigeria. In Nigeria, the idea of a woman being in a powerful position very quickly becomes ordinary once she has attained that position. But I find that in this country, there are always ways to disguise it, that even the women have to perform in ways that diminish their own power, if that makes sense, because they have to make people feel comfortable with it.

TH: Yes, yes, this whole cover. You also talk about this curse of being like-able . . .

CNA: Yes.

TH: . . . and this obsession with being likeable. We get to talk more about this at the City Lit Festival a week from Saturday, and I look forward to it.
CNA: So do I, so do I.

TH: It's been great to meet you, thank you so much.
CNA: Thank you, thank you.

The Novelist as Therapist: A Conversation with Chimamanda Ngozi Adichie

Daria Tunca / 2018

Interview conducted in London on 11 October 2018.

Daria Tunca: I wanted to start this conversation—which, as you know, is due to be published in a book of interviews—by talking about precisely this: interviews. The first interview with you that I was able to find dates back to 1999; it was conducted by a journalist named Howard Altman and published in the *Philadelphia City Paper*.[1] Was this your first interview in the United States?
Chimamanda Ngozi Adichie: Yes, I'm sure it must have been.

DT: Can you remember anything about it?
CNA: I don't remember the content. But I remember that I was taking a class in media at Drexel University, and we were supposed to interview somebody who worked in the media. I knew the *City Paper*—a free newspaper in Philadelphia—because that's what I would use to look at the employment sections when I was looking for a babysitting position. So that's how I met Howard Altman. He was the editor of the *City Paper*. I called him and I said, "I'm taking a class in media at Drexel and I need to interview an editor. Can I interview you?" And he said yes. I then did my class project on him. I don't remember details, but I think I must have gone in there, and then he decided to interview *me* because, you know, I was from Nigeria and I was a writer.

DT: One of the things that you are quoted as saying in this interview is: "I want to go home and start a TV show and write." What is this about? Did you really want to start a TV show?

CNA: I did when I was in secondary school. There were times when I liked the idea of having a TV show where I would interview politicians and change Nigeria. I mean, I don't think that I wanted to interview celebrities. It was rather a TV show as a political tool. But it was always something that was going to be on the side. Writing was always my main focus.

DT: Another thing that struck me about this *City Paper* interview is that a lot of the questions revolved around the political situation in Nigeria. In this sense the piece is quite typical of your early interviews in the US and Europe, where it seems that you were often put in the position of a "native informant." Today, I feel that you have rather become a therapist of sorts, especially in Q&A sessions with audiences. Do you think that this development has indeed occurred—that we are no longer speaking of "the novelist as teacher," as Chinua Achebe would put it, but of "the novelist as therapist"?
CNA: [*laughs*] But what you have done here is compare interviews with journalists on the one hand with Q&As at public events on the other. That's kind of different, right?

DT: Yes, true.
CNA: So, what do you think has changed in interviews with journalists now? I'd be curious to know. Am I still a "native informant"?

DT: Hardly, I think. Sometimes when you are interviewed by big news channels, perhaps. But what I find is that, in the past five years or so, people have tended to move away from your work to focus more on the politics of it. I also feel that the range of topics that you are asked about has shrunk, and that the discussion often comes back to feminism . . .
CNA: . . . which concerns me a little. Obviously, I feel very strongly about feminism, but there are times when I have the impression that people don't want to hear anything else from me. But then I feel conflicted, because I think it's so important that it should be talked about. Still, it can be very limiting. I remember that I went through a period of wanting to go back to read the Holocaust books that I had read years ago—I have a bit of an obsession with Holocaust books and films. An editor had asked me to write something and I replied that I wanted to write about that subject, but he said, "No, we want you to do feminism." And I remember being upset by that. I said, "No, I'm not doing it." But it made me really stop and think, and realize that there is a cost to being a "feminist icon." It can become a single story of who I am.

But to come back to your question about the "novelist as therapist": I think it's true. It's also a role that I like. In my family, I am everybody's therapist. My friends tease me about wanting to fix the lives of the people I love, because I would always say to them, "What can we do to make this better now? Let's have a plan." But as I writer, I also think that the "novelist as therapist" idea speaks to a need in people, mostly young women. I did an event in Cheltenham yesterday, and the last question came from a young girl in the audience. It made me feel almost emotional, because she said to me, "I'm black and I'm female, and I feel that I constantly have to fight to make myself feel that I'm not inferior." It made me so sad. I felt a kind of protective anger on her behalf, and I said to her, "You matter. Don't you ever let anybody put you down." So she came to my event because she sees me as a possible source of validation. Obviously, I feel very grateful and honored, but I hate that we live in a world where she needs that.

DT: Does it put pressure on you that so many young women look up to you? Do you feel a sense of responsibility?

CNA: Do I feel a sense of responsibility? Not really, no. Does it put pressure on me? No. Because I like it. I mean, I don't mind it at all. I have a bit of a messiah complex—I want to save the world. I particularly want to save women and vulnerable people, so I feel that it's important to make people feel better. I think that a sense of responsibility suggests a kind of duty that one feels one *must* do certain things; I never felt that. I mean, this is the honest answer: I like feeling that I'm useful, because sometimes I talk to those girls and I see in their faces that something has happened. Once a young woman said to me, "You make me feel more courageous." It moved me very much. Of course there are times when I feel that I don't really have the answer to people's questions, but I try to be honest and tell them that I don't know.

Sometimes in Nigeria people tell me that I'm a role model, but I don't really like that label. "Role model" suggests that you have to be a certain way, because of people's expectations of you. I'm not going to do that. I'm going to be me—if it works for you, that's wonderful; if it doesn't, sorry, but I'm not going to change me. So in that sense, I don't feel a sense of responsibility, because I'm doing what feels true to me.

DT: Another thing that has become obvious over the years is that interviews get you into trouble. I mainly refer here to conversations with journalists, several of which have given rise to controversies, but also to the interview that you conducted with Hillary Clinton at the PEN America World Voices Festival in April 2018, when you questioned her use of the word "wife" as the first descriptor in her Twitter profile. It seems that many people, particularly in Nigeria, considered your question to be disrespectful of the institution of marriage. At a recent public event in Lagos, you mentioned that the ensuing controversy had become so fierce that it had affected even people close to you, such as your mother. You then said something that I found heartbreaking: "It [that controversy] made me start thinking that self-care might in fact be creating space between me and Nigeria" . . .

CNA: Yes. One of the decisions that I have made lately, knowing I'm now a famous person, is that I'm going to be an honest person, publicly. This means that I don't want to pretend that things that hurt me don't hurt me. I have many friends and relatives who think that I shouldn't let people know that something is getting to me, because it means giving those people power. But I disagree. It's the reverse: I don't want to give them the power of my having to pretend that something that hurts me doesn't hurt me. When I started writing, in Nigeria the reception was very different to what it is now; it was mostly positive. When I became a feminist voice, it changed very sharply. As someone once said to me, "Nigerians want you to shut up and write; they just don't want you to talk about feminism." The Hillary Clinton controversy was a turning point, because fundamentally I did not understand why it happened. And it was *huge.* I went back to Lagos the day after the interview, and on the car radio, I heard people saying, "How dare Chimamanda ask Hillary Clinton about this; Chimamanda has no respect for marriage . . ." I had to tell my driver to turn the radio off. When I got home, my poor mother told me that everyone was talking about it in the Whatsapp group of the church that my parents belong to. It was also in the newspapers, and I just . . . I don't know, it did something to me, and I really started to think, "It must be that I don't understand my country after all." This kind of ugly negativity is not worth it. So I cut my visit short. I was supposed to stay in Lagos for a month, but after a week and a half I just packed my things, took my child, and went back to America. And for the first time in my life, I started to question how I felt about my country. I've always been a good daughter of Nigeria; I've always deeply loved Nigeria; I've always felt that Nigeria would work—and not just as an Igbo person, as a Nigerian person. I've always believed that we have problems, but that we can make it happen. After that, I really started to question it. I'm still questioning it. The only other time that I felt very negatively about Nigeria was when my father was kidnapped. But it was a different kind of negativity, one that was really directed at the government and the failed infrastructure that couldn't protect my father. When my father was kidnapped, I had to reach out to the American Consul General to help us, and it made me start thinking, "I need to get an American passport," which for a long time I have not gotten by choice, because I want to feel what it's like to have only one passport, which is Nigerian. I still do, but I think that's going to change. And the Hillary Clinton noise has really been the catalyst. It did something to me. I know how marriage is overvalued in Nigeria, and I think that's very, very danger-ous, particularly for women. I remember hearing from friends who told me that, the whole day at work after the interview with Hillary Clinton, people were insulting me—calling me arrogant, saying I had no right to question marriage—and they were also insulting my friends because my friends were close to me. I mean, the ugliness was shocking, and the worst part is that I did not understand what the problem was.

DT: Did you have support as well?
CNA: There was almost no support. And this I know because my friends would tell me about the things they had heard. A friend told me about a woman in Nigeria who is strongly feminist and who usually supports me, but who that time was among those saying, "How dare she?"

DT: There were also other topics discussed in that conversation with Hill-ary Clinton. One of the things that you mentioned is how you had written a piece about her for *The Atlantic*, an op-ed that you had wanted to call "Why Is Hillary Clinton So Widely Loved?" However, you were censored, and the title ended up being "What Hillary Clinton's Fans Love about Her," which is something quite different . . .
CNA: Very different. Very different.

DT: Is this censorship from editors something that you have often encoun-tered? Why do you think it happened in this case?
CNA: Because it was Hillary Clinton. I can't even tell you that I've ever really been censored by editors before. I mean, I can tell you that I've been edited in stupid ways. And I feel that the more prestigious the publication, the worse the editing, quite frankly.

DT: Really?
CNA: Yes. Because I think that often they have a tone that they want to maintain, and so they want to take out the things that, in my opinion, make

my voice my voice. Sometimes I let that go, especially with op-eds because I'm trying to make a point about something, and I'm willing to concede certain things. But sometimes, I would say "No, we need to put that back in." But this was the first time I had been censored. What the editor had done, I felt, was really change my points. I had written that piece because I felt so frustrated at how the media was constantly pushing the story of how nobody likes Hillary, how they hate her. But I love her, and I'm surrounded by people who love her—not people who think she's only just okay, no: people who are passionate about her. So I thought that we needed to start to try to change this narrative. That's why I chose the title "Why Is Hillary Clinton So Widely Loved?" And just to show you how biased I think the entire American media establishment was: this editor very quickly said no to using my title, arguing that it was not objective fact. I replied: "And the idea that she's disliked *is* objective fact?" Then, my manager looked at *The Atlantic*'s history of op-eds, of their coverage of Hillary Clinton. Many articles had lines that are anything but objective. In the end, after a lot of back and forth, *The Atlantic* said that they couldn't use my title, and that the best they could do was, "What Hillary Clinton's Fans Love about Her."

DT: Considering this atmosphere of censorship, it's actually rather funny that you were able to publish two short stories about Melania Trump, "The Arrangements" and "Janelle Asked to the Bedroom," without being sued for libel.
CNA: I know!

DT: How did you get away with that?
CNA: Well, actually, the *New York Times* would have been sued, not me. And I'm sure they have very good lawyers.

DT: But did you have to ask anyone for permission?
CNA: No. The *New York Times* wrote to me saying that they were doing something that they had never done before, which is to publish fiction. They wanted to publish fiction about the American presidential campaign, and they wanted me to write a piece. Of course I was very honored—the *New York Times* is asking *me* to write their very first fiction special? Yes! And they told me that I could write about anything that I wanted to, but that it had to be about the campaign. Of course, there was already a character that was just made for fiction, but that was so fictional as to be almost unbelievable in fiction. Actually, I did think very briefly about writing about Hillary Clinton, who I loved very much, but I thought that there just wasn't enough

for fiction to work. The *New York Times* editor said to me, "You don't need to check with me about what you want to write about, just write." I thought, "Great!" So I went and did some research on Melania Trump, just some general research on the family. Then I wrote the story, which I really enjoyed doing, and I sent it to the editor. She loved it, but said that she would of course have to run it through the paper's lawyers. And, apparently, what needed to be done was to make it very clear from the beginning that it was fiction. So "The Arrangements" was subtitled "A Work of Fiction."

DT: You wrote two pieces involving Melania Trump. I thought that the follow-up, "Janelle Asked to the Bedroom," was quite different to "The Arrangements." In an interview, you said about the first story that you had wanted to humanize Melania, without being overly sympathetic to her. In the sequel, she is quite a different character to the one in the first story: she is depressed and sad, but she is also slightly unhinged—obsessively looking at photos of Michelle Obama—and she is spoilt, racist, and self-centered.
CNA: Trump had won, hadn't he, when I did the follow-up?

DT: Yes, he had.
CNA: It has to be about that. If you had asked me, "Were you consciously aware that Melania Trump the character had darkened in the follow-up?" I would have said no. But clearly, it must be that my own view of her had darkened. And also, I was writing in a different space where this man was now president.

DT: Was that piece commissioned?
CNA: No, I chose to do a follow-up. This was for the *New York Times Style Magazine*. They wanted me to do a little story to go with their "Greats" issue, and it really started from a bit of laziness; I just didn't know what else to write about. So I thought, well, let's go back! But also, I do think that not just the president and his family, but the entire Trump administration, are racist. I think that they're antiblack racist and anti-Hispanic racist, and so I wanted to make a point. It's also interesting that despite this racism, Melania Trump, I hear, has a kind of obsession with Michelle Obama.

DT: Really? So that part of the story is true?
CNA: Yes, I have read about this. She follows her. I just exaggerated it. I learnt about it, I think, when Melania gave that speech where she pretty

much repeated Michelle Obama's speech. I read that Melania was sort of a "fan" of Michelle Obama's and followed her fashion choices. So I thought, why not turn this into something even bigger, exaggerate it and make it into a slightly fetish-like obsession.

DT: That is exactly what it is in the story. It's hilarious.
CNA: But I have to say, I do have a certain sympathy for that woman. I think that she's a tragic figure. She's so sad.

DT: But she's also a very powerful woman.
CNA: Yes, she's benefiting from ugly, corrupt, evil power. I understand that. But I think that you can do that *and* also be a tragic figure. She's benefiting, but at what cost? She's powerful, but she's also quite clueless. I mean, she went to Ghana and Egypt and Kenya wearing a pith helmet! I couldn't even be angry. I was just laughing. I was just thinking, this is so sad. I mean, somebody told her that this was the right way to look in Africa—*really*? You have to be really out of touch to believe that. I find a deep sadness in her, which existed even before Trump won. But now I think that this is not at all what she asked for. Again, I'm not saying she's a good person; I don't know enough to make that judgment. I also think that she backs up a lot of her husband's racism. When Trump kept insisting that Barack Obama had not been born in the US, Melania supported her husband, saying that Obama should show his birth certificate, which made me think, "Darling, *you* should show your birth certificate."

DT: Yes—some people say that she entered the country illegally, don't they?
CNA: We still don't know. We haven't seen Trump's tax returns; we don't know what Melania's immigration story is. Her parents apparently are US citizens now. Trump tells us that immigrants shouldn't file for families, but how did her parents become citizens? With Trump, the conversation is not about immigration, it's about not wanting people who are not white. That's fundamentally what it is. The US media will say that it is about immigration, but it's not. It's about race.

DT: You mean that America will accept certain kinds of immigrants and not others, right?
CNA: Yes. Trump tells us very nicely that they can come from Sweden, but not from what he calls the "shithole" countries.

DT: Let me now move on to some questions that I have as a long-time reader of your fiction. I was wondering about your process of revision, and more specifically about the previously published short stories that you revised for your collection *The Thing around Your Neck*. How much of that revision was yours? To what extent were you asked to revise your stories for the book?

CNA: I worked with an editor. I think that there were some changes that she felt worked and I wasn't really sure about, but she made the case for them, so . . .

DT: Can you remember any details?

CNA: No. But I can tell you I don't really like that book.

DT: Really? Why?

CNA: I think it's the one book of mine that had a little cynicism to it, which is to say that my editor suggested that we should do a collection, because we felt—and I think *I* felt—that it was time for me to gesture to the American audience. I had a bunch of stories that we looked at, and my editor kind of selected the stories for the collection, but I went along with it because in my mind I felt that, yes, this is good for the American readership, as many of the stories were about America. Afterwards, I didn't like myself for doing that. And I think that's why the book didn't do well—I mean, *The Thing around Your Neck* is the book of mine that's been the least successful.

DT: But it's a book of short stories, as opposed to a novel . . .

CNA: Yes, but I really think it's the cynicism. I do. That's also why I've said to myself, I will never do that again, because it doesn't work. I feel that I should have resisted more. I don't even like looking at that book. I still like some of the stories; I mean, as individual stories, I'm quite proud of some of them. But as a book, I don't know. So I've learnt my lesson. *Americanah*, on the other hand, is a novel that I wrote thinking, "They're not going to like it." Actually, my editor hated it.

DT: Why is that?

CNA: Oh, there was a lot. She said that I should take out all the blogs because they were too obvious; she said that there was no nuance, that I should take out certain sections, that some passages were unbelievable, that I had just staged them so that I could say something about race . . . We had this battle, and I said, "No, this is the book I want to write." Had *Americanah* ended up like *The Thing around Your Neck*, I would have been fine with it.

I really did think that they were going to hate this book. And the opposite happened. I mean, with *The Thing around Your Neck*, I thought, "Wow, Americans will love it." But nobody really cared about that book! [*laughs*]

DT: That's an exaggeration!
CNA: Yes, but that book is also a product of more than just literary considerations. That's why I had mixed feelings about it. I don't think I've ever actually gone back to read it. So I can't even tell you what changes I made and didn't make . . . But I do think some of the stories are a bit flattened, no?

DT: I would say that some of them are narratively more explicit—there are fewer gaps that the reader needs to fill.
CNA: That was my editor. She would say things to me like, "An American reader . . ." But actually, I have to say that I did fight back about quite a few things. For example, she wanted to change the word "Vice-Chancellor" to "University President." I refused. I said, "Americans aren't stupid, and they will learn what a Vice-Chancellor is." I guess this shows you what the editing process was like. It was very much about, "This is the book that we're doing for Americans."

DT: But I feel that some of the changes that were made also had literary significance. For example, the story "The Thing around Your Neck" was first published in 2001 under the title "You in America." In the first version, the protagonist goes back to Nigeria at the end of the story, and she says "thank you" to her white American boyfriend when she hugs him goodbye. In the revised version, the "thank you" is gone: she just hugs him and leaves. I thought that this actually worked better, because one could wonder why she should be grateful to him.
CNA: Hmm. I don't actually remember. That might have been me, because I think my editor would want the "thank you"!

DT: I have a different question, this time about Ugwu in *Half of a Yellow Sun*. You have commented on the fact that, even as the writer of the novel, you were shocked that the character committed rape—I think that Ugwu's act comes as a surprise to the reader as well. In completely different circumstances, you have commented on how unforgiving you can be with people. Yet at the end of *Half of a Yellow Sun*, Ugwu becomes the voice that speaks for Biafra. Does this mean that you forgave Ugwu?
CNA: That's a very good question. Yes, I think I forgave him. But it's very interesting for me to talk about this now, in 2018. It's not that I was any less of

a feminist when I wrote *Half of a Yellow Sun*, but I'm only realizing how anti-feminist the world is. Actually, I've realized it now. I don't think that I would write the book differently, because I'm just in a different world when I write fiction. But afterwards, when I think of Ugwu, I don't know. I think the truth is that I forgave him because, for me, Ugwu raping that girl wasn't so much a crime of Ugwu's as it was a crime of war. I felt that that scene was about how terrible war is, about how it turns human beings into monsters. Ugwu just slipped into being a monster, even if briefly. But it was important for that to happen. It is obvious that he is the character that the author of the book loves from the beginning, and I think it would have been not just disingenuous but also too simplistic to have him experience the entire war and still emerge as our beloved champion. It just wouldn't be true. He needed to be complicated in a way that would be difficult for the reader. I mean, it was difficult for *me*. I rewrote that rape scene many times. I felt that the first version was too dramatic—it was very hard to find a balance. And I also remember my uncle telling me about a Biafran girl who had been raped by Biafran soldiers, and that broke my heart more than anything. It's kind of stupid, obviously, because rape is rape. However, had she been raped by Nigerian soldiers, I would have said, "Oh, it's rape as a weapon of war." But she was raped by her Igbo brothers. I remember my uncle saying something like, "She was never the same." Rape isn't something that people really have the language to talk about. My uncle used the word "rape" in English but added, in Igbo, that after that she was never the same again. And that was all he said. For some reason I became almost obsessed not just with the idea that the woman was raped, but that she was raped by the people who were supposed to protect her.

DT: The young woman that Ugwu rapes appears very briefly in the book. She is raped, she stares back at him, and she disappears. Did you think about her after that moment?
CNA: Yes . . . but in some ways, as Ugwu's sister. When Ugwu sees his sister after the war, the entire passage is really about that bar girl that Ugwu raped. So I did think about her quite a bit. But to have her reappear would have been really melodramatic; I wasn't going to have her do that. Still, clearly, when Ugwu sees his sister, it is really about that girl that he raped. But I think I forgave him.

DT: In an interview with Radhika Jones, you talked about the fact that audiences had not responded to particular scenes or characters in the way that you had hoped. You said, there are "[t]hings that I have written and liked

that have not been liked the way I wanted them to be liked." I remember raising a similar issue with you when I first attended one of your events in 2006. I asked you whether you felt that anything in your fiction had been underappreciated. Back then, your response was: Father Amadi in *Purple Hibiscus*. You said, "I wrote this sexy character and no one seems to care . . ."
CNA: [*laughs*] I still stand by that, by the way.

DT: Now, there is a particular passage in *Americanah* where Ifemelu goes to the house of a tennis coach and is abused. After this incident, she stops communicating with her boyfriend Obinze. This doesn't make logical sense, but it makes emotional sense. I was wondering if that passage had meant anything to you. I haven't seen it discussed by journalists or audiences, but maybe people approach you in private to talk about it?
CNA: No, and it actually kind of bothers me. I was hoping that it would be a thing and that people would go looking for the tennis coach in Ardmore.

DT: What you wrote about is a complex case of sexual abuse, right? Ifemelu apparently goes to his house willingly, but one wonders whether she really has a choice . . .
CNA: . . . and then afterwards she's savagely questioning herself. The easy kind of story about a woman being assaulted is, "Oh, she was very resistant, he forced her, he pushed her down." This happens, obviously, but I feel that the most common stories are much more complicated. For me, the complication doesn't make it any less of sexual assault. Clearly, Ifemelu was assaulted by this man, and it wounded her spirit in a way that made her punish herself. In a certain kind of way, she's thinking, "I no longer deserve Obinze, I no longer deserve love." Actually, I've been surprised: nobody talks about it. I don't think I've ever been asked about it. When *Americanah* first came out, I remember thinking that this passage was going to be the thing. And I actually thought, "Oh my God, they're going to ask me if it's based on my life." And it sort of, *kind of*, is, but not really. I wanted to be honest if they asked me, so I was thinking, "What am I going to say?" If I wanted to talk about my personal life, I would write a memoir. I wrote a novel. But I do want to talk about what assault means, and how it affects people. Maybe that incident wasn't discussed because there is just so much in the book? People were like, "Oooh, let's talk about race and hair!"

DT: Exactly. And in a way, perhaps race and hair were "sexier" topics?
CNA: Yes, but I think there is also the idea of a novel bringing news. Writing

about women who have been assaulted is something that people have done. Writing about race in that "in-your-face" way was the "news" of the novel. Then people started to talk about hair—which I didn't mind, because I did want to talk about hair and race. I guess that looking at more subtle, nuanced emotional passages requires a different kind of reading.

DT: I wanted to ask you what is perhaps a more difficult question. In March 2018, you took part in an event at the Southbank Centre with Reni Eddo-Lodge, the British author of *Why I'm No Longer Talking to White People about Race*. One of the things that you and Eddo-Lodge both expressed irritation about is white fragility, and more specifically the fact that white people constantly need to be reassured that discussions about racism are not personal attacks against them. The conversation then moved to issues of class, and you mentioned how defensive you were when your social privilege in Nigeria was brought up. You said that, whereas you were not among the privileged in terms of gender and race, you were in terms of class, and that you felt defensive when you were attacked about it. Part of the audience that you were saying this to were white. I was wondering: doesn't telling white people that you are defensive about class indulge white fragility? I mean, aren't you saying, "Look, I'm like you: I'm as defensive about class as you are about race"?

CNA: You know what: the fact that I am defensive about class is true. The problem with academics is that you people don't want to see life as it is. You have a point, but the truth is I *do* feel defensive about class. In some ways, me admitting to this means acknowledging the complexity of these things. I feel defensive about class, and I'm consciously telling myself not to be as defensive. Growing up in Nigeria, I had class privilege, being a university professor's daughter. Even within the campus in Nsukka, I had privilege: my father was Deputy Vice-Chancellor, we lived in the big house, we had a driver. Recently my friend Chioma was telling me, "You don't actually know that life was not that easy on campus, because it was easy for you people." I remember an almost automatic defensiveness. I was going to say to her, "Come on, what do you mean?," but I made myself walk it back. Seven or ten years ago I would have been very defensive. My point being that acknowledging the defensiveness is also a way to start working on it.

Part of the reason I say this is because I'm increasingly uncomfortable about the idea that if you're part of an oppressed class, then it makes you a saint. I don't like that. I deal with a lot of crap for being a black person and a woman in the world—and sometimes, I'm very frustrated by the way white women will start crying when you tell them about racism. It gets very annoying, and you realize they're crying because somehow they think it's about them. But then, when I realize how I react when it comes to class, I think, "Oh, I'm starting to understand you people." It's the same way I felt when I was suddenly told that I was transphobic. I was so defensive for a short while. Honestly, I felt such sympathy for white people for about a week. I thought, "Aaah, so that's why you people do that!" Because, sometimes when a white person is told that what they did was racist, suddenly they start telling you that their great-grandfather's best friend was black.

DT: [*laughs*]

CNA: But anyway, to answer your question—and I do think it's a fair question—is it excusing white fragility? No. It's acknowledging that to be black, to be in various oppressed groups, doesn't make me perfect. Being the oppressed in certain places doesn't mean that I'm not capable of being the oppressor in other places. And I think there's something about being the oppressor that just makes people react in a certain way. So, it's not to say that white fragility is fine; it's to say that I kind of get it, but that you all need to do something about it. There are some people who don't even think that white fragility exists. There are many white people who deeply feel, "Oh my God, I'm not terrible," in the same way that when people tell me that I thought Nsukka was easy when it really wasn't, I think, "But how can you think I'm a bad person?"

I've also realized that, increasingly, I'm almost uncomfortable in certain situations. I'm uncomfortable with wide inequality, and I get awkward. My brother Okey teases me that when we are in Nigeria with people who are really poor, I sometimes overcompensate, because I'm so sorry. Even in that, there is condescension. My brother Okey is very different. He doesn't think that there is anything to be sorry for, so he treats everyone the same. I, on the other hand, have been poisoned by a certain kind of liberalism, so in Nigeria I'm so sorry around very poor people that I sometimes do stupid things. When they say something like, "Oh, you like eating fresh salad," I'm like "No, no, no"—but it's a lie. At the same time, I can't deny that I like being privileged.

DT: Let me pick up on that. I like your honesty, but then it also depresses me to hear someone like you say that they like their privilege and that they would give away *some* of it for a better world, but maybe not all of it. What hope is there for racism to disappear from the world if privilege is something that people hang on to?

CNA: Well, here is the thing. The answer is to have a world where everyone has access to that privilege. Quite frankly, I don't want a world where we're all starving and poor. I want a world where we can all have salad and kale. Because I like salad and kale. I just am not prepared to lie to you and say that I don't like that I have a big house in Lagos, because I do. It's important for me to say this because, if I met me, I would need to know that I wasn't lying about my privilege to be able to engage me about that privilege. Telling the truth opens the door to being more honest when talking about privilege.

DT: Indeed.

CNA: White privilege is just inconceivable to many white people because they would say, "I can't pay my rent." They're so steeped in enjoying their white privilege that they don't even acknowledge it. I feel that we need to be honest for people to be able to have those conversations. Especially in the US right now, I don't think that we're having conversations about anything. But if we create a space where decent white people—not Trump voters— can start to see how it's different for black people because they're black, and how it's better for white people because they're white, and then maybe we can meet halfway somewhere, and white people can say, "Let's give up half of our white privilege." [*laughs*]

DT: That would be a start.

CNA: Because I'm willing to give up half of my class privilege. Honestly, I really don't like inequality; as I said, it makes me uncomfortable. But what's interesting about my class privilege in Nigeria is that often it clashes with the fact that I'm female and kind of young-looking; I don't look like a "Madam." I don't often get immediate respect. Gatemen can be quite disrespectful when they see me, so then I overdo the "Madam": I raise my voice, I say "Open the door for me!" And in doing this, I assert class, because I say it in proper English. Right afterwards, I start feeling guilty, thinking about how this poor guy is underpaid. At the same time, he's functioning from a place of a certain privilege because he has a penis. I remember going to a passport office, and a man started touching me, stroking my arm and saying "You're very fresh, I'll marry you." I was so taken aback. That hadn't happened to me in a long time, because the "Chimamanda privilege" had covered some of that. This man didn't know who I was; I was just somebody who came into the passport office asking to see the *oga*. I was so appalled that I wanted to throw up. I then said, "Are you mad? Leave me alone!" I could tell that he was taken aback, probably thinking, "My God, she must be somebody for her to raise her voice to me." Now, in that case, I didn't feel guilty; I was outraged. And I realize that part of my outrage was also that I felt that I hadn't gained from my privilege. Ten years ago, this kind of incident happened to me all the time. I remember going to the American embassy once, and the guard, even as he clearly saw that we were not from the same class, told me "I like this your body, see your breasts." It's such an ugly feeling . . . But because this hadn't happened to me in a long while, to go into that immigration office and have that nasty man touch my arm with his dirty stubby fingers, I felt so violated. I mean, this is just to say that it's complicated because, obviously, I have power over him, but at the same time, because he's male, he felt entitled to my body.

DT: To end this interview, I wanted to discuss another difficult topic—religion. More precisely, I have a question about Pope Francis. In 2015, you wrote an essay about him, in which you mentioned how inspired his progressive attitude made you feel. At the time you wrote your piece, one of the issues that Pope Francis had been known to be progressive about was homosexuality. But recently, discussing this subject, he said that "When it [homosexuality] shows itself from childhood, there is a lot that can be done through psychiatry" . . .
CNA: He said that?

DT: Yes, you didn't know?
CNA: No! What I have in my head is him saying, "Who am I to judge?"

DT: He did say that too, much earlier. But since you didn't know about the incident I've just referred to, let me perhaps rephrase the question. It is not uncommon to hear supposedly progressive Christians—not just Catholics—say that God loves homosexuals, but that He does not like homosexuality. What do you think about that?
CNA: I think that's absolute nonsense. God made homosexuals *and* homosexuality. But let me come back to what you said about Pope Francis. My friend Dave Eggers once said to me that sometimes, when you're on stage, and you're hyper, you just start to talk rubbish . . . But the problem is, it stays forever. Someone picks apart that rubbish, and then they bring it up twenty-five years later, not to ask you, "Is this something you've rethought?" or "Is this just something you said on the spur of the moment?" No, they criticize you for the thing you said. The reason I mention this is that I just don't believe that Pope Francis believes that. Was he speaking to a group

of ultraconservative Catholics and did he feel that he needed to say that? Because, you know, the Pope has to be a politician.

DT: Hmm ... [*looks doubtful*]
CNA: You're looking at me because you're thinking, "You don't want to believe that he believes that."

DT: Yes.
CNA: I've read enough about him. Social justice matters to him, but there is a kind of practicality to him. I feel like he is the sort of person who looks at the world as it is, not as he thinks it should be. But anyway, now I feel compelled to go and read what he said. It's a bit depressing. But can he change his mind? Can he walk that back?

DT: I hope so ... But I mean, my question is also about whether Pope Francis saying something like that would change what your faith is now. I don't know if you believe in God right now, in this moment?
CNA: Sort of . . . –ish. I haven't been to Mass in a while, but we're raising our daughter Catholic. My husband was raised Presbyterian, but now he goes to Catholic Church. Other denominations are not as anal as Catholics about where they go to church—whereas I, even when I was deeply resistant to Catholicism, would not go to another church. Pope Francis is the Pope I longed for when I started questioning the Church. He felt human to me. It wasn't even because he doesn't like the Popemobile or doesn't wear red satin shoes. I couldn't care less about those things because I think people are different; you can like red satin shoes and also be humble. But it was the way he said "Who am I to judge?"; it was reading some of his writing, watching him speak; and just feeling the humanity that I never felt with Pope John Paul. Pope John Paul was so popular, but I always found him quite cold, about the magisterium of the Church. Pope Francis, I just felt, was saying to people, "Come, let's love." He made me feel that maybe there is hope.

Religion bothers me on many levels, but I also find it beautiful in other ways. My father, who I adore, is very Catholic, in a very beautiful way. He believes deeply, not just in God but in the Roman Catholic Church, in its traditions. He says his rosary, and he always has his rosary in his pocket. He is very gentle and very kind—even if he has a very dry sense of humour that has become worse as he's gotten older. But I love it, I love that he's sarcastic now. So anyway, when I started really questioning the Church, I still couldn't entirely separate myself from it because of my father. And there are things I still cannot say in my father's presence about how I feel about the Church because I don't want to hurt him. So that piece I wrote about Pope Francis, I kind of hoped he wouldn't read it; actually my brothers said, "Let's just hope Daddy doesn't see this because he wouldn't like it." I mean, he knows that I question the Church. When I was a teenager, I was a fierce Catholic apologist; he knows that I'm no longer that, and that I don't really go to Mass anymore. I go once in a while. When he comes to stay with us in the summer, I go maybe one Sunday out of four, mostly to make him happy, because he loves when we all go to Mass together. In Lagos, I never go to church, partly because church there is all about dressing up, and I haven't found the right Catholic church that isn't about what people are wearing, whether they are wearing gold.

DT: Is it spirituality, then, more than religion, that you are looking for?
CNA: Yes.

DT: I suppose that this is also what you see in your father?
CNA: Yes, and it is also what I see in Pope Francis, and in my friend who is a priest in Nigeria, Father Amaechi. I often say to him, if many more priests were like you, I would never have left the Church. He's so practical, so true, and so genuine, and he can say "I don't know." Once he said to me, "You don't have to accept everything"—which, I'm sure, his bishop would be horrified to hear. I found it very moving, him saying that you don't have to accept everything, because obviously I cannot accept many of the Catholic Church's teachings. I think it's nonsense, really. But on the other hand, because it's the tradition in which I grew up, I don't see myself ever making peace with another Christian church. This is what Catholicism does to you. It's like a poison.

DT: Interesting choice of word, "poison" . . . You're raising your daughter Catholic!
CNA: Yes, but it's like a poison that doesn't quite kill you. I want my daughter to know the beauty of Mass, because Mass is like drama, it's like theatre. The singing is beautiful; there are times I'm moved to tears, particularly at Easter. Easter has this incredible tradition, the Pascal Mass. The day before, you light the candles. Half the time I'm crying, because there is a part of me that loves drama, and I just think "Oooh, I want my daughter to have that." But also, I'm going to raise my daughter to question everything. If she wakes up at fifteen and says to me, "I'm done with the Church," I'll say, "Ok." If she

wakes up at fifteen and says, "I want to convert to Islam," I'll say, "Ok." But I will say to her, "Have you read everything about Islam?" The point being that I want her to be a questioning human. But . . . am I Catholic? When I'm asked that, I still don't know what to say. I'm too guilty to say no, but . . .

DT: That's very Catholic, right?

CNA: Yes, yes. But I'm also still too questioning to say yes. There are two priests in the church that I occasionally go to in the US: there is one that I love, who talks about love and how we can't be judgmental; he makes me feel lighter. But there is also another one that I can't stand, who talks about Catholic dogma. The last time we went to church—my parents, my husband, me, my daughter—it was the priest who speaks about Catholic dogma. He started talking about having to pray for all the unborn children who are killed, and he just lost me there. I don't see myself ever accepting that a woman does not have the choice to do what she wants with her body. I just cannot accept it. And so, that's the kind of thing that makes it impossible for me to say "yes" fully. I don't know . . .

DT: It's an ongoing process . . .

CNA: It's ongoing, yes. You know, when I was growing up, I really loved the idea of the Blessed Virgin Mary. I felt, "Oh, it's wonderful that this woman figure is important in the Church." Increasingly now, I don't know, because she's kind of . . . limp. You know? I mean, there's a lot that the Church needs to change. I think it will be forced to change, I really do. Membership in seminaries is dropping everywhere in the world. If the Church is going to continue, they have to change: priests have to marry, women have to become priests. When that happens, I'll be dead. But if I were alive, then I would probably say I'm fully Catholic, because I can tell you that if women become priests, the Church's rigidity will change. When I hear now that we have to pray for the unborn children, I think, but what about the women? I feel that in the abortion debate, the humanity of women is completely forgotten.

DT: Thank you very much for sharing these thoughts, Chimamanda.

Notes

This interview was not published as a Q&A, but as a short "profile" piece. It is still available online. See Howard Altman. "Amanda's Voice." *Philadelphia City Paper*, 10–17 June 1999. http://mycitypaper.com/articles/061099/feat.howcol.shtml.

Key Resources

An extensive bibliography is available on the Chimamanda Ngozi Adichie Website at http://www.cerep.ulg.ac.be/adichie.

Interviews (in chronological order)

Anya, Ike. "In the Footsteps of Achebe: Enter Chimamanda Ngozi Adichie, Nigeria's Newest Literary Voice." *Nigerians in America*, 10 October 2003. Repr. *Sentinel Poetry* 12, November 2003, http://www.sentinelpoetry.org.uk/magazine1103/page11.html.

Vawter, Norah. "Author Explores Faith and Country in Acclaimed New Novel." *allafrica.com*, 13 October 2004. http://allafrica.com/stories/200410130920.html.

Salu, Jide. "Chimamanda Ngozi Adichie with Jide Salu." *YouTube*, uploaded by Jide Salu on 10 April 2004. http://www.youtube.com/watch?v=SWM1VRxU1oI.

Kotzin, Miriam N. "Miriam N. Kotzin with Chimamanda Ngozi Adichie." *Per Contra* 2, Spring 2006. http://www.percontra.net/archive/2adichie.htm.

Elliott, Debbie. "Capturing Biafra's Brief Day in the 'Yellow Sun.'" *All Things Considered*, NPR, 17 September 2006. http://www.npr.org/templates/story/story.php?storyId =6088156.

Birnbaum, Robert. "Chimamanda Ngozi Adichie." *Morning News*, 23 October 2006. http://www.themorningnews.org/article/chimamanda-ngozi-adichie.

Shea, Renee H. "An Interview with Fiction Writer Chimamanda Ngozi Adichie." *Poets & Writers Magazine*, 8 August 2007. http://www.pw.org/content/interview_fiction _writer_chimamanda_ngozi_adichie.

Adagha, Ovo. "How Does It Feel to Be Home?" *Vanguard*, 12 August 2007. http://allafrica .com/stories/200708130686.html.

Segundo, Bat. "Chimamanda Adichie." *The Bat Segundo Show* 141, 5 October 2007. http://www.edrants.com/segundo/bss-141-chimamanda-adichie/.

Bolonik, Kera. "Memory, Witness, and War: Chimamanda Ngozi Adichie Talks with *Bookforum*." *Bookforum* 14, no. 4 (2007–2008): 37.

Lang, Kirsty. *Front Row*, BBC Radio 4, 3 April 2009. http://www.bbc.co.uk/programmes /boojbs2d.

Shea, Renee. "Chimamanda Ngozi Adichie." *Kenyon Review*, April 2009. http://www .kenyonreview.org/conversation/chimamanda-ngozi-adichie.

Koval, Ramona. "In Conversation with Chimamanda Ngozi Adichie." *The Book Show*, ABC Australia, 26 May 2009. http://www.abc.net.au/radionational/programs /bookshow/in-conversation-with-chimamanda-ngozi-adichie/3147314.

Mustich, James. "Chimamanda Ngozi Adichie: A Conversation with James Mustich." *Barnes and Noble Review*, 29 June 2009. http://www.barnesandnoble.com/review /chimamanda-ngozi-adichie.

Wainaina, Binyavanga. "Chimamanda Ngozi Adichie with Binyavanga Wainaina." *Lannan Foundation*, 28 September 2011. http://podcast.lannan.org/2011/10/01/chimamanda -ngozi-adichie-with-binyavanga-wainaina-conversation-28-september-2011-video/.

Parks, Sheri. "Worldwise: Arts and Humanities Dean's Lecture Series: Chimamanda Adichie." 19 February 2013. *Vimeo*, uploaded by UMD College of Arts and Humanities on 1 March 2013. http://vimeo.com/60861516.

Allfrey, Ellah. "Humanising History and Connecting Cultures: The Role of Literature." *Royal Society of Arts*, 10 April 2013. http://www.thersa.org/discover/podcasts/2013 /04/humanising-history—connecting-cultures-the-role-of-literature.

Bannister, Matthew. "Chimamanda Ngozi Adichie on Life in US." *Outlook*, BBC World Service, 22 April 2013. http://www.bbc.co.uk/programmes/p0175w3t.

Klarl, Joseph. "Chimamanda Ngozi Adichie's Continental Divides." *Interview Magazine*, 14 May 2013. http://www.interviewmagazine.com/culture/chimamanda-ngozi-adichie -americanah#.

Tepper, Anderson. "Interview with Chimamanda Ngozi Adichie." *goodreads*, May 2013. http://www.goodreads.com/interviews/show/857.Chimamanda_Ngozi_Adichie.

Sylvester, Kevin. "*Americanah* with Author Chimamanda Ngozi Adichie." *Sunday Edition*, CBC Radio, 7 July 2013. http://www.cbc.ca/player/play/2395840969.

Kamal, Soniah. "Q&A: Chimamanda Ngozi Adichie Tackles Race from African Perspective in *Americanah*." *ArtsATL*, 4 March 2014. http://www.artsatl.com/qa-chimamanda -ngozi-adichie-americanah/.

Gray, Emma. "Chimamanda Ngozi Adichie on the TEDx Talk Beyoncé Sampled and Why We Should Forget Feminism's 'Baggage.'" *Huffington Post*, 6 March 2014. http:// www.huffingtonpost.com/2014/03/06/chimamanda-ngozi-adichie-feminism_n _4907241.html.

Kasbekar, Asha. "Hair-raising Histories." *Live Mint*, 8 March 2014. http://www.livemint .com/Leisure/vohbaIky54ajloIzhoGFCP/Chimamanda-Ngozi-Adichie—Hairraising -histories.html.

Woetzel, Damian. "Chimamanda Ngozi Adichie in Conversation with Damian Woetzel." *YouTube*, uploaded by The Aspen Institute on 11 March 2014. http://www.youtube .com/watch?v=1eoJ24rTTu4.

Schulz, Kathryn. "Chimamanda Ngozi Adichie: Tenement Talk from March 12, 2014." *YouTube*, uploaded by Tenement Museum on 8 April 2014. http://www.youtube .com/watch?v=yY1RK6aAPws.

North, Anna. "Chimamanda Ngozi Adichie: 'When You're Not a White Male Writing about White Male Things Then Somehow Your Work Has to *Mean* Something.'" *Salon*, 13 March 2014. http://www.salon.com/2014/03/13/chimamanda_ngozi_adichie _when_you%E2%80%99re_not_a_white_male_writing_about_white_male_things _then_somehow_your_work_has_to_mean_something/.

Jones, Kima. "The Rumpus Interview with Chimamanda Ngozi Adichie." *Rumpus*, 17 June 2014. http://therumpus.net/2014/06/the-rumpus-interview-with-chimamanda -ngozi-adichie.

Jouwe, Nancy. "We Should All Be Feminists | Chimamanda Ngozi Adichie—Atria." *You-Tube*, broadcast live by Atria Kennisinstituut on 15 October 2016. http://www .youtube.com/watch?v=Ligb8wICe9w&.

Panych, Sophia. "Chimamanda Ngozi Adichie on Why You Can Be a Feminist and Love Makeup." *Allure Magazine*, 18 January 2017. http://www.allure.com/story/chimamanda -ngozi-adichie-feminism-makeup.

Macdonald, Cathy. "Cathy Talks to Best-Selling Author Chimamanda Ngozi Adichie." *Sunday Morning with . . .* , BBC Radio Scotland, 5 March 2017. http://www.bbc.co.uk /programmes/po4w67dl.

Bascaramurty, Dakshana. "Author Chimamanda Ngozi Adichie on Living and Teaching Feminism." *Globe and Mail*, 6 March 2017. http://www.theglobeandmail.com/arts /books-and-media/author-chimamanda-ngozi-adichie-on-living-and-teaching feminism/article34226410/.

Begley, Sarah. "Ten Questions with Chimamanda Ngozi Adichie." *Time*, 6 March 2017. http://motto.time.com/4690165/chimamanda-ngozi-adichie-dear-ijeawele-10 -questions/.

Begley, Sarah. "Chimamanda Ngozi Adichie Discusses Her New Feminist Manifesto, *Dear Ijeawele*." *YouTube*, uploaded by Bustle on 9 March 2017. http://www.youtube .com/watch?v=H5yxrXzKNIc.

Eddo-Lodge, Reni. "Chimamanda Ngozi Adichie and Reni Eddo-Lodge in Conversation." *Soundcloud*, uploaded by Southbank Centre: Think Aloud on 11 March 2018. http:// soundcloud.com/southbankcentre/chimamanda-ngozi-adichie-in-conversation-1.

Cornish, Audie. "Chimamanda Ngozi Adichie, *Dear Ijeawele*." *YouTube*, uploaded by Poli-tics and Prose on 24 March 2017. http://www.youtube.com/watch?v=PaCRkyKJar4.

Slaughter, Anne Marie. "In Conversation: Chimamanda Ngozi Adichie and Anne Marie Slaughter." *YouTube*, uploaded by New America on 22 May 2017. http://www.youtube .com/watch?v=7_A8UWXk76k.

Marchese, David. "In Conversation: Chimamanda Ngozi Adichie." *Vulture*, 9 July 2018. http://www.vulture.com/2018/07/chimamanda-ngozi-adichie-in-conversation.html.

Books

Emenyonu, Ernest N., ed. *A Companion to Chimamanda Ngozi Adichie*. Martlesham: Boydell and Brewer, 2017.

Onukaogu, Allwell Abalogu, and Ezechi Onyerionwu. *Chimamanda Ngozi Adichie: The Aesthetics of Commitment and Narrative*. Ibadan: Kraft Books, 2010.

Journal articles and book chapters

Cooper, Brenda. "Breaking Gods and Petals of Purple in Chimamanda Ngozi Adichie's *Purple Hibiscus*." In *A New Generation of African Writers: Migration, Material Cul-ture and Language*, by Brenda Cooper, 110–132. Woodbridge and Scottsville: James Currey and University of KwaZulu-Natal Press, 2008.

Cooper, Brenda. "An Abnormal Ordinary: Chimamanda Ngozi Adichie's *Half of a Yellow Sun*." In *A New Generation of African Writers: Migration, Material Culture and Language*, by Brenda Cooper, 133–150. Woodbridge and Scottsville: James Currey and University of KwaZulu-Natal Press, 2008.

Eisenberg, Eve. "'Real Africa' / 'Which Africa?': The Critique of Mimetic Realism in Chimamanda Ngozi Adichie's Short Fiction." *African Literature Today* 31 (2013): 8–24.

Hallemeier, Katherine. "'To Be from the Country of People Who Gave': National Allegory and the United States of Adichie's *Americanah*." *Studies in the Novel* 47, no. 2 (2015): 231–245.

Hewett, Heather. "Coming of Age: Chimamanda Ngozi Adichie and the Voice of the Third Generation." *English in Africa* 32, no. 1 (2005): 73–97.

Hodges, Hugh. "Writing Biafra: Adichie, Emecheta and the Dilemmas of Biafran War Fiction." *Postcolonial Text* 5, no. 1 (2009): 1–13.

Krishnan, Madhu. "Abjection and the Fetish: Reconsidering the Construction of the Postcolonial Exotic in Chimamanda Ngozi Adichie's *Half of a Yellow Sun*." *Journal of Postcolonial Writing* 48, no. 1 (2012): 26–38.

Leetsch, Jennifer. "Love, Limb-Loosener: Encounters in Chimamanda Adichie's *Americanah*." *Journal of Popular Romance Studies* 6 (2017): 1–16.

Masterson, John. "Posing, Exposing, Opposing: Accounting for Contested (Corpo) Realities in Chimamanda Ngozi Adichie's *Half of a Yellow Sun*." In *Expressions of the Body: Representations in African Text and Image*, edited by Charlotte Baker, 137–160. Oxford: Peter Lang, 2009.

Ngwira Emmanuel Mzomera. "'He Writes about the World That Remained Silent': Witnessing Authorship in Chimamanda Ngozi Adichie's *Half of a Yellow Sun*." *English Studies in Africa* 55, no. 2 (2012): 43–53.

Norridge, Zoe. "Sex as Synecdoche: Intimate Languages of Violence in Chimamanda Ngozi Adichie's *Half of a Yellow Sun* and Aminatta Forna's *The Memory of Love*." *Research in African Literatures* 43, no. 2 (2012): 18–39.

Novak, Amy. "Who Speaks? Who Listens? The Problem of Address in Two Nigerian Trauma Novels." *Studies in the Novel* 40, no. 1–2 (2008): 31–51. Partly deals with Chimamanda Ngozi Adichie's *Half of a Yellow Sun*.

Ouma, Christopher E.W. "Childhood(s) in *Purple Hibiscus*." *English Academy Review* 26, no. 2 (2009): 48–59.

Ouma, Christopher E.W. "Composite Consciousness and Memories of War in Chimamanda Ngozi Adichie's *Half of a Yellow Sun*." *English Academy Review* 28, no. 2 (2011): 15–30.

Phiri, Aretha. "Queer Subjectivities in J.M. Coetzee's *Disgrace* and Chimamanda Ngozi Adichie's 'On Monday of Last Week.'" *Agenda* 29, no. 1 (2015): 155–163.

Phiri, Aretha. "Expanding Black Subjectivities in Toni Morrison's *Song of Solomon* and Chimamanda Ngozi Adichie's *Americanah*." *Cultural Studies* 31, no. 1 (2017): 121–142.

Simoes da Silva, Tony. "Embodied Genealogies and Gendered Violence in Chimamanda Ngozi Adichie's Writing." *African Identities* 10, no. 4 (2012): 455–470.

Stobie, Cheryl. "Dethroning the Infallible Father: Religion, Patriarchy and Politics in Chimamanda Ngozi Adichie's *Purple Hibiscus*." *Literature and Theology* 24, no. 4 (2010): 421–435.

Stobie, Cheryl. "Gendered Bodies in Chimamanda Ngozi Adichie's *Purple Hibiscus*." In *Literature for Our Times: Postcolonial Studies in the Twenty-First Century*, edited by Bill Ashcroft, Ranjini Mendis, Julie McGonegal and Arun Mukherjee, 307–326. Amsterdam: Rodopi, 2012.

Toivanen, Anna Leena. "Spaces of In-between-ness and Unbelonging: The Hotel in Short Stories by Sefi Atta and Chimamanda Ngozi Adichie." *English Studies in Africa* 60, no. 1 (2017): 1–11.

Tunca, Daria. "The Confessions of a 'Buddhist Catholic': Religion in the Works of Chimamanda Ngozi Adichie." *Research in African Literatures* 44, no. 3 (2013): 50–71.

Tunca, Daria, "The Danger of a Single Short Story: Reality, Fiction and Metafiction in Chimamanda Ngozi Adichie's 'Jumping Monkey Hill.'" *Journal of Postcolonial Writing* 54, no. 1 (2018): 69–82. Repr. in *Minor Genres in Postcolonial Literatures*, edited by Delphine Munos and Bénédicte Ledent, 69–82. Abingdon: Routledge, 2019.

Uwakweh, Pauline Ada. "'Breaking Gods': The Narrator as Revelator and Critic of the Postcolonial Condition in *Purple Hibiscus*." In *Emerging African Voices: A Study of Contemporary African Literature*, edited by Walter P. Collins III, 53–74. Amherst, NY: Cambria Press, 2010.

VanZanten, Susan. "'The Headstrong Historian': Writing with *Things Fall Apart*." *Research in African Literatures* 46, no. 2 (2015): 85–103.

Wenske, Ruth S. "Adichie in Dialogue with Achebe: Balancing Dualities in *Half of a Yellow Sun*." *Research in African Literatures* 47, no. 3 (2016): 70–87.

Index

About the Editor

Daria Tunca works at the University of Liège, Belgium, where she is a member of the postcolonial research group CEREP. Her research focuses on stylistics and African literatures, with a particular emphasis on contemporary Nigerian writing. She is the author of *Stylistic Approaches to Nigerian Fiction* (2014).

CPSIA information can be obtained
at www.ICGtesting.com
Printed in the USA
BVHW072224170720
583717BV00001B/4